THIRD EDITION

Sciencing

An Involvement Approach
to Elementary Science Methods

Sandra E. Cain, Central Michigan University
Jack M. Evans, Central Michigan University

Merrill, an imprint of
Macmillan Publishing Company
New York
Collier Macmillan Canada, Inc.
Toronto
Maxwell Macmillan International Publishing Group
New York   Oxford   Singapore   Sydney

Cover Photo: Kevin Fitzsimons

This book was set in Korinna.

Administrative Editor: Jeff Johnston
Developmental Editor: Linda Scharp
Production Editor: Mary M. Irvin
Art Coordinator: Vincent A. Smith
Cover Designer: Russ Maselli
Photo Editor: Gail Meese

Photo credits: All photographs by Brenda Hunt, David Brittain, Flint Horton, Jack Evans, Sandra Cain, and Susan Day Brown except for p. 42, 72, 91, 98 by Donald Birdd/Merrill; p. 85, 366 by John T. Harlan/Merrill; p. 168 by Charles Quinlan; p. 189 by Greg Miller/ Merrill; p. 206 by Paul Conklin.

Library of Congress Catalog Card Number: 89–62301
International Standard Book Number: 0–675–20869–6
Printed in the United States of America
2 3 4 5 6 7 8 9—94 93 92 91

PREFACE

This text is designed to offer elementary science methods instructors, preservice teachers, and inservice teachers an exciting and challenging alternative to the traditional lecture-discussion format prevalent in most college classes. Direct involvement is used throughout to guide students in acquiring the specific skills necessary for teaching science in the elementary school. The program is structured to provide flexibility, interaction, individualization, and personalization.

Each of the eleven chapters contains an introduction, overall goals, a list of objectives, reading material, activities, and a list of background and supplementary reading material. The core of each chapter is a set of activities arranged and designed to guide the students toward the acquisition of the stated objectives. Space is provided for recording and organizing information gathered during the activities.

Several major changes have been made in this third edition. A new technology component has been added to the science components of content, process, and attitudes in Chapter 1. This additional component focuses on involving children in using science to solve real-world problems, a vital aspect of sciencing.

Although ESS, SCIS, and SAPA materials are not used as much in the schools as they once were, the concept and the teaching strategies are still very important; therefore, Chapter 2 has been modified to emphasize this. A full review of the programs is still available in Appendix A. The original activities are maintained to provide an overview of the type of activities found in the programs as well as to provide examples of ways to create science lessons for daily use in the classroom.

Chapter 3 has been rewritten to include the text-kit approach and the textbook approach to sciencing. Most of the new textbook series have made an effort to incorporate activities into their programs, and kits are now available for most, if not all, textbook series from either the publisher or Delta Education. New activities provide a more complete review of the textbooks and supplementary materials such as computer supplements, enrichment activities, and special help for the exceptional student.

Units 3 and 5 from the second edition have been updated and combined to form Chapter 4. This new chapter provides an opportunity to examine the role of the sciencing teacher in relation to decision-making and management skills.

The "Classroom Methodology" chapter (Chapter 5) has been revised to include a brief overview of the Hunter Model of effective instruction. This model is integrated into the strategies and format for effective lesson planning presented in this chapter.

Computers and quality software are becoming common in the classroom. Chapter 8 has undergone a major revision to emphasize the use of the computer in the science classroom. Information on basic computer literacy has been expanded. There are more suggestions for using the computer, as well as activities to (1) help develop computer skills and (2) provide guidelines for evaluating and selecting software.

Chapter 10, "Projects and Science," is a revised and expanded version of the Involvement Projects found in the second edition. It includes information on science fairs, class projects, state and national programs, and resources. The concept of short term activities and long term projects is included. The life science activities have been retained as examples of long term activities. New activities include opportunities to plan and participate in a science fair, inventory resources, and collect activities.

A final chapter, "Looking into the Future," was added in this third edition. It focuses on the challenging opportunity that elementary teachers face—providing students with experiences that will lead to their scientific literacy. Project 2061 is discussed and its implications for sciencing are drawn. A brief review of the text material is also included to help students begin to integrate the ideas presented and use the skills gained to formulate a sciencing action plan.

These major changes, along with the normal updating of the remaining chapters, make this text meaningful for today's students.

Sciencing offers preservice and inservice teachers a chance to become directly involved in sciencing. Students are exposed to science education philosophy, direct, first-hand experience involving science equipment and materials, and science concepts. Generally, the program encourages students to be active participants in the learning process. Representative commercial programs are included to acquaint students with the laboratory and textbook approaches to sciencing. No particular program is advocated, and the cross application of concepts, skills, and methods between various commercial programs and traditional materials will be evident.

This textbook is based on the philosophy of student-instructor involvement. The students read informational materials, try hands-on as well as mental activities, discuss reactions with peers and instructor, record information gathered, and apply what they learn to an evaluation task or exam. The instructor usually initiates each chapter with an introductory presentation to individuals, small groups, or large groups, confers with students during the course of activities, modifying or prescribing as necessary, and participates in summarizing the learning experience upon completion. The instructor also evaluates the student's performance on the evaluation task and prescribes remediation if warranted. The student and instructor are partners in a learning experience, actively working together to analyze individual needs and use the text to meet those needs. Students are also able to modify or adapt portions of the text for their use.

Acknowledgments

The authors wish to thank their students at Central Michigan University who have contributed their time and energy to provide valuable suggestions during the preparation of this third edition. We are indebted to the teachers and students in the Mt. Pleasant Public Schools who made significant contributions to the text by allowing photographs to be taken while they were engaged in sciencing activities. We also appreciate Susan Day Brown's help in updating Chapter 7, "Sciencing with Special Needs Children," and the aid of Jan Hansen, who typed the manuscript. Mary Irvin provided significant help and expertise during the production process at Merrill. Finally, we thank our families for their continued support and understanding of the many long hours that were necessary to complete this third edition.

CONTENTS

CHAPTER 1
PROCESS-ORIENTED SCIENCE

CHAPTER 3
TEXTBOOK APPROACH TO ELEMENTARY SCIENCE 111

CHAPTER 4
THE SCIENCE TEACHER 139

CHAPTER 5
CLASSROOM METHODOLOGY   **169**

CHAPTER 6
QUESTIONING TECHNIQUES   207

CHAPTER 7
SCIENCING AND CHILDREN WITH SPECIAL EDUCATION NEEDS   227

APPENDIX A
SUPPLEMENTAL BACKGROUND
MATERIAL FOR ESS, SCIS, AND SAPA II

335

APPENDIX B
INDIVIDUAL EDUCATION PROGRAM:
SUPPLEMENTAL MATERIAL FOR CHAPTER 7 ACTIVITY 7.1

395

Process-Oriented Science

Goals

After completing this chapter, you will demonstrate competence in the following:

1. Describing the relationship of the nature of science, the nature of learning, and the nature of the child to the teaching of elementary science

2. Assimilating and accommodating Piaget's theory of mental development

3. Acquiring the process-inquiry skills

Objectives

In completing this chapter, you will do the following:

1. Identify and describe the four components of science

2. Identify and describe the three domains of learning

3. Identify and describe Piaget's four stages of mental development

4. Explain how Piaget's theory of mental development has influenced elementary science curriculum

5. Identify and demonstrate the ability to utilize the following process-inquiry skills:
   A. Observing
   B. Classifying
   C. Measuring
   D. Using spatial relations
   E. Communicating
   F. Predicting
   G. Inferring
   H. Using integrated processes

INTRODUCTION

How do teachers decide what to teach? What criteria should teachers use for making decisions about what students will learn in science? These questions, which concern both inservice and preservice teachers, are very complex questions with no easy answers.

Chapter 1, "Process-Oriented Science," seeks to provide insight into the teaching and learning of elementary science. The focus will be on

1. The nature of science
2. The nature of learning
3. The nature of the child

Information gleaned from each of these areas provides the teacher with valuable criteria and the rationale needed in making decisions about what to teach and how to teach it.

THE NATURE OF SCIENCE

How would you define or describe science? What is science? What would you teach if you were responsible for a third-grade science lesson tomorrow? What would your third-grade students do during the science lesson? These questions are designed to help you to begin to think about the *nature* of science. It is extremely important that you are aware of and understand the nature of science to successfully involve elementary children in appropriate sciencing experiences. In the past, science has been approached as a body of knowledge, or facts, to be memorized and repeated later on a test. The 1960s saw a movement in science away from the product, or content, emphasis and toward a process orientation. Science was becoming more of a "doing" thing. Science educators began using the term *sciencing* to focus on this change of approach. The hands-on, process-oriented kit approach to elementary science was introduced into many elementary schools. The new curriculum projects were among the most exciting things that had ever happened to elementary science.

Support from the National Science Foundation (NSF) and the United States Office of Education made it possible for scientists, science educators, teachers, and children to be directly involved in the development of these process-oriented programs. The research and theories of such well-known child development psychologists as Jean Piaget, Robert Gagné, and Jerome Bruner provided direction and guidance for the new science approach.

Consequently, heavy reliance on the textbook and the teacher for information gave way to a more direct, hands-on approach. Science, or sciencing, began to be seen as a *means* rather than an end product. Elementary children became involved in generating, organizing, and evaluating science content, not merely in memorizing it.

The 1980s saw a renewed interest in science by our elementary and middle schools. The current theme seems to be "Science for All." Realistic science instruction in the early grades that emphasizes the interrelatedness of science and everyday life is the new focus. Preparing children for life in the increasingly technological world that they face now and in the 21st century is an important task. What science knowledge and skills will be needed to live and work successfully in the scientific and technological world of the future? Teachers have a responsibility to the children they teach to involve them in seeking the knowledge needed to make informed science-related decisions.

It is important, then, to prepare for teaching science by exploring the nature of science. What is science? What science do I teach? These are questions that one must ask in order to become aware of the following components of science:

1. Content or product
2. Process or methods
3. Attitude
4. Technology

A successful science program must include all of these components.

These students are involved in hands-on science.

Science as Content or Product

You are probably most familiar with science as content or product. This component includes the accepted facts, laws, principals, and theories of science. At the elementary level, science content can be separated into three areas: physical, life, and earth.

Physical science is the examination of nonliving phenomena. Typical topic areas include air, magnets, electricity, changes, energy, matter, sound, simple machines, and light. *Life science* is the investigation of living things. Three basic divisions of this content area include zoology, the study of animals and humans; botany, the study of plants; and ecology, the study of the interaction of plants, animals, and the environment. Typical topics from these divisions are our bodies, different types of animals, life cycles, seeds, parts of a plant, molds, communities, and pond life. *Earth science* content is drawn from the areas of astronomy, meteorology, and geology. Astronomy topics include day and night, the planets, seasons, stars, the moon, and the sun. Typical meteorology topics are solar energy, clouds, and weather and weather instruments. Crystal formations, rocks, erosion, and fossils are some geology topics usually studied at the elementary level.

Science as Process

In grades K through 8, the emphasis in science is placed on the process component. This component focuses on the *means* used in acquiring science content. As an elementary science teacher, you must think of science not as a noun— a body of knowledge or facts to be memorized—but as a verb—acting, doing, investigating; that is, science as a *means* to an end. At this level *how* the children acquire scientific information is more important than their committing scientific content to memory. They need hands-on experiences that involve them in gathering, organizing, analyzing, and evaluating science content. This is the core of sciencing. A sciencing approach necessitates a change in the traditional roles of both the elementary teacher and the elementary student. No longer is the elementary student to be merely a sponge "soaking up" the information given. The sciencing approach demands the active participation of the student, with the teacher serving as guide and resource person. This approach fosters growth and development in all areas of learning, not just in the memorization of facts.

To be successful with the sciencing approach, the learner must develop the following process-inquiry skills:

1. **Observing:** Using the senses to find out about subjects and events
2. **Classifying:** Grouping things according to similarities or differences
3. **Measuring:** Making quantitative observations
4. **Using spatial relationships:** Identifying shapes and movement

5. **Communicating:** Using the written and spoken word, graphs, drawings, diagrams, or tables to transmit information and ideas to others

6. **Predicting:** Making forecasts of future events or conditions based upon observations or inferences

7. **Inferring:** Explaining an observation or set of observations

8. **Defining operationally:** Creating a definition by describing what is done and observed

9. **Formulating hypotheses:** Making educated guesses based on evidence that can be tested

10. **Interpreting data:** Finding among sets of data patterns that lead to the construction of inferences, predictions, or hypotheses

11. **Controlling variables:** Identifying the variables of a system and selecting from the variables those that are to be held constant and those that are to be manipulated to carry out a proposed investigation

12. **Experimenting:** Investigating, manipulating variables and testing to determine a result

The first seven skills listed are considered basic skills. The student must acquire them to perform skills 8–12. These last five skills (8–12) are considered integrated skills. Several of the basic skills are integrated within skills 8–12.

In Grades K through 3, emphasis is given to the first seven basic skills. This does not mean that younger children should not be provided with an opportunity to acquire the higher level integrated skills if they are capable of handling them.

In Grades 4 through 8, the higher level integrated skills receive more focus. The basic skills must often be reviewed, since they are incorporated within these higher level skills.

Process-inquiry skills are basic to all later learning. They are not separate from science content; rather, they are the tools of scientific investigation. The utilization of these skills in gathering, organizing, analyzing, and evaluating science content is an ongoing goal of sciencing.

Science as Attitudes

The elementary teacher must encourage children to develop a need for seeking rational answers and explanations to natural and physical phenomena. As a teacher, capitalize on children's natural curiosity and promote an attitude of discovery. Focus on the students' finding out for themselves how and why phenomena occur.

Developing objectivity, openness, and tentativeness as well as basing conclusions on available data are all a part of the scientific attitude. The concept of intelligent failure should be developed at the elementary level. Children should not be afraid to stick their necks out and make intelligent mistakes. Much scientific knowledge has resulted from such mistakes. Science can be fun and stimulating. Children should be involved in "messing about" activities as well as structured experiences.

Science as Technology

During the 1980s we have seen the beginnings of a new focus in science education. That focus emphasizes preparing our students for the world of tomorrow. The development of technology as it relates to our daily lives has become a vital part of sciencing. The usefulness of science applications in solving "real world" problems is the theme seen in new curricula. In these curricula, students are involved in identifying a real-world problem, formulating a solution or alternative solutions, and then actually taking action. In this approach, students use technology to solve real-world problems. This experience builds an understanding of the role of science in the development of technology and gives the student confidence in using technology. The link is made between sciencing and everyday life. Science is seen as practical, useful preparation for everyday life. Elementary students must become involved in realistic science instruction that emphasizes the interrelatedness of science and everyday life and focuses attention on their using science to solve real-world problems. This component also involves them in understanding the impact of science and technology on our society.

Summary: The Nature of Science

These four science components—content, process, attitude, and technology—provide structure and guidance for the elementary teacher in planning appropriate science experiences for children. The first component identifies the physical, life, and earth science content that children should explore. The second component identifies the process-inquiry skills that children must develop to be directly involved in gathering, organizing, analyzing, and evaluating the content. The third component concerns the way children "see" science or feel about science. It involves developing a scientific attitude that includes openness and objectivity. The fourth component focuses attention on the need to involve children in realistic science instruction. Children must recognize the interrelatedness of science and everyday life. They must be given opportunities to identify and solve real-world problems by using technology.

In preparing to teach science, one must explore and understand the nature of science in order to make decisions about what and how to teach. In answering the question "What is science?," one must describe science as content, process, attitude, and technology. The first three components provide the teacher with the appropriate structure needed to make decisions about *what* a student should learn in science, *how* a student should learn it, and the *attitudes* that a student should develop. The fourth component, science as technology, provides the vital link between "pure" science and the student's everyday life. It is the *application,* or the practical use, of science. Together these four components help to explain the nature of science and are vital in answering the questions "What is science?" and "What science do I teach?"

THE NATURE OF LEARNING

Now that we have identified the basic components of the nature of science, we will examine the nature of the learning process itself. An effective teacher cannot ignore the impact of the learning process on the learning outcome.

Domains of Learning

There are three areas, or domains, of learning that an elementary teacher must consider: cognitive, psychomotor, and affective. All learning can be classified according to these three domains. Each area is reviewed briefly here. (For more information on these three domains, see the books by Bloom, Hastings, & Madaus; Krathwohl, Bloom, & Masia; and Harrow in the "Suggested Readings" at the end of the chapter.)

Cognitive.   The cognitive domain encompasses all learning concerned with the acquisition of facts, concepts, and generalizations. There are two methods for

These children are learning by combining touching and questioning.

obtaining knowledge. One method involves gaining knowledge almost solely from reading, listening to lectures, and other secondary sources. The other method of obtaining knowledge is through direct, firsthand experience. This approach uses empirical procedures involving process-inquiry skills.

Most science educators agree that both approaches are necessary for effective learning to take place. Secondary sources are legitimate sources of scientific information, but they do differ from direct, firsthand manipulation of equipment and materials.

Psychomotor. The psychomotor domain deals with physical skills. In science, we are concerned with providing opportunities for elementary children to manipulate equipment and materials in performing laboratory tasks. They are expected to be able to manipulate laboratory equipment with some facility so that they do not hurt themselves or others and do not damage the equipment.

Affective. The affective domain involves attitudes, interests, and feelings. Most science teachers hope that their students will like science. In addition, they hope that students will develop and accept certain attitudes associated with scientific inquiry. The acceptance and utilization of the processes of scientific inquiry—observing, measuring, hypothesizing, formulating generalizations, and designing and conducting experiments—by elementary children is considered an important goal of science instruction.

Elementary teachers are responsible for providing learning experiences for children that will help them grow and develop in each of the three domains of learning.

Stages of Development

Science curricula have been influenced by the research of many noted child development theorists. Jean Piaget, a Swiss psychologist, has been a major influence in promoting the theory that the ability to think and learn is itself a growing thing. Educators who accept this theory see their role as that of providing learning experiences to help children develop their mental capacity.

Piaget's research (Inhelder & Piaget, 1964) in the area of mental development in children has resulted in four identified stages of mental development.

1. Sensorimotor
2. Preoperational
3. Concrete operations
4. Formal or abstract thought

These stages are sequential. Each child passes through each stage in the same order, but not necessarily at the same rate. The attainment of formal, or abstract, thought—the highest level of development—is not achieved by most children until around the age of 11 or 12. But to reach this final stage, children must be provided with opportunities to develop the prerequisite skills of the preceding stages. You can begin to see how important curricular decisions—what to teach, how to teach, when to teach—are affected by a child's particular stage of development.

The science curriculum is a vital and important part of an elementary school program. It can offer elementary children many experiences that are essential for attaining formal thought. Let's look briefly at some characteristics associated with each stage of development.

Sensorimotor Stage. At birth, an infant does not possess even the simplest sensory or motor skills. No directed, purposeful motor activity or well-focused sensory activity is observable in the newborn human. But the capacity to develop these basic skills is present (Furth, 1970, p. 23). Reflex action and random movement characterize the early part of this stage. Gradually, by interaction with the environment and the passage of time, the young child begins to develop control of motor and sensory skills. During this stage, the child cannot "separate thinking from external action; he 'thinks' in external action" (Furth, 1970, p. 25). That is, he cannot think about actions prior to carrying them out.

As children progress through the sensorimotor stage, they develop the ability to

1. Focus on an object
2. Move toward an object in a coordinated manner
3. Manipulate an object
4. Repeat an action

These actions reflect the development of what Piaget calls sensorimotor schemes. Such schemes are not present at birth but are the product of time and children's interactions with their environments. These preceding abilities are also dependent upon outside stimuli.

Children in the sensorimotor stage are easily distracted by new stimuli and quickly forget original intentions. When children begin to exhibit behavior that indicates greater attention and more goal-oriented activity, and when they can initiate some action of their own, they are beginning to move out of the sensorimotor stage.

Preoperational Stage. The first characteristic of children who have progressed beyond the sensorimotor stage is the recognition of object permanence, or that objects exist even when they cannot be seen or touched. Children who have developed this capability will look for a desired object when it is hidden from them.

Another characteristic of the preoperational stage is symbolic behavior. Children begin to demonstrate things through symbolic actions without depending on physical events. For example, they may pantomime the actions involved in eating without actually eating. It is this capacity to *think* about actions that distinguishes a preoperational child from a sensorimotor child.

Verbal language development also takes place during the preoperational stage. Children are now able to describe their thoughts and the things around them. They base their thinking on their own personal perspectives and experiences. However, they cannot see things from another's point of view; their behavior reflects a self-centeredness. This should not be interpreted as selfishness. It means that a child's understanding, or knowing, is dependent upon personal experience and background. For example, a child who has a pet dog has a different understanding of the word *dog* than a child who has only seen pictures of a dog.

There are other characteristic behaviors of preoperational children. Children in this stage focus on only one property or variable to the exclusion of others, give contradictory or magical explanations, depend upon trial and error for most actions, and lack the ability to reverse actions mentally.

Concrete Operations Stage.   Typically, children between the ages of 7 and 12 acquire the ability to perform elementary logical operations, but only through concrete means. They are unable to engage in hypothetical reasoning but can perform *mentally* what has been performed *physically*. Because of this newly acquired ability, the concrete operational child, unlike the preoperational child, can reverse actions mentally.

During this stage, a child can be given two identical containers of juice with exactly the same amount of liquid in each. Then the juice in one of the containers can be poured into a much shorter but wider container. Ask the child, "Is there more, less, or the same amount of juice in the two containers?" A concrete operational child who has physically experienced the reverse action should be able to mentally reverse the action and reply that there is the same amount in both. If the child has not concretely experienced the reversal, she will probably reply differently. When the child is given the opportunity to experience physically the reversal action—pouring the juice from the shorter, wider container back into the original one—she sees that the amount is the same as before and equal to the other. With many experiences of this kind, children begin to develop the concept of conservation (usually in this order: number, matter, length, area, weight, and volume).

During the concrete operational stage, children also develop the ability to isolate variables and are able to think in steps without relating each step to all the others. They begin to be aware of contradictions and will try to resolve them. However, concrete operational children cannot yet go beyond that which is empirically given and are able to deal only with ideas and thoughts that result from direct personal experience. The ability to *think* about one's own thought is not yet present.

Formal or Abstract Thought.   Typically, a child begins to develop the ability to think in abstract terms—beyond one's own personal experiences—around the

At the concrete operational stage, this child will know
whether the beakers contain the same quantities of juice.

age of 11 or 12. The thought processes begin to be markedly different from those of a concrete operational child. At the formal stage, the child can carry out *mental* experiences as well as actual ones.

The child can deal with the possible and is not satisfied with simply the empirical event given. Deductive reasoning—the ability to consider all possible combinations—and controlled experimentation are ably performed at this stage.

Behavioral View

Piaget's research examines the learning process from a developmental framework. It describes the mental processes or operations that enable a child to acquire knowledge.

Another approach taken by researchers interested in the learning process focuses on *external* factors rather than internal processes. These two views of the learning process are complementary, rather than contradictory. As a teacher,

At the formal stage, children experience mentally.

you must understand the internal factors that govern learning as well as the external techniques that you can use to enhance the acquisition, retention, retrieval, and transfer of knowledge.

The *behavioral view* of the learning process stresses a stimulus, response, reinforcement approach. Research in this area typically focuses on manipulating environmental factors (*stimuli*) to cause a specific observable *response,* which is *reinforced.* Behavioral researchers of the past include Ivan Pavlov, who is remembered for the salivation experiments with dogs (classical conditioning), and E. L. Thorndike, who concentrated on learning that occurs through trial and error (instrumental conditioning).

The most dominant of the behavioral researchers today is B. F. Skinner. Skinner tends to avoid the internal processes that Piaget suggests govern learning and concentrates instead on identifying optimal reinforcement contingencies to guide and direct children's learning. Research in this area provides teachers with many specific techniques that can be used to increase instructional effectiveness and that influence the quality of learning. (For more information, see the books by Skinner and by Fester and Skinner in the "Suggested Readings" at the end of the chapter.) Some of these techniques will be identified and discussed in later chapters.

Summary: The Nature of Learning

Teaching involves not only understanding the nature of the discipline, in this case science, but also understanding the nature of the learning process. We know that learning occurs in three areas, cognitive, psychomotor, and affective. Learning experiences in science must provide for growth and development in each of these areas. Piaget's research in the area of mental development provides teachers with information about the *internal* processes, or operations, that enable a child to acquire knowledge. His research has shown that these processes develop sequentially. Therefore, curricula and instructional decisions—what to teach, how to teach, when to teach—are directly influenced by a child's particular stage of development. *External* factors must also be considered in instructional decision making. B. F. Skinner and other behavioral researchers have identified external factors that affect the learning outcome and provide teachers with many specific techniques to increase instructional effectiveness.

Teachers cannot ignore the impact of the learning process on the learning outcome. The domains of learning, the internal processes that enable a child to acquire knowledge, and the external factors that affect learning outcome, all must be understood and utilized in making decisions about what to teach, how to teach, and when to teach.

THE NATURE OF THE CHILD

So far we have explored the nature of science and the nature of the learning process. We have established that these two are vital elements in instructional decision making. We must consider one other element: the nature of the child. Elementary school children, ages 6 to 12, are usually thought of as being in middle childhood. Physical growth continues at a steady rate. Motor abilities improve and skillful manipulations of equipment and materials increase. Cognitive abilities are expanding and reasoning becomes possible. Socially, the elementary school child begins to pull away from parental influence and seek peer group approval (Havighurst, 1972).

According to Piaget's stages of cognitive development, children tend to enter school using preoperational thought processes. By Grade 2, most will have developed concrete operational thinking skills. Therefore, information must be presented in a concrete form in order for them to take it in, deal with it, and understand it. For learning to be effective, elementary children need actual contact with materials. They need to have firsthand physical and visual contact with information, not merely to read about or listen to another's experiences.

Erik Erikson (1963) identified eight psychosocial stages that one passes through from infancy to late adulthood. At each stage there is some psychosocial crisis that must be resolved in a positive way for healthy personality development to take place. During the elementary school years the crisis involves industry versus inferiority. If children are to develop a sense of industry as opposed to feelings of inferiority, teachers must provide them with many opportunities to develop and refine skills needed for successful school experiences. The development of a positive concept of self and of a sense of productivity is crucial during this period.

Thus, the nature of the child, along with the nature of science and the nature of the learning process, must be considered a vital element in science instructional decision making. Science has four components—content, process, attitude, and technology—but the emphasis at the elementary school level is on the process of science. The process-inquiry skills are the tools of sciencing, and students employ them in gathering, organizing, analyzing, and evaluating science content. Research in the nature of learning and the nature of the child supports the need for process-oriented sciencing. As teachers, if we wish to help children learn to reason and develop their mental capacities, we must provide many opportunities for concrete experiences.

The activities that follow relate to specific process-inquiry skills designed to help you review your own competence in these areas. You might want to modify or adapt them for use with your students. Remember that children need many concrete experiences in which they use their senses individually and collectively in gathering information. These activities are designed to help you become more aware of the specific process skills and to use them in gathering, organizing, analyzing, and evaluating data.

These activities were designed to help mesh theory with practice by involving you with ideas, materials, and experiences that will help you acquire knowledge, skills, and attitudes necessary for achieving competence in sciencing.

ACTIVITY 1.1: INTERVIEWING

A. Interview some young children (ages 5 to 7). Ask them (1) "What is science?" (2) "What does a scientist do?" (3) "What would you do if you were studying science at school?" and (4) "Are you a scientist?" Record the conversation, and play it for the class. How do young children see science? How do you see science? What did you learn from this experience?

B. Interview several elementary teachers. Ask them to define their "philosophy of science." Ask them how much time they spend teaching science and what they generally do in science. Share your findings with others in the class. What did you learn from this experience?

☐ **Comments**

ACTIVITY 1.2: THE PROCESS-INQUIRY SKILLS

The first seven activities (1.2a–1.2g) in this section are designed to give you some appropriate practice in using the basic process skills of observing, classifying, measuring, using spatial relationships, communicating, predicting, and inferring. Activity 1.2h provides an opportunity to summarize and apply the insights of the seven activities. Activity 1.2i involves you with the integrated processes of defining operationally, formulating hypotheses, interpreting data, controlling variables, and experimenting. Since each of these skills was briefly defined early in this chapter, you may want to refer to that list of definitions while completing these activities to satisfactorily mesh the theory with the application. These activities are designed to be free of content so that the *process* becomes the focal point.

Activities 1.2a through 1.2f, dealing with the basic processes, may be completed in any order you choose. Activity 1.2g, inferring, should be completed *after* the observing activity. Activity 1.2i, which involves the integrated processes, should not be done until all of the first seven are completed. Your instructor should be available for feedback. You will be expected to maintain a continuing dialogue with the instructor as well as with your classmates. This constant interaction is essential for successfully attaining the specified skills.

Space is provided for recording your reactions, questions, and comments regarding the various activities. (If necessary, use additional paper.) This written record will provide valuable insights and lend structure to the many small group discussions included in this part.

Activity 1.2a: Observing

A. In this activity you are to select an object from those provided and to list at least 10 properties of the object that you can observe. Record your answers and reactions. You may work with a partner or small group in completing this activity.

The criteria presented in the following self-check can be used to evaluate the quality of observations.

☑ **Self-Check**

1. Review your list to see that it contains only those properties that can be directly observed. In other words, you must have *firsthand knowledge* of

all properties listed. For example, if you listed "it will float," you must have *directly* observed this. You must not use past experience. Cross out any properties listed that you did not directly observe.

2. Now check your list to see if you used all of your senses in making observations about your selected object. Most people tend to rely on sight. If you find your list heavily weighted toward visual observations, try using your other senses of hearing, touching, and smelling. You may omit tasting the object. Remember, even if the object makes no sound while stationary, that is an observation! Make additional observations and add them to your list.

3. Did you include an observation that required quantitative measurement? How long is it? How wide? How much does it weigh? Check over your list. If you find you did not include an observation based on quantitative measurement, please add one now.

4. Do your qualitative observations have a reference point? If you listed qualitative properties such as large, hard, or smooth, you need to give a reference point. Larger than what? Harder than what? Smoother than what?

5. Make sure that you have included at least one observation in which you acted on the object. Will it roll? Does it burn? Will it dissolve? If you did not, add that now.

6. Check over your revised list and make sure the properties listed are those that are unique to the object being observed. Could someone else identify the object by reading your list of observations? Make sure that the final list of observations is specific enough to identify the specific object being observed.

7. It should be clear to you now that there really is a difference between making observations and making good observations. You may wish to select another object and try listing your observations again now that you are more aware of the criteria for good observations. You are also encouraged to share your experience with your classmates and to exchange ideas and insights gained in this activity. Your instructor is also available to give help and feedback if you need it, or to offer encouragement and moral support.

B. The second part of this observing activity is designed to give you more practice in using your senses to gather information. Since people tend to rely so heavily on the sense of sight, other senses become less useful. In fact, many people find it very difficult to accurately describe an object without the benefit of seeing the object. Therefore, in the second part of this activity you are to select a container from those provided and list as many observations as you can (at least seven) about the object(s) *inside* the container. The container is opaque and is sealed, and you are not to look inside it or damage it in any way. Use your senses other than sight and the criteria from the self-check in making observations. *Remember to list only those properties that*

can be directly observed. Do not list inferences or conclusions.
Container selected:

Observations:

☑️ **Self-Check**

Make sure no observations are included that would require the use of your sense
of sight. You may not, for example, include an observation such as "the object in
the container is round." This observation would require you actually to see or
feel the object. Neither of these avenues is available to you since the object is
sealed in an opaque container. What you can observe are sounds made by the
object(s), the weight of the object(s) plus the container, and other observations
made using your senses of hearing, touching (through the barrier of the container), and smelling. Cross out any observations that do not meet the criteria,
and add any necessary additional observations. Compare your observations with
those of others, and jot down any problems, questions, or comments that you
want the instructor to explain or discuss.

☐ **Comments**

You may now wish to go directly to Activity 1.2g, which continues this activity by
asking you to make *inferences* about the object(s) inside the container.

Activity 1.2b: Classifying

A. In this activity you will select a container from those provided and separate
the contents into groups. You are to identify and label each group according
to the property you used to separate the groups.

These students are using their sense of hearing to make observations.

1. Separate the contents of the container you selected into two groups. Record the property used to make the separation in the following space.

2. Find another way to separate the contents of the container into two groups. Label the two new groups.

3. Take about 3 minutes and see how many different ways you can divide the contents of the box into two groups. Label each group.

✓ **Self-Check**

4. Check over your list to see that all the objects in the container fit into one of the groups in each set. But make sure that no *one* object could fit into both groups of one set. You might want to have a classmate check over your list while you check his or hers. Discuss any problems you are having, and ask your instructor for feedback.

5. Look over your sets of groups to see if you have any set that would allow the inclusion of additional objects not included in the set of objects provided for you. Put an asterisk beside any such set. If none of the sets of groups formed thus far would allow for any other objects to be included, then form two groups that *will* allow for the inclusion of an additional object. For example, if you have grouped objects on the basis of color, and if your groups are "red objects" and "black objects," then yellow objects will fit in neither group. By making your groups "red objects" and "non-red objects," you allow *any* object to fit into one of the groups. Use the following space to record your explanation of what you did.

B. Now that you have had some practice in grouping, or classifying, objects into two sets, try to separate the contents of the container into three groups. Make as many sets of three as you can and label them in the space below.

C. Compare your responses with those of your classmates. Use the same criteria given for the groups of two to evaluate the quality of your work.

1. If you were trying to help children develop the skill of classifying, what questions might you ask to encourage the learners to investigate the various properties that could be used in grouping the objects?

2. Jot down questions and comments for later discussion.

☐ **Comments**

Activity 1.2c: Measuring

This activity will involve you in the process of measuring. You will make linear measurements, liquid measurements, and mass/weight measurements. Work with a small group in completing this activity.

A. Linear Measurement

Select a nonstandard measuring device, identify it by some means, and have each group member measure the same object or distance in the classroom using the selected device. You may choose a device from those provided by your instructor or create your own. Body parts such as hands, feet, or arms make good measuring devices. Record your data.

Linear measurements can be made without a ruler.

1. Identify your measuring device.

2. Identify what was measured.

3. Identify the distance measured.

4. How does your measurement compare with those of the other members of your group?

☑ **Self-Check**

5. Is the recorded measurement consistent with the type of measuring device used? For example, if you selected a paper clip as the measuring

device, the object or distance measured should be recorded as so many paper clips in length.

6. Did everyone in the group use the same device for measuring? For example, if your group chose to use a hand as the measuring device, then the same hand must be used by all. Hands come in different sizes, as do other devices that might be used in measuring distances. It is very important that a standard be established so that measurement can be related.

B. Liquid Measurement

Select two containers from those provided. One should be much larger than the other. Identify each by some means and have each group member use the smaller container to determine the amount of liquid that the larger container holds. Record your data.

1. Identify your measuring device.

2. Identify what was measured.

3. Identify the amount measured.

4. How does your measurement compare with those of the other members of your group?

☑ **Self-Check**

5. Is the recorded measurement consistent with the type of measuring device used? For example, if you identified the measuring device as "a small orange juice can," then the amount recorded should be in so many small orange juice cans.

6. Did you establish a way to handle the problem of describing the amount measured when the measuring device was only partially filled? If not, do so now.

C. Mass/Weight Measurements

1. Select an object and measure its mass/weight using the equal-arm balance.

2. Place the object to be measured on one side of the balance and measure its mass/weight by placing paper clips on the other side until it balances. Record your data.

   a. Identify the object to be measured.

   b. What was the mass/weight of the object?

☑ **Self-Check**

3. Is the mass/weight of the object recorded so that it is clear that paper clips were the standard?

4. What other things could you use as a standard for measuring mass/weight?

5. Be ready to discuss the following with your small group when you have completed the three parts of this activity:

   a. How were you involved in the process of measuring?

   b. Can you explain this process?

   c. How important is it to identify a standard when making measurements?

Use the following space to record comments, questions, and conclusions that resulted from your discussion of this activity.

Using paper clips as a standard, these children compare
the mass/weight of various objects.

☐ **Comments**

Activity 1.2d: Spatial Relationships

A. In this activity, you will be working with four geometric shapes: squares,
rectangles, parallelograms, and triangles of different sizes.

   1. Using the set of seven shapes provided, select any two and produce a
third geometric shape (that is, either a square, rectangle, parallelogram,
or triangle). Draw the shape, indicating component shapes with dashed
lines.

2. Try some other combinations of two shapes to see the result. Draw your results.

3. This time, use four of the shapes to construct a square, rectangle, parallelogram, or triangle. Draw your results.

4. Try some other combinations of four shapes. Draw your results.

5. This part will be a little bit harder, but it *can* be done. In fact, there are several ways to do it. Take all seven shapes and construct either a square, rectangle, parallelogram, or triangle. Don't give up. Try to apply what you learned in the first two parts of this activity. If you have trouble, try making half of a rectangle or square, and then match the remaining shapes on top of these. The bottom part will give you a concrete picture of what you will need to form the entire rectangle or square. Then just slide the top pieces off and you should have the whole shape. Work on this first by yourself, then with another person or small group if you have trouble. Draw your completed shape in the following space and indicate the component shapes with dashed lines.

This child is learning that geometric shapes can be constructed from other geometric shapes.

B. Discuss any difficulties and frustrations with your classmates. Share your hints with a classmate who is having problems with this activity, but don't show how you did it! Record comments and questions for later discussion.

☐ **Comments**

Activity 1.2e: Communicating

This activity is designed to extend the skills acquired in the observing activity. If you have not completed Activity 1.1, do so before beginning this activity. *Communicating* in science refers to the skill of describing simple phenomena. A written or oral description of physical objects and systems and of the changes in

Learning how to describe what you see is important in science.

them is one of the most common ways of communicating in science. Constructing graphs and diagrams for observed results of experiments is another form of communicating.

A. Using the solid substance provided, describe it by listing at least 10 observations. *Remember the criteria for good observations.* Record your responses.

☑ **Self-Check**

1. Does your list include observations in which you used four of the five senses (excluding taste)?

2. Did you act upon the object?

3. Did you include an observation in which you gave some quantitative measurement?

B. Mix the substance with one of the liquids that are provided and observe. Describe as many physical changes as you observe.

☑ **Self-Check**

1. Did your observations include all of the criteria mentioned in the first part of this activity?
2. Did you include changes in the liquid as well as in the substance?

C. Describe any characteristic you observed that remained unchanged.

☑ **Self-Check**

1. Did you include the state of the liquid, its color, level, and temperature?
2. Compare your reactions with those of others and discuss the application of this skill for elementary children. Record any comments or questions.

☐ **Comments**

Activity 1.2f: Predicting

Making a prediction is very different from just guessing: predictions should be based upon selected data. Two types of predictions are possible using graphically presented data: (a) interpolation, within the data, and (b) extrapolation, beyond the data. In both types of predictions, data are gathered and recorded in graph form. A pattern should emerge and the prediction is made. The following activity is designed to help you engage in the process of predicting.

A. Equipment

Use the set of beakers provided. You will notice that they are labelled 1, 2, 3, and 4. A large candle, matches, and several smaller candles are also provided. Light the larger candle, and use it in lighting the smaller candles throughout the activity. This way you will conserve the number of matches you use.

B. Procedure

1. Using the lighted larger candle, light one of the smaller candles and place Beaker 1 over it. Record how long the candle will burn. Make three trials and obtain an average time. Record the data.

Measurements for Beaker 1

first trial	second trial	third trial	average

These students are gathering data to use in making a prediction.

2. Relight the smaller candle and place Beaker 3 over it. Be sure you use Beaker 3. Measure the burning time and record as for Beaker 1.

Measurements for Beaker 3

first trial	second trial	third trial	average

3. Use the following bar graph to record your data for Beakers 1 and 3. On the left side, the time is indicated so that each set of horizontal blocks represents a specific number of seconds. Space is provided at the top for you to continue the graph if necessary. The grid provides space for recording the burning time of the candle for each beaker in bar graph form. Notice that space is provided for both *predicted* and *actual* time for Beakers 2 and 4. You will be able to see the results better if you choose a different color for marking the predicted and actual times.

4. Using the data gathered thus far, *predict* the length of time the candle will burn under Beaker 2. Record this prediction below and on the graph. Tell how the data were used to make your prediction.

   a. Predicted time the candle will burn under Beaker 2.

   b. How were the data used to make your prediction?

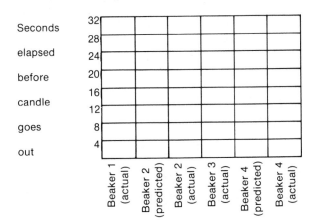

5. Light the smaller candle and record the actual time it takes for it to go out when Beaker 2 is placed over it. Make three trials and then average the results. Record the data below and on the graph.

Measurements for Beaker 2

first trial   second trial   third trial   average

6. Using the data gathered, predict the length of time the candle will burn under Beaker 4. Record your prediction below and on the graph.

   a. Predicted time the candle will burn under Beaker 4.

   b. How were the data used to make your predictions?

7. Light the smaller candle, and measure the actual time it takes for it to go out when Beaker 4 is placed over it. Record the data below and on the graph.

Measurements for Beaker 4

first trial   second trial   third trial   average

☑ **Self-Check**

Review your results. Are they recorded so that others could understand them? Check your predictions against the actual measured times. How close were they?

If there is more than 2 seconds' difference, how do you account for the discrepancy? What could you do to make your predictions more accurate? Record your response under comments.

☐ **Comments**

Activity 1.2g: Inferring

Inferences differ from observations. An inference is a conclusion or judgment based upon observations. It is arrived at *indirectly* rather than directly. For example, you see the sun shining on your car. You know that your car has been parked in the sun for 3 hours. You can feel that the air around you is very warm. You *infer* that the hood of your car will feel very warm to the touch. You have not experienced this directly as yet, but based upon your observations, you can infer that the hood will feel warm when you touch it. You can test this inference by actually touching the car.

In this activity, you will use the same sealed containers that are used in the observing activity. You will now make *inferences* about the object(s) inside the container. To help you become more aware of the process of observing, you will also list the properties *observed* that you used in making the inferences.

A. Select two of the sealed containers used in the second part of Activity 1.1 and make inferences about the object(s) concealed in the container. *Remember, inferences should be based upon the observations you make.* Record your inferences and observations.

    1. Container _____

      Observations   *Inferences*

These students are learning to make inferences from what they observe.

2. Container _____

Observations   *Inferences*

B. When you have completed the activity, open the sealed containers and check to see how accurate your inferences were.

☑ **Self-Check**

1. Were your inferences based on the observations you listed? If not, how did you determine the identity of the concealed objects?

2. If others read your list of observations, could they make the same inferences that you made about the objects' identity?

3. Compare your results with those of others, and discuss any problems or questions that arise. Record your comments or questions for later discussion.

☐ **Comments**

Activity 1.2h: Basic Skills Summary

The activities you have just completed were designed to give you some firsthand experiences with the basic process-inquiry skills. For the most part, the activities were void of content in order to help you see clearly the process involved. Science activities that you plan for children will probably include content as well as process. The two should be meshed so that elementary children not only understand the content of science, but also develop ease in using the process skills to investigate natural phenomena. You should examine science curricula materials carefully to see that process is included and that science is not merely memorizing facts and repeating them back on a test. Piaget tells us that children need firsthand experiences in which they use the process skills in order to advance from one developmental stage to the next and to reach the final stage of formal thought.

A. Examine some prepared activities from elementary textbooks. Select activities that involve children in observing a phenomenon and discovering certain concepts related to it. Find other activities that focus on discriminating likenesses and differences of objects and grouping them on the basis of the identified properties. Share these with the class.

B. Review the activities completed so far. Form a small group with your classmates and discuss these activities. Share your reactions with your instructor. If you feel that you have mastered the basic process-inquiry skills, you may do Activity 1.2i.

☐ **Comments**

Activity 1.2i: Experimenting

Elementary science activities should involve children in many types of investigations in which the process-inquiry skills are used in gathering, organizing, analyzing, and evaluating science content. At the early grades these activities tend to focus on *observational* investigations. The children use their senses to gather information about phenomena and discover the related concepts. *Classification* investigations—those that focus the child's attention on discriminating similarities and differences and on grouping objects on the basis of identified properties—are also used in the early grades.

In the middle and upper elementary grades, a heavier emphasis should be placed on *experimental* investigations. Experimental investigations involve children in designing and conducting an investigation in order to answer a question or solve a problem. In true experimenting, children must not already know for certain what the outcome of the investigation will be. There is always a *control* and a *variable*. The child must plan the strategy, identify the control(s) and the *one* variable that will be manipulated, then systematically investigate and record the results. A tentative conclusion is reached, based on the information gathered in the investigation.

Questions such as "Does the *temperature* of water affect the time it takes for a sugar cube to dissolve?" or "Does the *shape* of a piece of clay affect its ability to float?" provide the format for experimental investigations. These kinds of questions can be given to a small group of children who are then told to design and conduct an experiment (investigation) to find the answers. The general *format* for conducting such an investigation is found in this activity. The last activity is designed to involve you in the *process* of experimenting.

In this activity, you will use the necessary process-inquiry skills involved in designing and conducting an experiment to answer a selected question. The extent to which one is able to use the integrated processes (defining operationally, formulating hypotheses, interpreting data, controlling variables, experimenting) depends on one's stage of mental development. Many elementary children will not be able to utilize the integrated processes to a great extent. This does not mean that elementary children should not be provided with any opportunities to use the various integrated processes. It does mean that the teacher must be *selective* and *structure the experiences* so that elementary children work with *limited* variables and are given the opportunity to manipulate *concrete materials* in solving problems.

A. Select a question from those provided, and design and conduct an experiment to answer it. Decide on operational definitions, if any are needed, to clarify terms that will be used in answering the question. Use the space provided to record your plans for solving the problem. You may wish to work with a small group in completing this activity.

   1. Question or problem:

   2. Method or strategy to be used in answering question:

**Applying their new skills, these students conduct an
experiment.**

3. You need to construct a hypothesis (a tentative answer to your selected
   question, based upon previous knowledge and experiences) to be tested.
   State your hypothesis.

4. In designing the experiment, you must consider all variables that could
   affect the outcome or results. List all possible variables.

5. To conduct the experiment, you must manipulate only one variable at a time. The other variables must be controlled, or the outcome may be contaminated. Identify the one variable that you feel is most likely to cause the outcome you indicate in the hypothesis.

6. You must now design your experiment so that all the other variables are controlled. Record the data gathered in the experiment.

7. Review your data. Relate these data to your stated hypothesis. Are the data you gathered sufficient to answer the selected question? Is your hypothesis supported or not supported? If your data are not sufficient to answer your question, you must continue the experiment using the other possible variables. Remember to allow only one possible variable to vary at a time. You should also examine your hypothesis and reevaluate your design. If you have trouble with this, ask the instructor for help. If your data are sufficient to answer your question, you can make generalizations and conclusions based upon the gathered data. State your generalizations and conclusions.

8. Indicate what implications there might be for further experimentation.

B. Arrange to meet with your instructor for a brief presentation of your experiment. This presentation should include a description of the method or strategy used, hypothesis constructed, variables considered, variable manipulated, data gathered, and generalizations and conclusions reached. A demonstration involving the equipment and materials used in conducting the experiment should also be included.

☐ **Comments**

SUMMARY

In completing this chapter, you were involved with ideas, materials, and activities designed to help you acquire specific information and skills necessary for achieving competence in sciencing. The chapter provided you with insight into the nature of science, the nature of learning, and the nature of the child. The ideas and information presented in those areas should provide you with a rationale for the process-oriented science approach. As a teacher of elementary science, you must understand the relationships among these three areas in order to provide experiences that will enable children to be active participants in all types of science investigations.

You were confronted with these questions: What is science? What is sciencing? What science do I teach? To answer those questions, we examined science as content, process, attitude, and technology. All four of these components must be included in a sciencing program.

The emphasis at the elementary school is on the processes of science. The process-inquiry skills are the tools of sciencing. Elementary children are involved in learning experiences in which they use process-inquiry skills in gathering, organizing, analyzing, and evaluating science content. This process emphasis is

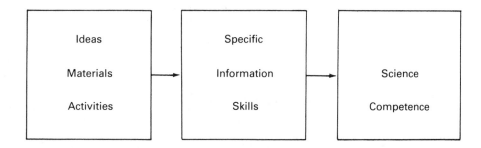

reflected in a change of name, from the noun *science* to the verb *sciencing.* Science is no longer defined as a body of knowledge but as what scientists *do.*

Sciencing is active, doing, investigating. It is direct involvement with science content. It involves acquiring the tools of scientific investigation—observing, classifying, measuring, using spatial relationships, communicating, predicting, inferring, defining operationally, formulating hypotheses, interpreting data, controlling variables, and experimenting. Sciencing is dynamic.

The nature of learning and the nature of the child are also essential elements for instructional decision making. Research in these areas supports the need for process-oriented sciencing. As teachers, if we wish to help children learn to reason and develop their mental capacities, we must provide many opportunities for concrete experiences. We must help the child develop a sense of industry, productivity, and self-confidence. A sciencing approach provides those kinds of experiences.

As you review this chapter, look over the questions and comments you recorded after the various activities. You may wish to get together with a small group of your classmates and discuss your reactions. If you have specific questions, share them with your group. Together you might be able to answer them.

REFERENCES

Erikson, E. H. (1963). *Childhood and Society.* New York: W. W. Norton.

Furth, H. G. (1970). *Piaget for Teachers.* Englewood Cliffs, NJ: Prentice-Hall.

Havighurst, R. J. (1972). *Developmental tasks and education* (3rd ed.). New York: David McKay Co.

Inhelder, B., & Piaget, J. (1964). *The early growth of logic in the child.* New York: Harper & Row Publishers.

SUGGESTED READINGS

Anderson, R. D. (1983). Are yesterday's goals adequate for tomorrow? *Science Education, 67*(2), 171–176.

Bloom, B. S., Hastings, T., & Madaus, G. F. (1971). *Handbook on formative and summative evaluation of student learning.* New York: McGraw-Hill.

Carin, A., & Sund, R. (1989). *Teaching science through discovery* (6th ed.). Columbus, OH: Merrill Publishing Co.

Esler, W. K. (1972). Putting it all together—Inquiry process, science concepts, and the textbook. *Science Education, 57*(1), 19–23.

Fester, C., & Skinner, B. F. (1957). *Schedules of reinforcement.* New York: Appleton-Century-Crofts.

Gega, P. C. (1977). *Science in elementary education* (3rd ed.). New York: John Wiley & Sons.

George, K. D. (1974). Chapters 1 & 2. In *Elementary school science: Why and how.* Lexington, MA: D. C. Heath & Co.

Harrow, A. J. (1964). *A taxonomy of the psychomotor domain.* New York: Longman.

Koballa, T. R., Jr., & Rice, D. R. (1985). Six strategies for improving attitudes toward science. *Science and Children, 22*(7), 32–34.

Krathwohl, D. R., Bloom, B. S., & Masia, B. B. (1964). *Taxonomy of educational objectives, Handbook II: Affective domain.* New York: David McKay Co.

Labinowisz, E. P. (1980). *The Piaget primer.* Menlo Park, CA: Addison-Wesley Publishing Co.

McAnarvey, H. (1972). What is the place of product and process in the development of generalizations in elementary school science? *Science Education, 56*(1), 85–88.

National Science Foundation. (1981). *Annual science and technology report to the Congress, 1980.* Washington, DC: U.S. Government Printing Office.

Piltz, A., & Sund, R. (1974). *Creative teaching of science in the elementary school* (2nd ed.). Boston: Allyn and Bacon.

Reeder, W., & Adams, B. (1977). Selection of an elementary science program: Process and criteria. *Science and Children, 14*(8), 8–10.

NSTA-CBC Joint Committee. (1982). Outstanding science trade books for children in 1981. *Science and Children, 19*(6), 47–50.

Simon, S. (1982). Using science trade books in the classroom. *Science and Children, 19*(6), 5–6.

Skinner, B. F. (1968). *The technology of teaching.* New York: Appleton-Century-Crofts.

Sund, R. B., & Bybee, R. W. (1973). *Becoming a better elementary science teacher: A reader.* Columbus, OH: Merrill Publishing Co.

Yager, R. E., & Penick, J. E. (1984). Science at work in the real world. *Educational Leadership, 42*(1), 93.

CHAPTER 2

Laboratory Approach to Elementary Science

Goal

After completing this chapter, you will demonstrate competence in the identification and use of equipment and curriculum materials that could be useful in a laboratory approach to elementary science.

Objectives

In completing this chapter, you will do the following:

1. Identify and describe the *Elementary Science Study* (ESS), *Science Curriculum Improvement Study* (SCIS) and its revisions *SCIIS* and SCIS II, and *Science . . . A Process Approach II* (SAPA II) as laboratory science programs.

2. Identify and describe the teaching strategy of ESS, SCIS and its revisions *SCIIS* and SCIS II, and SAPA II.

3. Identify and describe the role of the teacher and the role of the student in the laboratory approach to elementary science.

INTRODUCTION

Over the years, much effort has been directed toward making science more relevant to students and their environment and toward helping teachers do a better job of teaching science. Millions of dollars have been invested in science curriculum projects by governmental agencies, private corporations, and local schools. Two types of elementary teaching programs have evolved: the textbook approach and the laboratory approach. Each will be discussed in this chapter, but the emphasis here will be on the laboratory approach, represented by three of the better known commercial kits. The textbook approach is examined separately in Chapter 3.

TEXTBOOK APPROACH

The textbook was the "first generation" or traditional content approach to teaching science. The laboratory approach became the "second generation" of science education. Using the concept of *doing* science rather than only reading about it, textbooks have evolved into a "third generation" and are presently the most widely used teaching program. Current textbooks serve as a curriculum guide, reader, and resource. Hands-on science activities and the teaching of process skills are stressed. Unfortunately, many of these textbooks really do not do process science, but are traditional textbooks in disguise. Science activity kits are available for almost all of the major texts. These kits supply most of the necessary materials and equipment to perform the suggested activities. A listing of current textbook series will be found in the activities section of Chapter 3.

LABORATORY APPROACH

The laboratory approach, or "second generation," is based on a kit that usually contains almost all of the materials needed to teach the program, including an instructor's manual. Typically, very few reading materials are provided for the student. Science process, or "how to do science," is stressed. The child learns by doing, not by reading about science. Examples of this approach are ESS, SCIS (and its revisions SCIIS and SCIS II), and SAPA II.

Many programs have been developed over the years, some of which have been very successful. Almost all of them have been a variation of the original laboratory programs, stressing hands-on sciencing. Project AIM has developed a series of science activities that can be used in conjunction with an existing program or used alone. The present emphasis on science is sure to produce other new programs that will find their way into the classroom and will incorporate all of the new knowledge we have about how children learn. This chapter and the one that follows introduce you to the laboratory approach and to the textbook approach. Sample activities from the programs will enable you to obtain a hands-on understanding of the materials used and the methodology employed.

In this chapter you will be actively involved in examining, analyzing, and evaluating three of the better known commercial kits:

1. *Elementary Science Study* (ESS)
2. *Science Curriculum Improvement Study* (SCIS, SCIIS, and SCIS II)
3. *Science . . . A Process Approach II* (SAPA II)

It is important to study these specific kits even though you may not have them available where you teach and much of the material is no longer commercially available. There are several reasons. First, ESS, SCIS, and SAPA are historically important in the field of education. They resulted from the desire of science educators to break away from traditional methods of teaching elementary science. The programs incorporated the most current information in child development and learning theories and thus contain unique ideas and teaching strategies. These ideas and strategies are what you will learn from the programs and adapt to your own teaching. You may also be able to adapt a number of the activities from the programs to your classroom. Moreover, since most ESS, SCIS, and SAPA materials are now in the public domain, they are incorporated into various new publications, textbooks, and science programs available to the public schools. Thus, you will see these materials repeatedly employed outside their original kits.

As you review the three laboratory approaches to science, you will find that they are quite different from each other. At the same time, you will recognize common bonds that produce similarities. The similarities and differences will become apparent as you examine the programs.

This chapter introduces you to the nature and structure of the laboratory approach in general and how it applies to the three representative programs— ESS, SCIS, and SAPA II. A short overview of each program is also presented. A more detailed presentation of the three programs can be found in Appendix A. Generally, though, you will learn about the laboratory approach and about the three specific programs by engaging in the activities provided in this chapter.

You are now ready to learn about the laboratory approach. As you go through the programs, notice how they are alike and how they are different. Mentally compare what each has to offer the classroom teacher and, perhaps more important, what each has to offer the students. In working through Chapter 2, you will follow a sequence of four steps:

1. Read the background information. This will help you become familiar with the concept of the laboratory approach. Remember, read everything before starting anything.

2. Review the teacher's manual or guide from each program, which may be obtained from your instructor. This is the first step in getting your hands on the actual material used by a particular program. The guides will give you insights not available in the background readings. Do not try to see how many you can look at or how fast you can look at them. A small number of manuals seriously reviewed will be much more beneficial.

3. You will actually do some of the activities found in the program under consideration. The activities have been selected as samples of the types found in the programs and how they are used. They have been modified somewhat to make them appropriate for your use and for use in a shorter time span, but they still reflect the teaching strategy of the program from which they came. Your hands-on involvement in the actual teaching materials should add to your insight into the program.

4. You will be involved in self-checking and instructor feedback throughout. At various stages, the chapter presents self-check questions and suggestions to help you judge your progress. The instructor will also be available to answer your questions or to direct you to new lines of thought as you look into the programs.

As you go through these steps, you must look for some specific information:

1. What is the basic teaching strategy, and how can you adapt this strategy to your teaching style?
2. What kinds of concrete materials are used in the activities? Where would you obtain similar materials for your classroom?
3. What do you think of each program as a whole? Would you like to teach that program? Why or why not?
4. How could you adapt some of the activities to your classroom? Pick one activity, and show how you would use it.
5. Chapter 1 heavily emphasizes the process skills and sciencing. Find evidence of these concepts in the three programs you are reviewing. What implications do these ideas have for your personal teaching strategy?

If you seriously look for answers to these questions while you are doing this chapter, you will learn much more than just the names of some science programs. You will learn new ways to teach science to elementary children. As you go through this chapter, you will be involved in some individual, some group, and some individual-group-instructor activities. Each type of activity should help you learn and reinforce what you learn. Do not try to do the entire chapter alone. Feedback and interaction are very important. Remember to read the background material before you start an activity and to read the directions before you try to answer the questions.

History

You can best understand the concept of the laboratory approach to teaching elementary science if you look at the way it developed. Prior to the late 1950s, science generally was not taught in the elementary school. Science, if taught at all, was usually some form of nature study. The textbooks that did exist were usually science readers that described Jack and Sue's visit to the zoo and what they saw, or described a particular experiment and its result. Clearly, not much student involvement took place in the science program.

In 1957, an event destined to change American education occurred: the Soviet Union launched Sputnik—the world's first artificial satellite. The immediate reaction of the United States was to question our science programs from kindergarten to college. We found that most science programs, especially elementary programs, were inadequate, that most teachers did not have much science background, and that textbooks were obsolete.

The National Science Foundation (NSF) was established by the federal government to provide financial help for science projects and to improve science education. Ideas and projects designed to improve science in the elementary school were advanced by many sources. Individuals, public school systems, universities, private companies, and scientific organizations were funded to develop programs. Some were successful; a great number were not. Three programs—*Elementary Science Study* by the Education Development Center, *Science Curriculum Improvement Study* by Robert Karplus, and *Science . . . A Process Approach* by the American Association for the Advancement of Science—emerged as the most successful. It is interesting to note that of these programs, one—ESS—was developed by a private company; another—SCIS— by a private individual working with a local school system; and the third—SAPA— by a scientific organization.

At about this same time, Jean Piaget, and soon after, Jerome Bruner, Celia Stendler, Robert Gagné, and other psychologists published work indicating that children in elementary school learn best by manipulating concrete objects. This became the basis for the laboratory approach and is reflected in all three of the major programs discussed in this chapter.

The National Science Foundation recognized that even the best science program is of little value if it is not available to the public. Consequently, NSF invited private publishing companies to bid for the rights to market many of the science programs. The company would publish, promote, and market the program. In return, the company would be given exclusive marketing rights for a predetermined period of time, after which the programs would be in the public domain. Of the elementary programs funded by NSF, three—ESS, SCIS, and SAPA—were accepted for major commercial publication.

Upon expiration of the exclusive marketing period, publishers developed revised programs to protect their investments. SAPA gave way to SAPA II, and SCIS became *SCIIS* and SCIS II. ESS underwent no major revision. None of the original publishers involved continue to publish the materials. ESS,

SAPA II, *SCIIS,* and SCIS II materials are now supplied exclusively by Delta Education.

Today, the laboratory approach is not as widely used as before, but its influence on elementary science programs has been great. Most science programs are no longer restricted to nature study or read-about science. New textbooks have been developed that, borrowing from the work of the 1960s, encourage student involvement with hands-on experiments and activities. Even though many teachers never used ESS, SCIS, or SAPA, they do use the concepts and teaching strategies found in the programs.

Definition of the Laboratory Approach

The laboratory approach is a hands-on, learn-by-doing approach to science. Students are given or are asked to develop a problem to be solved; then they attempt to solve it. There may be very little structure, as in ESS, or a lot of structure, as in SAPA, but the student learns by actually doing activities or experiments to solve the problem. The teacher directs the experience. The concrete experience is the focal point of the laboratory approach.

Common Characteristics

Several common characteristics become apparent upon examination of the three programs. First, although three distinct approaches to teaching elementary science emerge, one goal is common to all three: children should learn how to *do* science, not merely memorize subject matter. The science processes are stressed as a way to accomplish this goal. The underlying assumption for these programs is that we all—children and adults—use science daily, whether we know it or not, and we should be prepared to meet any problem we encounter.

A second common characteristic is the use of a hands-on approach to teaching and learning science. Piaget and other psychologists indicated that children in elementary school learn best by manipulating concrete objects. All three programs, therefore, try to get materials into the hands of children as much as possible for concrete experiences and reinforcement. Involvement with materials allows children to be partners in the learning process by actually doing what scientists do.

Many children have reading problems that penalize them in all of their school work. They cannot read the materials; therefore, they cannot do the work. This problem is minimized in a hands-on, laboratory approach. Children who cannot read can participate in almost all of the activities. They learn by doing rather than by reading. Success in science might encourage some of the slower readers to want to become better readers so that they might supplement what they are learning.

The three programs are also physically similar; they are all kit programs, each consisting of a teacher's guide and materials to be used by the students. Usually a kit provides everything necessary to teach the lesson, except common classroom supplies. Consumable items may be replaced by purchasing refill kits provided by the publisher or by purchasing replacement items locally.

Teaching Strategy

Probably the most important difference between traditional science programs and the laboratory programs is the teaching strategy employed. Each project developed a unique teaching strategy, but they all shared one characteristic. The roles of the teacher and student changed. The teacher became a guide and resource rather than a dispenser of knowledge. The student became an active participant instead of a passive receptor in the learning process.

The lesson or activity is usually initiated through a discussion, demonstration, or question. Students then develop problems and design solutions. The teacher raises questions but does not answer them. He may verify answers or ask leading questions to provoke thought or to challenge data and solutions, but he is always trying to get students to think and to understand what they are thinking about. A major problem, however, is that many teachers do not know how to teach this way. They must be retrained to teach the laboratory programs properly. More than one of these programs have failed because a teacher did not know how to use it. Preservice and inservice workshops, which may vary in format or length, are recommended for all three programs. When the teacher knows his or her role, the students can perform accordingly.

Students also have a new role. They are actively involved in the learning process, assuming responsibility for what they learn and how they learn it. What is learned depends on what the student does, not on reading material or the teacher's lectures. Students are expected to raise questions, then devise methods of answering them. They develop experiments, collect data, and interpret their findings. Most importantly, they can determine the depth and direction of their efforts. General instructions are suggested by the teacher's guide, and the teacher directs the investigations, but the curiosity and ability of the students ultimately determine what is done in each unit or lesson. Teacher flexibility allows curious students to explore any of the many problems that arise during the course of the unit. The students' active participation makes them partners in the learning situation on a level of involvement equal to that of their teachers. They become part of the teaching-learning team.

Each of the programs follows a specific teaching strategy that differentiates it from the others. ESS follows a four-step tactic.

1. **Discussion:** An opening discussion about a topic or phenomenon arouses curiosity and raises questions. This discussion may either be student- or teacher-directed.

2. **Speculation:** Students begin to wonder about the problem and to speculate on possible solutions. Hypotheses are formulated and examined in open discussion or in the child's mind.

3. **Experimentation:** Experiments are devised and carried out to give the student a hands-on involvement in answering the question.

4. **Application:** The knowledge gained is reinforced by being applied to new situations.

SCIS uses a three-step strategy.

1. **Exploration:** The teacher places material in the hands of the students to arouse their curiosity and allow them to find out what they can do with the materials. Students learn through their own spontaneous activities and experiments.

2. **Invention:** This is the structured teaching phase of the learning cycle. The teacher brings the students together to discuss their explorations and "invent" the concepts that are being taught.

3. **Discovery:** Students "discover" new applications, usually in a variety of situations, for the concepts they have just invented.

SAPA uses a very structured three-step strategy, following specific directions in the teacher's guide.

1. **Introduction:** The teacher introduces the concept through a discussion or demonstration.

2. **Activities:** The students do the activities described in the teacher's guide following the teacher's instructions.

3. **Appraisal and Evaluation:** A group activity determines if the students have acquired the behaviors expected of them. Test items are provided that can be administered to individual students for further evaluation of progress.

As you review some of the teacher's guides, be sure to look for examples of these teaching strategies. Also, remember to look at the role of the teacher and of the student.

Evaluation of the Laboratory Approach

The laboratory approach is not a traditional content-oriented program and cannot be evaluated as such. Evaluation is very important in all three programs, and appropriate techniques have been devised. In general, two types of evaluation have emerged. First, and most widely used by ESS and SCIS, is an ongoing, informal evaluation. Constant feedback allows the teacher to judge the students' progress and, even more importantly, to determine the students' needs. This forms the basis for the teacher's participation in the teaching-learning experience. She knows what the students are doing and what input to provide to ensure maximum performance from each student. This might be called the "honest appraisal" approach. The teacher does not rely on a test score. Rather, she may obtain feedback from the observations of a student's behavior, work habits, attitudes, and classroom participation. Written work on lab sheets or in the student's manual can also provide clues for the teacher, as can the student's response to the teacher's questions. This is a very subjective method of evaluation, but if the teacher is conscientious, it probably is the most accurate and most helpful. The effects of these programs may be long-term, showing up later in the child's development.

The second method of evaluation used in the laboratory approach is to assess the accomplishment of behavioral objectives. This method forms the basis of the SAPA competence appraisal. ESS and SCIS also have established objectives as well as teacher-formulated objectives that lend themselves to this type of evaluation. Checklists that can be marked "achieved" or "not achieved" help the teacher keep track of students' accomplishments and needs.

Evaluation in the laboratory approach is more than determining a grade for a report card. It is a teaching device. In evaluating progress, the teacher must use every means available to learn as much about each child as possible. Tests are helpful, but so are checklists, classroom observations, written work, parent conferences, student conferences, question-answer sessions, and observation of classroom participation and behavioral changes. Evaluation is an honest effort to find out what a child knows or can do, so that a teacher can prescribe new learning experiences to further the child's education.

SPECIFIC PROGRAMS

You have been reading about the three programs that are the most common examples of the laboratory approach—ESS, SCIS, and SAPA II. This section provides an overview of each program. If you wish to obtain more detailed information about any or all of these programs, please refer to Appendix A. You will also learn more about each specific program by doing the activities in this chapter.

Elementary Science Study (ESS)

The *Elementary Science Study* (ESS) program was developed by Education Development Center and published by the Webster Division of McGraw-Hill. Work on ESS began in and continued through the 1960s and 1970s. There has been continual internal revision of the program but no major supplementing revision. The original publisher no longer produces the materials, but Delta Education supplies some kits and materials for the program.

ESS is a modular program that can be tailored to fit any school requirements. There were approximately 56 units available (the number changed as revisions were effected), a variety of topics being found under four headings: Earth Science, Physical Science, Biological Science, and Mathematics. A complete list of these units can be found in Appendix A. Schools select appropriate units (usually five or six) for each grade level to form a science program. Individual units can be used with existing programs if a school does not want to use the entire program. Topics for units are derived from common experiences, as illustrated by unit titles such as *Balancing, Animal Tracks,* and *Kitchen Physics.* ESS is a nonstructured program, allowing the teacher to guide the direction and depth of each unit. The units may be easily adapted to different grade levels as well as different student abilities. ESS has also developed the *ESS/Special Education Teacher's Guide* (Ball, 1978), consisting of specially selected and adapted units appropriate for children with learning difficulties, especially the educable mentally retarded (EMR).

ESS kits can be simple or complex, expensive or inexpensive, depending on your choice of units. Generally there is a teacher's guide and a kit containing the materials needed to teach the unit. Some kits, such as *Bones* and *Batteries and Bulbs,* are very complete, requiring nothing more than what is furnished. Other kits, such as *Animal Tracks,* supply very little material. Nonconsumable materials or hard-to-find materials are usually supplied, whereas "supermarket items" are not supplied. This is not always true, however, but depends on the unit. Consumable materials can usually be purchased as a replacement kit from the publisher.

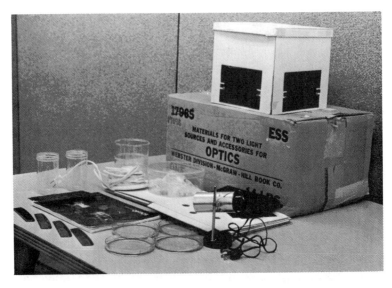

Basic equipment for the ESS *Optics* activity.

Science Curriculum
Improvement Study (SCIS)

In 1962 Robert Karplus obtained an NSF grant to develop an elementary science program and formed the team that produced the *Science Curriculum Improvement Study* (SCIS) program. Rand McNally became the publisher and distributor of the completed version. In 1978, two revisions of SCIS were introduced. *SCIIS* was written by members of the original writing team and marketed by Rand McNally. SCIS II was written by a team who had worked primarily in the field-testing and implementing stage of the original program; it was marketed by American Science and Engineering (AS&E). Only minor changes can be found in either of the two revisions. In 1982 Rand McNally and AS&E stopped producing SCIS, *SCIIS,* and SCIS II materials and turned over publication and distribution rights to Delta Education.

The SCIS program (and each of its revisions) is a sequential program for Grades 1 through 6; a kindergarten program is also available. The goal of the SCIS program is *scientific literacy,* which is defined as a functional understanding of scientific concepts. The teacher uses the strategy of *exploration-invention-discovery* to develop scientific literacy. Two units per grade level, one on life science and one on physical science, are taught, with emphasis placed on the concept of interaction. A listing and description of these units can be found in Appendix A. Students are encouraged to learn through experimentation and to maintain their curiosity. There is very little material to be read by the students, but supplemental reading is encouraged. Teachers are urged to use convergent (factually oriented) and divergent (theoretical) questions to create curiosity and give direction to the students' experimentation as well as to obtain feedback for evaluation.

SCIS kits supply almost everything needed to teach the units. Living organisms are supplied, but they must be ordered as they are needed. Refill kits are available to replenish consumable materials and to facilitate sharing of kits by teachers of the same grade level. Sharing kits can effectively reduce costs. Most of the items found in the SCIS kit are common items that are easily found around the home.

Science . . . A Process
Approach II (SAPA II)

In 1961 the American Association for the Advancement of Science (AAAS) formed a commission to determine the best way to teach science to school-age children. After two years of research and development, the commission recommended a process-oriented curriculum for Grades K through 12. The National Science Foundation then funded a trial program, but only for kindergarten through sixth grade. Six years later, after writing, testing, and rewriting, *Science . . . A Process*

Approach (SAPA) was ready to market. The need for revision became apparent after several years of use, resulting in the development of SAPA II. The revision centered around the format of the teacher's guide and teaching flexibility. Ginn and Company was the publisher of SAPA and SAPA II until 1981, when Delta Education became the exclusive manufacturer and supplier of all SAPA II materials. The old SAPA program is no longer commercially available.

SAPA II is a sequential, K-through-six program, with 15 modules (or units) for each grade level. A list of these modules can be found in Appendix A. SAPA II does not use subject matter as its base, but uses the science processes as the basis for the program, with subject matter, or content, introduced as needed. The assumption is that if elementary children can learn the processes, they can understand and use the content. For a listing of these processes, see Appendix A.

A module can be described as a unit of work involving a specific phase of a specific scientific process. The specific process taught may be any one of the eight basic skills or five integrated processes. Each module is designed to achieve specific objectives that are listed at the beginning of the teacher's guide, along with a rationale, list of materials, vocabulary, activities, and evaluation procedure. The teacher needs only to follow the instructional procedure outlined in the teacher's guide to teach SAPA II, but he may supplement the activities if he chooses. The students learn the processes by actual experience followed by discussion of their experiences. Peer teaching is also encouraged by having students help each other with the activities. There are optional activities for the faster students who want to extend their understanding. At the end of each module is an appraisal activity and a competency measure that the teacher uses to determine if the objectives were reached.

Various SAPA II instruction booklets.

SAPA II kits contain most of the materials necessary to teach the modules. Usually all of the laboratory equipment—such as balances, containers, and chemicals—are supplied, but living organisms, perishable materials, and common classroom items are not. Printed materials—such as pictures, charts, transparencies, and spirit duplicator masters—are also included as part of a kit. Replacement kits for expended materials are available.

Summary of ESS, SCIS, SAPA

The laboratory approach is designed to teach science using hands-on activities rather than reading material. Three programs—*Elementary Science Study* (ESS), *Science Curriculum Improvement Study* (SCIS), and *Science . . . A Process Approach* (SAPA)—and their revisions were developed using this concept. Each program consists of a kit containing a teacher's guide and the materials necessary for the activities. Very little reading material is supplied for the students because learning occurs as students do activities to solve problems. The teacher assumes the role of guide and resource person, and the student becomes an active participant in the learning process. Although the programs are not as widely used now as they were in past years, the teaching strategy and the hands-on concept are well worth knowing and should be incorporated into all science programs.

Before you begin these activities, be sure that you have read the background information for the laboratory approach. You may want to refer to the background information found in Appendix A. You should now have some understanding of the approach. In keeping with the philosophy of learning by doing, you are going to be directly involved with some of the materials used in ESS, SCIS, and SAPA II programs.

The first step will be to review some of the teacher's guides. See your instructor for directions in obtaining these. You can get the feel of the programs by reading through the same material that the teacher would in preparing to

These preservice teachers are familiarizing themselves with the ESS activities.

teach. What you have read about the program can be compared with the real materials. Remember, the background information serves as a guide and provides additional information; refer to it as you go through these activities. After you have reviewed several guides from each program, you will do some representative activities. These will give you the opportunity to see what kinds of materials and activities can be used. Keep in mind that soon you will be teaching; be alert to any ideas or activity you could use in your own classroom. Think about what you see and do and how these experiences can help you be a better teacher.

As you go through these activities, remember that the content is not as important as how it is being used. Look at the material from the student's point of view as well as from the teacher's. Be sure to discuss your thoughts with your group and with your instructor. You are responsible for what you learn in this module; the instructor will act as a guide and resource person.

ACTIVITY 2.1: REVIEW OF ESS, SCIS, AND SAPA II TEACHER'S GUIDES

A. The teacher's guide is the key to all of the laboratory programs. It gives information about the program, materials needed, and ideas for teaching. Your objectives in reviewing some of the guides are

1. To familiarize yourself with the guides
2. To understand better how the programs are structured
3. To understand better the teaching strategy used by reading the suggestions for teachers found in the guides
4. To get ideas from the examples in the guides about how you can use everyday materials to teach children how to do science

Try to keep these purposes in mind as you go through the teacher's guides. Obtain several guides to review. You should review one program at a time to avoid confusion, but later you may want to compare them. Try to select guides that will give you a good cross section of the program. Your instructor might want to set a minimum number of guides from each program to be reviewed, but you should review several for a more complete understanding of the program.

Review the guides alone or in small groups. If you review alone, plan to meet with your group for information sharing. Do not underestimate the value of group interaction, either as a student involved in it or as a teacher using it as a teaching device.

B. Now that you have made your choice of guides to review, note the title, subject area, and grade level of each before you start. As you read through them, look for the following information:

Teacher's guides for SCIS

1. How is the information in the guide organized? Compare several guides. Are all of them organized in the same manner? What type of information is available to the teacher? Is the information adequate to help you teach the module or unit?

2. Find the activities. Are they written as you expected them to be? How are they taught? Look for examples of student discovery. How are the students involved in the act of discovery? How could you adapt any of these activities to your classroom?

3. Look at the types of materials used. Could you find the necessary materials if you wanted to teach any part or all of the module?

4. What is the teacher's role? Does the manual describe it? Can you find evidence of the teacher's acting as a guide or a resource person? See if you can determine the student's role.

5. Find suggested methods of evaluation. Are they what you expected? What is the teacher really trying to find out in an evaluation? How could you use this type of evaluation technique in your classroom?

6. What is the module really trying to teach? Look beyond the title and try to determine the real science skills being taught. Are the science processes (observing, classifying, etc.) taught in the module?

7. Look closely for any information you can use to help you become a better teacher. Think about how you could adapt some of the ideas, suggestions, and activities to your classroom. Remember, one purpose of this exercise is to familiarize you with the ESS, SCIS, and SAPA II programs, but the

most important purpose is to give you the opportunity to improve your teaching repertoire.

C. You have looked at some ESS, SCIS, and SAPA II guides and should have some interesting comments to make. Here is the place to do it. Write down your thoughts. These comments should be for your own benefit, not necessarily for your instructor's, so say what you think. Remember, you are not expected to like every program you review. All programs have strengths and weaknesses; look for them.

D. Meet with your group to discuss the guides reviewed. You might want to invite your instructor to participate in the discussion. Share the ideas you have obtained and the concerns that you may have about the programs. If you have any questions, bring them up for discussion. Make some notes on your discussion.

☐ **Comments**

☑ **Self-Check**

Did you review several guides or only one? Each guide is different, and one guide cannot give you a true overall picture of the program. How well did you look at the guides? Skimming doesn't really help a lot. Did the guides help you understand how the teacher presents the material? Would it be difficult to obtain materials to teach some of the activities? It should not be, because almost all of the materials can be found around the school or community. Some materials are specialized and would require a special purchase. What ideas can you take with you? How would you like to teach one of these programs?

☐ **Comments**

Summary of Activity 2.1

In this activity you have reviewed some ESS, SCIS, and SAPA ll teacher's guides to help you better understand the laboratory approach to science instruction. The types of activities used, the kinds of materials used, the teaching strategies, and the student's role were examined. The objectives of this activity were to help you understand how the laboratory approach is taught and to develop new insight into your own concept of teaching science.

ACTIVITY 2.2: ACTIVITIES FOR ESS

Here are four activities taken from ESS material, one from each of the different subject areas. Do at least two of them. (Your instructor may choose to tell you how many to do or may do them with your class in an ESS-simulated lesson.)

Group interaction is important in doing ESS units.

These activities were selected because they provide interesting involvement using simple, easy-to-obtain materials.

In general, each activity represents the type of activities found in its subject area. Because of the individual nature of the modules, no activity can completely represent all of the other ESS activities. However, these activities will help you understand what the student does in the ESS science class. The activities are not taken directly from the program but are composites of several activities found in the teacher's guides. They have been modified to be appropriate for your needs and limited time.

Select the activities you are going to do by looking at all of them before choosing. Your group might want to decide on the approach you will take to complete these activities, whether you will work on them as a group or subdivide the work. Do not do them individually because you will miss out on the group interaction that is stressed in ESS activities. Furthermore, do not be afraid to extend the activities beyond what is required. If you think of something interesting, try it. If a "what-would-happen-if" situation occurs, find out. That is what ESS is all about.

As you go through the activities, think about what you read in the background information and in the teacher's guides. Combine the three elements to give yourself an understanding of the program and the philosophy behind it. Think about how a child might react to what you are doing. How would you present the same activity to an elementary student? And, most important, actually do the activities. You will miss out on the fun and the learning experience if you do not get your hands on the materials.

Activity 2.2a:
Biological Science—Mealworms[1]

This activity is a modification of the upper-grade unit *Behavior of Mealworms.* The most important thing a child can learn from this unit is how to carry out an investigation. See how well-developed your investigative skills are. As you do the structured activities, think of other investigations you would like to make. How would you set up the investigation, and what would you look for?

A. In this activity you will become familiar with mealworms. Mealworms are the larval stage of the grain beetle (*Tenebrio molitor*) usually found around flour mills or in grain warehouses and feed stores. They are commonly used as fishing bait. (This should give you a clue as to where to obtain a supply if you wish to use this activity with a class at a later date.) Locate the container of mealworms provided, and you will be ready to start.

Ode to a Mealworm

by Lora Fleming, Park School, Brookline, Mass.

Pity the poor mealworm
He is not an ideal
worm
In fact, he's not a real
worm
But a bug.
Ugh
And when he sought the bran
He couldn't escape my scan
No matter how hard he ran,
What a bug,
Ugh^2

B. Mealworms and Their Habitat

    1. Observe the mealworms in their natural habitat. Describe their habitat.

    2. Where do mealworms seem to prefer to stay?

    3. Find an example of each of the three stages of development. Identify and sketch each.

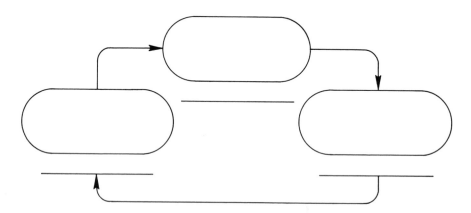

C. Structure of Mealworms

    1. Examine the structure of two or three mealworms. Hand lenses are available. Do not do anything that might injure the mealworms. Describe the structure of a mealworm; then draw a picture.

D. Learning About Mealworms

    1. Investigate at least two of the following questions. Keep in mind that a mealworm has chemical reactors over its entire body and putting a drop of irritating liquid on a mealworm is somewhat like having it poured into

**Many interesting observations can be made about
mealworms by using a hand lens.**

your mouth or nose. Irritating liquids should be dropped near, but not
directly on, the mealworms.

    a. How do mealworms move?

    b. How do mealworms eat?

    c. Can mealworms see?

    d. Can mealworms be made to back up?

    e. Can mealworms follow walls?

Record the questions selected and your answers to each.

2. What other activities can you suggest for elementary children to investigate mealworms?

☑ Self-Check

For the activity:

Did you have any trouble finding examples of each stage of development? Larvae move around and pupae do not. Were you squeamish about handling the organism? Some children (and teachers) are uneasy with mealworms at first but get over it as interest develops. Did you manage to answer two of the questions to your satisfaction? Did you try anything extra just to satisfy your own curiosity about something that came up during your investigation? You might want to refer to the *Teacher's Guide for Behavior of Mealworms* if it is available.

Implications for teaching:

How would you teach this module to your class? It is an easy, inexpensive way to have living organisms in your classroom. What other simple organisms might you use? There are many varieties available, such as earthworms, pill bugs (Isopods), or ants. Could you make up your own ESS activity? A good idea is versatile and can be adapted to almost any situation.

☐ Comments

Summary

A simple, easily maintained organism is used to teach children how to experiment with habitat, environment, and climatic conditions necessary for optimum development of an organism. This unit is inexpensive and requires very little equipment. Many teachers are using earthworms rather than mealworms, as they are more readily found by children. Other related ESS units are *Brine Shrimp, Butterflies, Crayfish, Eggs and Tadpoles,* and *Mosquitoes.* You might want to examine some of their manuals if they are available.

Activity 2.2b:
Physical Science—Colored Solutions[3]

Colored Solutions is a physical science activity best suited for grades three to six. Density and layering of liquids are used to help children learn how to answer questions using both physical materials and their own investigations. Two simple activities are provided here to introduce you to the unit. Remember, these are basic, introductory exercises, but the students in your classroom could do a lot more with this unit. Can you?

A. Dropping, Mixing, Watching

1. Fill a plastic cup with water.

2. Put one drop of food coloring in the water. Do not stir. Now, describe and draw what you see.

3. Add different colored drops, one at a time. Describe what you see.

4. Describe what happens if you stir the water after adding one color. After adding two or more colors.

Using colored solutions, students learn about the density of liquids.

5. Would there be any difference in the results if you used warm water or cold water rather than room-temperature tap water? Find out.

B. Layering

1. Four containers of liquid are used in this activity. They are numbered and colored. Three of the solutions are salt water of varying densities, and one is tap water. The salt solutions are made by adding 1 cup, $\frac{2}{3}$ cup, and $\frac{1}{3}$ cup of salt, respectively, to three one-quart containers of water. A fourth one-quart container has no salt added. Three of the containers are then colored with green, red, and blue food coloring; the fourth is left clear. Only your instructor knows which solution has no salt and what combinations of salt and water are in the other three colored solutions. You are going to find out for yourself.

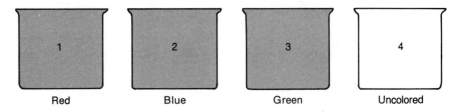

1	2	3	4
Red	Blue	Green	Uncolored

2. By carefully placing one solution on top of or underneath another, you can find out which is denser. A dropper or a straw can be used to add the color slowly and carefully.

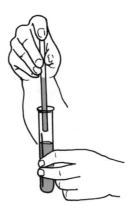

Special Hint: Use a small diameter vial or test tube rather than a large container like a plastic cup. Narrow containers work better and are easier to see the results in. Try using the red and blue solutions. Which is the more dense of the two? How do you know? Draw your results.

3. Float one color on another to make a "parfait." See if you can layer all four of the liquids. Which color is the most dense? Which is the least dense?

4. Sketch a picture of your parfait and label the colors. You should know which colored solution is what salt combination; indicate that on your drawing.

☑ **Self-Check**

For the activity:

Were you surprised by the pattern made by a single drop of food coloring placed on the water? Pretty, wasn't it? Did you wonder about the motion of the color in the still water? How could you account for this movement? You might think about molecular motion. Did your colored solutions layer, or did they mix? If you mixed them, try again, carefully. You might look at the *Colored Solutions* guide if it is available.

Implications for teaching:

Do you think that children would like this activity? Did you? Why or why not? How expensive would it be to use this activity? Salt and food coloring can be purchased at any grocery store. What else can you think of to do with this activity? Did you try anything not in the directions? Why not? You have time, and the equipment is available. Wouldn't you want your students to answer some of their questions if you were the teacher?

☐ **Comments**

Summary

Food coloring, salt, and water are used to teach children how to investigate density and molecular motion. The students learn how to experiment in order to answer questions that develop as they do science activities. Related units are *Drops, Streams and Containers; Kitchen Physics; Sink or Float;* and *Water Flow.* You might look at some of these guides if they are available.

Activity 2.2c: Earth Science—Mapping[4]

In the study of earth science, it is important that the student have some knowledge of physical geography. One important aspect of physical geography is knowing how to read and construct a map. Even though the study of maps and map skills is usually encountered in social studies, it can also be taught, with relevance, through the science program. ESS presents this material through a unit entitled *Mapping*. Several ideas are presented, such as playing games to develop map skills, constructing maps or models, and following and giving directions. This sample activity concentrates on following and giving directions.

A. Following Directions

    1. Obtain a set of directions from your instructor. This should be a handout prepared by your instructor with directions to one or more places in the building or to objects within the room.

    2. Follow the directions. Where do they lead you?

    3. Did you have any trouble following the directions? What changes would you make in the directions so that they are easier to follow?

B. Giving Directions

    1. Select one of the following locations:

        a. Your dormitory or apartment

        b. Your favorite local restaurant

        c. Registrar's office

        d. University bookstore

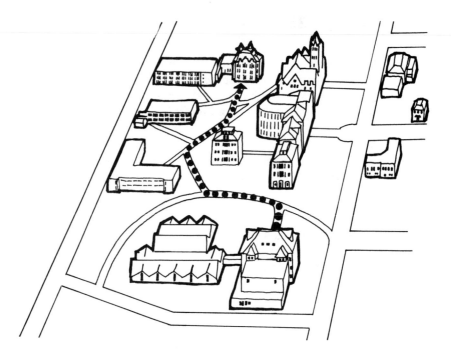

2. Write out a set of directions that would get you from your classroom to the destination. Pretend that someone who does not know where the location is must follow your directions. Use as many steps as you feel are necessary.
Location:

Directions:

3. Draw a map showing how to get from your classroom to the point selected.

4. Have other members of your group read your directions and look at your map. What suggestions did they make to improve either or both?

☑ **Self-Check**

For the activity:

Did you have any trouble following directions? Is this something you need to work on? Can you give good directions? Think about how giving and following directions are part of map usage. Be sure to compare your directions with those of other members of your group. Can you follow their directions? If the guide for *Mapping* is available, look through it.

Implications for teaching:

You can combine your science activities with other subject areas. *Mapping* is an example of combining science and social studies. Can you combine art, music, mathematics, and physical education, as well as reading, with your science program? A good teacher can. Here is something else to think about: Can you give clear instructions to your students? Teachers who give unclear instructions cause failures in assignments and frustrating situations in the classroom.

☐ **Comments**

Summary

Mapping helps students understand the physical relationships found in the earth's surface. In this unit students learn how to use directions and graphic representation to better group the concepts of location and symbols. Related ESS units are *Stream Tables, Match and Measure, Daytime Astronomy, Light and Shadow,* and *Geo Blocks.* You might be interested in reviewing some of these guides.

Activity 2.2d:
Mathematics—Peas and Particles[5]

A word of explanation about ESS mathematics modules is needed before you begin *Peas and Particles.* Spatial relationships, measuring, attributes, and the use of mathematics are the subjects of these modules, not numerical computation. You might want to refer again to the chart in Appendix A to see what titles are included in this category.

This activity is one in which children deal informally with estimation and large numbers in ways that may be new to them. They answer questions—how many? how big? how far away?—not with worksheet or arithmetic test precision, but as we tend to answer questions ordinarily, with wild estimates and educated guesses. For this activity, all you need is something to estimate, such as a pint of rice or peas, a container of marbles, a quart of macaroni, or a quart of beans. Your imagination is your guide.

A. Estimating a Handful of Peas

    1. You will need to work with at least one other person in this activity. One of you should take a handful of peas from the container of peas.

    2. Observe the handful of peas for a few seconds. Now, both of you are to

The teacher is introducing *Peas and Particles* **to his students.**

estimate the number of peas in the handful. Your guess: _____ Your partner's guess: _____

3. Count the peas and compare the actual count to the estimates. Actual number in the handful: _____ Who was closer, you or your partner? _____ By how many? _____

4. Do this again, letting the other person get the handful this time. Your estimate: _____ Your partner's estimate: _____ Actual count: _____

5. Did you come closer the second time? Why or why not?

B. Estimating a Jarful

1. With your partner, select one of the jars of objects provided for this activity. Which jar did you select?

2. Each of you should make a quick guess, without taking the objects out of the jar, as to how many objects are in the jar. Your guess: _____ Your partner's guess: _____

3. Now try some serious estimating to check your hasty guess. You may want to actually count the objects one by one, but do not do that just yet. Try to develop some more imaginative methods of estimating to check your guess. Devise some counting strategies that involve manipulating the objects. You are to describe your strategies and make your estimate based on each strategy.
   Strategy 1:

   Estimate:

   Strategy 2:

   Estimate:

Strategy 3:

   Estimate:

4. If you feel like counting the objects to check your guess and your estimating strategies, you may do so now.

☑ **Self-Check**

For the activity:

Did you find that your ability to estimate improved with practice? What caused
the improvement? Developing a point of reference, such as how many peas are
in a handful, gives you something concrete on which to base your estimate. Did
you have to resort to counting, one by one, to confirm your estimates, or were
you willing to trust your estimates? If you had a bushel of beans, would you trust
a carefully planned estimate, or count them one by one? If the guide is available,
you might refer to it at this time.

Implications for teaching:

You can use this activity to introduce either estimating or large numbers to a
class. How hard would it be for you to obtain objects to estimate? One teacher
actually used a bushel of beans to initiate the activity. Can you think of a better
attention getter than a contest to guess the number of beans in the bushel
container? What could you do with this activity?

☐ **Comments**

Summary

Many times a close guess is sufficient or even more desirable than an actual count. With this unit, children are taught to make estimates of large quantities of small objects, using household items. They can then expand into other areas of measurement. Large numbers are also considered and become more real when students can actually see the quantity represented by the numbers. There are no related units available.

ACTIVITY 2.3: ACTIVITIES FOR SCIS

The following four SCIS activities will give you a good idea of what the SCIS program is like. There are two life science activities and two physical science activities; you should do at least one of each. Simple equipment, usually found in any elementary classroom or easily obtainable, is used in all of the activities. Each one was adapted from actual SCIS activities and uses the same type of teaching strategy as SCIS. Look for examples of *exploration, invention,* and *discovery* as you do the activities.

These students are setting up the SCIS activity *Life in an Aquarium.*

Students can make observations by studying an aquarium.

You are to work with a small group or with your instructor and the entire class on these activities. You can work alone, but much better results will be obtained from group interaction. Before selecting the activities your group will do, read through all four of them. Your group might want to divide, if it is large enough, and have each subgroup do two activities so that you can share in all four of the activities. When working on the activities, do not be afraid to ask "What would happen if . . . ?" and then try to find out. You are not limited to the questions and procedures presented here.

How would a child react to each activity? Always remember the student's viewpoint. Refer to the material you have read and the guides you have reviewed to help you put the entire program into perspective. Talk to your group and to your instructor to be sure that you understand the SCIS philosophy and what is really being taught in an activity.

Activity 2.3a:
Life Science—Life in an Aquarium[6]

The aquarium is a central part of many life science activities throughout all grade levels of SCIS. It offers an ideal, controlled environment for observation and experimentation. This activity is used to introduce first-grade students to living organisms and to allow sixth-grade students to experiment with ecosystems. It is a very versatile activity, requiring only an aquarium (several small aquariums are used in the program) and a little imagination.

A. An aquarium is a common fixture in many elementary classrooms. It is not expensive and can easily be set up and maintained. You have, no doubt, seen an aquarium. But have you ever really looked closely at one? You will get a chance to do so in this activity. Find an aquarium and you will be ready to start.

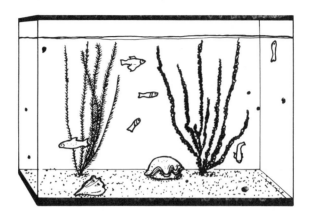

B. Observing an Aquarium

   1. Obviously, the first thing you will notice in an aquarium is the animal life. Usually, this will be the fish. Look closely at them. How many are there? _____ Are they all the same kind? _____ If not, how many kinds are there? _____ How do you know that they are not all the same species?

   2. Look for other forms of animal life. Do you find any? _____ What are they and what do they contribute to the system?

   3. Animal life is not the only kind of life found in an aquarium. Most aquariums also have plant life. How many forms of plant life can you find? Describe them.

4. Are plants really necessary for a well-ordered aquarium? What do you think the plants contribute to the system?

5. A certain amount of nonliving material can also be found in an aquarium. The most obvious, of course, is the water and the container. What other nonliving materials can you find? Describe each and tell what you think it contributes to the system

6. The container and everything in it make up a habitat for the animal life found there. Describe a system that makes up your habitat.

C. Observing a Specific Organism

   1. In Section B of this activity, you looked at the total system and its component parts. Now you are going to be more specific. Pick one organism and observe it. You may want to use a hand lens to help you see it better. Do not remove the organism from its habitat.

   2. Which organism do you pick? Describe it. (A sketch might be appropriate to aid your description.)

3. How does the organism move about?

4. How do you think it eats?

5. What does it eat?

D. Using the Aquarium in the Classroom

    1. Two problems are presented to you as a teacher. Read both of them. Then, with your group, choose one for discussion. After your group has discussed the problem, describe your course of action.

        a. What would you do if you came into your classroom and found a dead fish in your aquarium?

        Did your group perceive the dead fish as an asset or a liability? SCIS considers the event a teaching opportunity because the students can try to find out why the fish died. They can also leave the fish in the container or put it in a separate, special container and then watch decomposition.

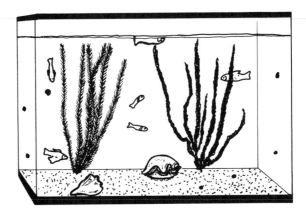

b. How could your students find out where the "black stuff" (detritus) on the bottom of the tank comes from?

The black stuff, or detritus, is waste material that comes from the organism(s) in the aquarium. Did you think to devise experiments to isolate each organism from all the others to see if it produced the black stuff? This activity offers a good opportunity to devise and carry out experiments.

2. Develop a problem of your own that you might use in your classroom.

☑ Self-Check

For the activity:

Have you ever looked closely at an aquarium before? There is more to it than pretty fish swimming. Did you use the observation skills presented in Chapter 1? Could you tell the difference between the male and female organisms? Some organisms have easily recognized differences, but others do not. You might want to look at the *Organisms'* guide now that you have completed the activities.

Implications for teaching:

What are some uses of an aquarium in your classroom? An aquarium, like animals in the classroom, can either be used as a teaching tool or as a pet with no real teaching purpose. The choice is up to you.

☐ **Comments**

Summary of Activity

Life in an Aquarium introduced you to the many possible uses of a common piece of classroom equipment. You were asked to make some observations and inferences to help you understand how SCIS uses a simple piece of equipment throughout the program.

Activity 2.3b: Life Science—Field Trip[7]

Field Trip is a combination of several SCIS activities modified to be used as a modular, self-directed exercise. In the actual SCIS program, the outside classroom is used quite often in both physical science and life science units, which are teacher-directed but student-oriented. As you do this activity, think about all of the ways you could use the outdoor laboratory in your school. Every school has one available, even those in the core of the city. It may be small or paved over, but it is there for your use.

A. You are going to go outside for this activity. A field trip does not have to be an elaborate venture, as you will see. You do not need much equipment for this activity, but you should have a hand lens. (Every child should have access to a hand lens.) You should have a small plastic container if you wish to collect specimens on your outing.

B. Seasons

   1. SCIS does not teach a unit on seasons as such, but children are aware of the changing seasons. Each season has its own characteristics; each living organism adapts, in its own way, to those characteristics. Life, or evidence of life, can be found in all seasons. Consequently, even if the ground is covered with snow rather than flowers, this activity is pertinent.

   2. What is the season?

Examining organisms in the outdoor laboratory is important to the SCIS program.

    3. What are the characteristics of this season?

    4. Which season is your favorite? Why?

C. Field Trip

    1. Go outside on a short walk with one or more members of your small group and select a small area for observation. This area need not be more than a few meters square. You might even do this activity on your way to or from class.

2. Look for organisms or signs of organisms. List some of your observations.

Organisms   **Signs of Organisms**

3. Can you find evidence of a food chain? Describe it.

4. Look for evidence of humans having visited your area. Describe the evidence.

D. Habitat

  1. A habitat is a place where a plant or animal lives. Many habitats can be found on your short walk.

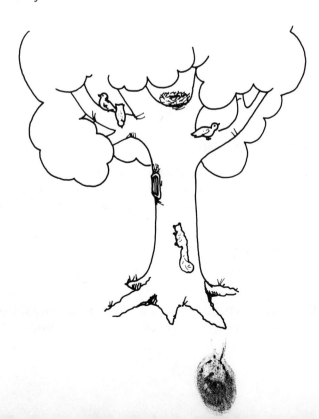

2. Locate a habitat, either plant or animal, and describe it.

E. Discussion

Share your observations with others in your group. Discuss the evidence presented.

☑ Self-Check

For the activity:

Did you have trouble finding a suitable site for your observation? You should not have had difficulty because any site is a good one. If you had difficulty collecting evidence of organisms, then you did not look closely enough. Such things as an insect's wing, a feather from a passing bird, or even a discarded can or cigarette butt indicate that some type of organism has passed through your site. Remember, look for simple signs.

Implications for teaching:

It is important to get your students interested in the world outside of the classroom. Think of variations of this activity that you might use with your class. What would the teacher be doing while the students are involved in this type of activity?

☐ Comments

Summary of Activity

You were asked to participate in an outdoor laboratory experience. SCIS uses many variations of this activity. Activities like this are inexpensive and have unlimited possibilities for the imaginative teacher.

Activity 2.3c:
Physical Science—Batteries and Bulbs[8]

SCIS uses electricity in several different activities, each one building on the previous one. Simple electrical circuits are introduced in the second grade to

This student is learning about electricity through direct experience.

illustrate interaction. More complex concepts are developed, building up to the sixth-grade unit, where electrical models are invented. Think about how you might use the simple act of lighting a bulb as a teaching opportunity. Flashlight batteries provide a safe, economical power source and are usually familiar to all of the students. *Batteries and Bulbs* is divided into two parts to illustrate two of the three SCIS teaching strategies: *exploration* and *discovery*. You will also be engaged in some invention as you discuss what you are doing with your group, but it will not be instructor-guided unless you ask your instructor to join you.

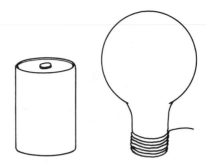

A. Lighting a Bulb

1. You will need a battery, a bulb, and two pieces of wire. Obtain these from the instructor or materials center.

2. Your first task is a simple one. You are to make the bulb light up. Use any or all of your materials. *Warning:* Stay away from wall outlets. Use only the dry cell battery for a power source.

3. On the next page, draw a picture of the way you arranged your equipment to make the bulb light up.

4. Can you devise an alternative method of lighting the bulb? *Hint:* It can be done either with one wire or two. If you used one wire in step 2, try using two wires or vice versa. Draw a picture of your second method.

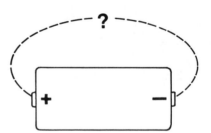

5. Look for a circuit in your two drawings. This is the path that the electricity travels to get from one end of the battery to the other. If you are not sure of what a circuit is, check with your instructor. Show the circuit on your drawings.

6. Compare your results with others in your group. How did you feel when you finally got your bulb to light up? Discovery is a great feeling, isn't it?

B. Solving a Problem

1. On your own, make a prediction about whether or not the bulb will light in each of the pictures on page 87. Don't check it yet, just predict.

2. Compare your predictions with those of the other members of your group. If you disagree, can you convince them that you are right?

3. Using your materials, go back and test each circuit. Mark those that you had trouble with. Have a group discussion about this activity.

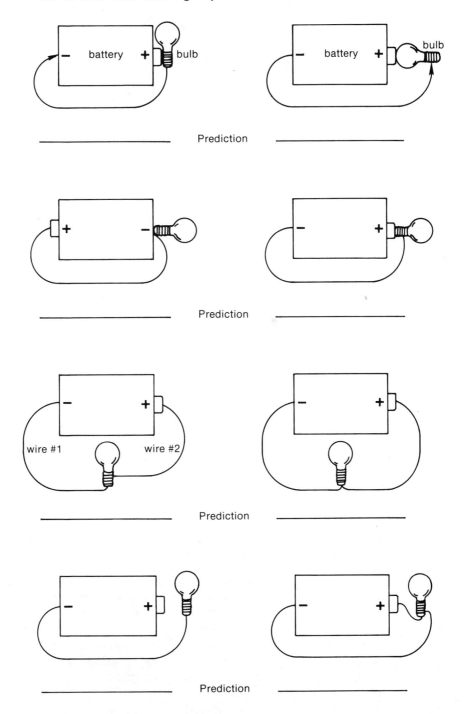

√ **Self-Check**

For the activity:

Did you have any trouble getting the bulb to light up? Wasn't it a great feeling when you finally did it? Did you check all of your predictions? It is easy to do when you have the actual equipment in your hands. You get much more positive feedback this way than when using an abstract answer sheet.

Implications for teaching:

Can you think of other ways to use this activity? Simple materials can be used in a variety of ways if you use your imagination. Think about safety as you plan activities for your students. This activity could be dangerous without safety warnings about using the proper power source, but it is harmless if proper precautions are taken. Safety is too often neglected in the classroom.

☐ **Comments**

Summary of Activity

Children use electricity all the time. You enter a room, flip a switch, and the light comes on; or you turn on a flashlight, and it produces light. But why or how? Here is a common phenomenon that nearly all children are familiar with. Why not use it as a teaching device? Electricity is used in the second grade, third grade, and sixth grade in the SCIS program.

Activity 2.3d:
Physical Science—Sorting Rocks[9]

The concept that the word object refers to a piece of matter and that objects can be described by their properties is the first thing taught to elementary children in the SCIS physical science program. In *Sorting Rocks* you will see how a child describes the properties of rocks and learns that a single object might be made up of more than one material. Language development is also stressed in this activity because the children are encouraged to discuss their observations and conclusions.

A. Describing Properties

  1. To begin this activity, each member of your group will need about five or six rocks. Obtain these from the rock box or wherever you can find five or six good rocks. Try to get a variety. A hand lens, if available, will be helpful.

  2. Carefully look at all of your rocks. Spend several minutes and really look closely.

  3. Pick out your favorite rock and describe it to the rest of your group. Summarize your description below.

  4. Some common properties that an elementary student might use to describe rocks are these: shape, size, color, and texture. See if you can sort

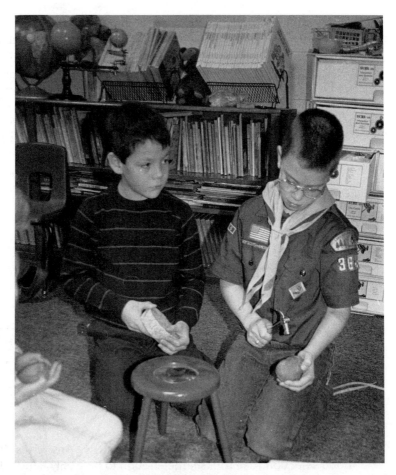

The unit *Sorting Rocks* **gives an introduction to one area of physical science.**

your rocks using some other identified properties. Make a list of these properties.

5. Show your list to the others in your group, along with your collection of rocks. Can they match each rock to your description of it? If not, modify your list of properties so they can.

B. Sorting Rocks

1. To start this activity, combine your set of rocks with those of the other members of your group. This will be a group activity.

2. Sort the rocks into piles according to various properties. Each member of the group will sort the rocks, using a specific property. You are to list the different properties used by your group.
   Note: For fun, each group member might sort the rocks into two or more piles using a property known only to her. The other members then try to determine what property was used. This is not a part of the SCIS, but it is an example of a variation that you might use to keep your children interested.

☑ **Self-Check**

For the activity:

In Section A, did you use only properties when you described your favorite rock, or did you sneak in some functional description? Did all of your rocks fit neatly into categories, or did you have trouble with some because of multiple characteristics? In Section B, did you have trouble thinking of a property not used by others? You might want to look at the *Material Objects* guide.

Implications for teaching:

Where would you obtain rocks for this activity? Any roadside or stone pile has a good selection. Use rocks large enough to be easily handled, about two or three centimeters in diameter. Devise an *invention* lesson to go with this activity.

☐ **Comments**

Summary of Activity

The first step in this physical science portion of SCIS is to learn what an object is and that it can be described by its properties. Rocks are used as objects to be described in this activity because they are easy to obtain and come in great variety.

ACTIVITY 2.4: ACTIVITIES FOR SAPA II

You are now ready to participate in some SAPA II activities. There are four activities presented, and you should do at least two of them. These particular activities were selected because they use simple, readily available material. Each

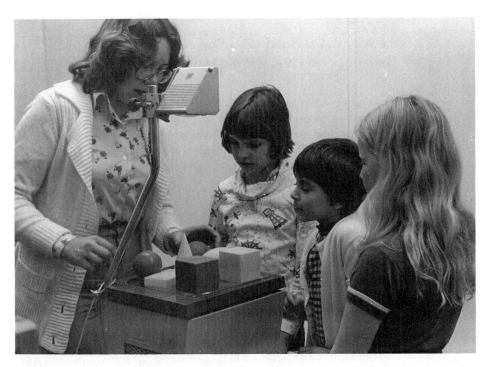

SAPA II activities emphasize the importance of student interaction.

one involves a different process and represents a different grade level. These are actual SAPA II activities, but they have been modified slightly to make them appropriate for your use.

Read over all of the activities before selecting the ones you are going to do. Discuss the choices within your group and decide which ones you are going to do. Your group may choose to do several, with all members participating in each activity, or it may choose to split into two groups, each doing two activities and then comparing the results. For these activities, it is better to work in small groups than to work alone. Interaction among students is important in SAPA II and in these activities.

These activities will teach you how a student sees the program. You will use the same materials the student uses and answer some of the same questions. You have already looked at SAPA II as a teacher, but not as a student. Try to think how, for example, a fourth grader might respond to such activities.

As you go through these activities, think about what you have read in the background information and in the instruction booklets. How does all this information fit together? What do you really know about SAPA II, and how can this knowledge help you to be a better teacher?

Activity 2.4a: Shadows (Module 29, Using Space/Time Relationships)[10]

Shadows is an adaptation of a first-grade activity. The children have already been exposed to three-dimensional shapes and objects in previous modules. They learned to identify shapes by touch and/or sight. Now they will begin to extend this ability by learning to recognize the relationship between two- and three-dimensional geometric shapes. Shadows are used to show the two-dimensional shapes for three-dimensional objects.

A. A shadow box is a simple device consisting of two basic components: a light source and a translucent screen. A filmstrip or slide projector is an ideal light source. Set it up about 1.5 meters from your screen for a clean, sharp shadow. A translucent screen can easily be constructed from a sheet of typing paper and cardboard frame to hold the paper steady. Place the object to be viewed between the light source and the screen; then view the shadow from the opposite side of the screen. You can draw on the screen, replacing it as you change objects. An overhead projector can also be used effectively as a shadow box. Simply place the object on the projection surface and turn on the light. The shadow will be projected. You might project a small image and have the children draw around the shadow. Your imagination is the only limiting factor in using the shadow box or overhead projector.

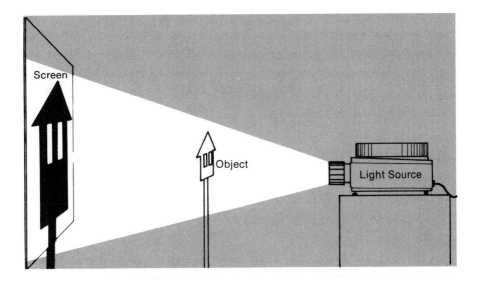

B. Have one member of your group operate the shadow box or overhead projector. The rest of the group should look at the shadows only, not at the object. You will need several simple three-dimensional objects. The operator does the first part of the directions, and the rest of the group records what they find out. The directions for this activity are as follows:

1. *Operator:* Place one of the objects in position and project the shadow.
   Group: Sketch the shadow. What do you think the object is?

2. *Operator:* Rotate the object to show another dimension.
   Group: Sketch the new shadow. Have you changed your mind about the identity of the object?

3. *Operator and Group:* Repeat the activity several times using different objects.

4. Do some objects have the same shadow no matter which way they are projected? Give an example.

5. Are the shadows of some objects similar if projected from one side but different if projected from another? Give examples.

C. You have looked at shadows and tried to picture the objects; now let's try a more abstract exercise. Here are some pictures of shadows. First, try to decide what three-dimensional shape was used to create each pair of shadows presented. Then, consider the shadow pairs again. One of the sets is incomplete for an accurate picture. Which one is it? Why?

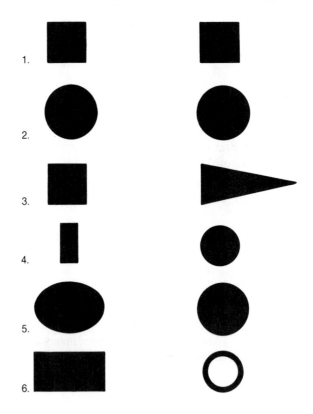

1.
2.
3.
4.
5.
6.

☑ **Self-Check**

For the activity

Did you peek at the object when you were looking at the shadows? Was the shadow what you expected? If you are unsure of your ability to visualize, try several objects on the overhead projector or shadow box. Look for objects that might reproduce the shadows in Section C. Is the shadow pair for number 3 from a pyramid or a wedge? If the instruction booklet for this module is available, you should refer to it.

Implications for teaching:

What are some variations of this activity that you could use? Could you adapt this activity to another grade level? Remember, a good idea is adaptable to many uses and situations. What materials would you need to teach a lesson such as this? How hard would it be for you to get them together? Think about the shadow box. It is a versatile piece of equipment that has many uses in subject areas other than science. Remember it when you start teaching.

Comments

Summary of activity

This first-grade exercise will help your students learn how to visualize an object from its outline or shape. Visualization skills are often neglected, but they should not be; they are an important step in developing abstract thinking. The shadow box used in this exercise is an excellent classroom teaching device that is easy to make and has unlimited potential.

Activity 2.4b:
About How Far? (Module 34, Measuring)[11]

In previous modules on measuring, you have learned how to make measurements by comparing an object directly to an arbitrary unit or standard. In this module, you will see that it is not always possible, or even desirable, to make these direct measurements. You will learn how to estimate linear measurements using mental images of standard units. You will need a meter stick or a similar measuring device. All SAPA II measurements are in metric units.

A. Metric Reference:
   You will need a few aids to help you estimate linear measurements. Using your meter stick, make the following measurements. You will have to decide on the proper units of measurement to use. Estimate these before you actually measure them.

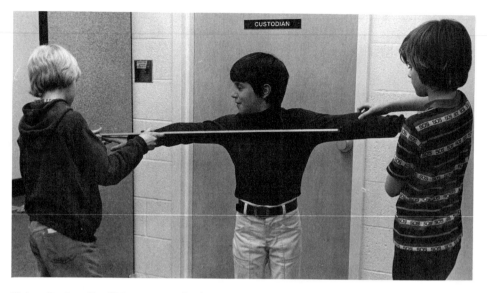

Using the length of his outstretched arms as a standard, this student will learn to estimate other linear measures.

1. Width of your finger _____

2. Length of your finger _____

3. Length of your hand _____

4. Length of your foot _____

5. Your height _____

6. Length of your pen or pencil

_____

7. Length of your pace or step

_____

8. Length of your arm _____

9. Length of your arms out-

stretched _____

10. _____

(your choice)

B. Try some more metric estimations. No fair using the meter stick yet. Do only the first column.

	Estimated	Actual
1. How high is your desk?	_____	_____

2. How long is the room?   _____   _____

3. How wide is your textbook?   _____   _____

4. What is the diameter of a quarter?   _____   _____

5. How tall is your instructor?   _____   _____

Now try a couple of your own choice.

6. _____   _____   _____

7. _____   _____   _____

C. Go back and actually measure the distances that you estimated. Compare your answers. How close were you in your estimations? If you were off by quite a bit, do a few more. SAPA II gives a general rule of plus or minus 20 percent as acceptable at this level. As adults, you should do much better.

☑ Self-Check

For the activity:

Did you have any trouble using metric measurement? Did you use your reference measurements to help you estimate distances? How many hands long is the width of the desk? How many paces long is the length of the room? What references did you use to estimate the height of your instructor? Were you within the plus or minus 20 percent allowance? If the instruction booklet for this module is available, you should look at it.

Implications for teaching:

How could you use this activity in your classroom? You will be teaching metric measurement; therefore, you should start collecting metric activities as well as becoming more familiar with the metric system.

☐ Comments

Summary of Activity

This exercise helps the student learn to estimate distances that cannot be measured directly. Mental images of common units help provide a reference base for estimations. The student is also learning to think in metric units rather than in the traditional units of feet and inches.

Activity 2.4c: Seeds and Soap
(Module 71, Controlling Variables)[12]

In *Seeds and Soap,* you will learn how to control variables. Students using the actual SAPA II sequence would have already been introduced to the terms *manipulated variable, responding variable,* and *variables held constant.* In this module, an experiment is described by the teacher and discussed. The elemen-

The *Seeds and Soap* program deals with controlling the variables in an experiment.

tary students must decide what the variables are, what kind each one is, and how they can modify the experiment to make it valid. You will get the same opportunity in this activity. Your students would have material to manipulate, but you will do your manipulating mentally.

A. You need some background information before you start. *Variables* are those factors that influence an experiment. All but two must be held constant. One is manipulated (*manipulated variable*), and the other responds to the manipulation (*responding variable*). Here is an example. You should be aware of the well-known experiment that demonstrates a plant needs light to grow. If you were to do this experiment, you would need to control variables such as

1. Size and variety of plant
2. Amount of water
3. Size of containers
4. Temperature

Now you are ready to manipulate a variable—how much sunlight each plant is to receive. One will be placed in the sun, the other in darkness. One plant grows; the other plant dies, or at least does not grow to be as strong and healthy as the first. Plant growth becomes the responding variable. Do you feel confident in your knowledge of variables? Go on to Section B and test your knowledge.

B. I am a curious person who enjoys a good experiment. The other day, I accidentally poured soapy water onto one of my house plants. I wondered if I had hurt it or helped it, so I decided to set up an experiment to find out if detergent had any effect on the growth of seeds. Please note the picture of my three-jar experimental apparatus.

1.
5 mm vermiculite
10 mm mung bean seeds
10 mm vermiculite
10 ml water

2.
30 mm vermiculite
25 mm mung bean seed
5 mm vermiculite
20 ml liquid detergent
(Ivory)

3.
20 mm shredded paper
50 radish seed
10 ml water
10 ml liquid detergent
(Joy)

Now, I will watch the containers for several days to see what will happen. The teacher would allow the students to decide whether or not this would answer the original question. Obviously it won't. Try to answer some questions about the variables in this experiment.

1. Are there any variables that have been held constant? Which ones?

2. List the variables in this experiment. According to SAPA, there are 14. You might be able to find more.

3. Which is the manipulated variable in this experiment?

4. Which is the responding variable?

5. Do you think that my experiment is any good? Why or why not?

C. Knowing that an experiment is invalid because the variables are not controlled is not enough. You have to be able to control the variables. Go back to your list of variables and choose five. Now, list them and tell how you would control them.

☑ **Self-Check**

For the activity:

How much trouble did you have finding 14 variables that were not controlled? Did you resort to some pretty unlikely ones? You did not have to. Have you discussed your list of variables with your group? Did all of you have similar lists? You should get some additional ideas from your discussions. The variables listed in the instruction booklet are

1. Kind of seed
2. Temperature
3. Number of seeds
4. Depth of vermiculite before adding seed
5. Depth of vermiculite after adding seed
6. Amount of light
7. Air movement
8. Amount of liquid added at start
9. Addition of more liquid
10. Concentration of detergent
11. Kind of detergent
12. Kind of container
13. Number of seeds germinating
14. Type of material in which all seeds are planted

Implications for teaching:

Did this activity give you some insight into the teaching of variables? Could you help your students devise valid experiments? You should think about valid experiments because you will be using experiments in any science program you teach. Does this activity suggest any teaching strategies to you? You might start a lesson with a hypothetical problem or story.

☐ **Comments**

Summary of Activity

An experiment is only as good as its controls. Students learn to identify and control variables that could invalidate an experiment. As an integrated process, this activity builds on the students' abilities to use the basic processes. The students are also preparing for the time when they have to set up experiments and defend their validity.

Activity 2.4d:
Eye Power (Module 98, Experimenting)[13]

The last ten modules of SAPA II are experimenting modules used to integrate all of the processes. In this module, the students investigate a common phenomenon—the resolving power of the eyes. Resolving power is the ability of the eyes to separate an apparent single light source into two or more separate sources. To illustrate this phenomenon, here is an example. At a distance, the headlights of an automobile appear as a single light, but as the automobile gets closer, two distinct lights are seen. As the students investigate this phenomenon, they practice the skills learned in previous SAPA II lessons. Begin this activity to learn about resolving power.

A. How well do you see? Do you always see what you think you see, or do your eyes deceive you? For this exercise, you will need a hand lens, a black-and-white newspaper picture, and a colored newspaper picture. (Colored pictures in textbooks serve the same purpose.) Try several.

    1. Look at a black-and-white newspaper photograph. Is everything either black or white, or are there shades of gray in the picture?
How can you print shades of gray using only black ink on white paper?

These students are performing Activity B in the *Eye Power* **unit.**

**By examining a newspaper through a hand lens, this child
is learning about the resolving power of his eyes.**

2. Now, take a hand lens and look at the same picture. What do you see,
especially in the gray areas?

Did your eyes deceive you?

3. Do the same thing with a colored picture. Describe what you see.

4. Why do you see a solid color when you look at the pictures unaided by
the hand lens?

5. If possible, look at the image on a television screen with a hand lens. You will find it quite interesting. What do you see?

B. You will now have the opportunity to see how your eyes resolve two dots of light. You will need a flashlight, a piece of onionskin paper, a construction paper disk, a pin, some tape, and a meter stick. You will also need several partners, so do this activity with your group.

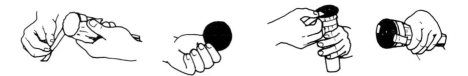

Cover the flashlight with the onionskin paper; then tape it in place. Use the pin to punch two holes, about two millimeters apart, in the center of the contruction paper disk. Tape the disk to the front of the flashlight, over the onionskin paper. If you have done everything correctly so far, you should be able to see two small light sources when the flashlight is turned on.

Find a test area about six or seven meters long, the darker the better. Have one member of the team stand at a marked spot at one end of the test area and hold the flashlight at eye level. Have another person start at the other end of the area and walk forward until he can see the two light dots. Mark the spot where the dots become distinct; then measure the distance from the light. Repeat the test several times with different people, then average the results of each person.

	Team Member	Team Member	Team Member
Trial 1	_____	_____	_____
Trial 2	_____	_____	_____
Trial 3	_____	_____	_____
Average	_____	_____	_____

1. How do you account for the discrepancy among different team members?

2. What variables are you manipulating? (You might need to refer to the previous activity for information about variables.)

3. Describe how you manipulate them.

☑ **Self-Check**

For the activity:

Did all of the little dots surprise you? Your eyes cannot resolve anything that small and close together without help. Did you have any trouble with the investigation? If so, were you able to get it straightened out? Did you need to refer to the previous activity *Soap and Seeds* (Module 71, Controlling Variables/c) for help with variables? If you didn't do that activity, it might be worth your time to look at it. If the instruction booklet is available, you should refer to it.

Implications for teaching:

Experimenting is an important part of teaching any science. Did this activity help you understand how to set up an experiment? Have you ever thought of using something simple like a newspaper picture and a hand lens to teach a concept? Sometimes simple equipment is the most effective.

☐ **Comments**

Summary of Activity

All of the basic processes are used when experimenting. The SAPA II modules for experimenting are used at the end of the program to help the child learn to use all of the processes together to really act as a scientist. You can use experiments to help your students understand complex technology as well as everyday phenomena.

SUMMARY

In this chapter you were introduced to three of the best-known laboratory approaches to elementary science: *Elementary Science Study* (ESS), *Science Curriculum Improvement Study* (SCIS), and *Science . . . A Process Approach II* (SAPA II). Each program consists of a kit containing a teacher's guide and the materials necessary for the activities. Little reading material is supplied for the students because learning occurs as students do activities to solve problems. The student is an active participant in the learning process; the teacher assumes the role of guide and resource person. Background information and hands-on activities were designed to give you a basic knowledge of each program, how it is taught, and what it is trying to teach. You were also asked to see how you could use some of the ideas presented in a classroom of your own. You must be able to draw from these programs (or from any source, for that matter) ideas and strategies that will enhance your own program and improve your teaching ability.

You have worked with both small and large groups, sharing ideas. If the only things that you shared were answers to questions, you have probably missed the point.

At the beginning of Chapter 2, three objectives were stated. Look at them again and ask yourself if you can

1. Identify and describe the *Elementary Science Study* (ESS), *Science Curriculum Improvement Study* (SCIS) and its revisions *SCIIS* and SCIS II, and *Science . . . A Process Approach II* (SAPA II) as laboratory science programs.

2. Identify and describe the teaching strategy of ESS, SCIS and its revisions *SCIIS* and SCIS II, and SAPA II.

3. Identify and describe the role of the teacher and of the student in the laboratory approach to elementary science.

Look at all of the information and notes you have accumulated from your activities, group seminars, and instructor contacts while completing this chapter. You are now ready to bring them all together. Your instructor will decide on the appropriate course of action, such as a large group (class) discussion, instructor summary, or small group discussion. Whatever form this synthesis takes, be sure that you participate.

ENDNOTES

1. Adapted from Education Development Center, ESS: *Teacher's Guide for Behavior of Mealworms* (St. Louis: Webster/McGraw-Hill, 1966). Adapted from *Behavior of Mealworms,* with permission of Delta Education, Inc., Nashua, NH.

2. Education Development Center, ESS: *Teacher's Guide for Behavior of Mealworms* (St. Louis: Webster/McGraw-Hill, 1966, p. 38. From *Behavior of Mealworms,* with permission of Delta Education, Inc., Nashua, NH.

3. Adapted from Education Development Center, ESS: *Teacher's Guide for Colored Solutions* (St. Louis: Webster/McGraw-Hill, 1968). Adapted from *Colored Solutions,* with permission of Delta Education, Inc., Nashua, NH.

4. Adapted from Education Development Center, ESS: *Teacher's Guide for Mapping* (St. Louis: Webster/McGraw-Hill, 1968, 1971). Adapted from *Mapping,* with permission of Delta Education, Inc., Nashua, NH.

5. Adapted from Education Development Center, ESS: *Teacher's Guide for Peas and Particles* (St. Louis: Webster/McGraw-Hill, 1966). Adapted from *Peas and Particles,* with permission of Delta Education, Inc., Nashua, NH.

6. Adapted from University of California SCIS unit *Organisms* (Chicago: Rand McNally, 1970). Adapted from *Organisms,* with permission of Delta Education, Inc., Nashua, NH.

7. Adapted from University of California SCIS unit *Environments* (Chicago: Rand McNally, 1970). Adapted from *Environments,* with permission of Delta Education, Inc., Nashua, NH.

8. Adapted from University of California SCIS unit *Models: Electric and Magnetic Interactions* (Chicago: Rand McNally, 1970). Adapted from *Models: Electric and Magnetic Interactions,* with permission of Delta Education, Inc., Nashua, NH.

9. Adapted from University of California SCIS unit *Sorting Rocks* (Chicago: Rand McNally, 1970). Adapted from *Sorting Rocks,* with permission of Delta Education, Inc., Nashua, NH.

10. Adapted from *Shadows* (Module 29, Using Space/Time Relationships/e) of *Science... A Process Approach II,* © Copyright, 1974, American Association for the Advancement of Science. Adapted from *Shadows,* with permission of Delta Education, Inc., Nashua, NH.

11. Adapted from *About How Far?* (Module 34, Measuring/e) of *Science... A Process Approach II,* © Copyright, 1974, American Association for the Advancement of Science. Adapted from *About How Far?,* with permission of Delta Education, Inc., Nashua, NH.

12. Adapted from *Soap and Seeds* (Module 71, Controlling Variables/c) of *Science... A Process Approach II,* © Copyright, 1975, American Association for the Advancement of Science. Adapted from *Soap and Seeds,* with permission of Delta Education, Inc., Nashua, NH.

13. Adapted from *Eye Power* (Module 98, Experimenting/c) of *Science... A Process Approach II,* © Copyright, 1975, American Association for the Advancement of Science. Adapted from *Eye Power,* with permission of Delta Education, Inc., Nashua, NH.

REFERENCE

Ball, D. W. (1978). *ESS/Special education teacher's guide.* St. Louis: Webster/McGraw-Hill.

SUGGESTED READINGS

Most of the older references are the original definitive works of those persons closely related to the specific programs. They provide insights into the ESS, SCIS, and SAPA programs that are not currently available.

Bruner, J. (1961). The act of discovery. *Harvard Educational Review, 31* (Winter), 21–32.

Henson, K. & Janke, D. (1984) Chapter 3. Organizing the science program. *Elementary science methods.* New York: McGraw-Hill.

Wolfinger, D. M. (1984). *Teaching science in the elementary school* (pp. 298–311). Boston: Little, Brown and Company.

Elementary Science Study (ESS)

Aho, W., Alberti, D., Perkes, V., Sheldon, R., Thomas, T., & Ward, R. (1974). *McGraw-Hill evaluation program for ESS.* St. Louis: Webster/McGraw-Hill.

Ball, D. W. (1978). *ESS/Special education teacher's guide.* St. Louis: Webster/McGraw-Hill, 1978.

Elementary Science Study. (1971). *A working guide to the elementary science study.* Newton, MA: Educational Development Center.

_____ . *ESS sample packet.* Nashua, NH: Delta Education.

Science Curriculum Improvement Study (SCIS)

Karplus, R., & Lawson, C. (1974). *SCIS teacher's handbook.* Berkeley: University of California. Limited copies available from Delta Education, Nashua, NH.

Karplus, R. & Thier, H. (1967). *A new look at elementary school science.* Chicago: Rand McNally.

Science Curriculum Improvement Study. (1974). *Evaluation supplements.* Berkeley: University of California. Limited copies available from Delta Education, Nashua, NH.

_____ . (1976). *SCIS final report.* Berkeley: University of California. Limited copies available from Delta Education, Nashua, NH.

_____ . *SCIS II sample packet.* Nashua: NH: Delta Education.

_____ . SCIS teacher's guides. Berkeley: University of California. Now supplied by Delta Education, Nashua, NH.

Science . . . A Process Approach II (SAPA II)

American Association for the Advancement of Science. *Curriculum catalog.* Nashua, NH: Delta Education.

————. *Program guide: Science . . . A process approach II.* Nashua, NH: Delta Education.

————. *Sample packet: Science . . . A process approach II.* Nashua, NH: Delta Education.

CHAPTER 3

Textbook Approach to Elementary Science

Goals

After completing this chapter, you will demonstrate competence in the ability to evaluate various elementary science textbooks.

Objectives

In completing this chapter, you will be able to do the following:

1. Evaluate elementary science textbooks using the criteria presented in this chapter.

2. List and explain the strengths and weaknesses of an elementary science textbook program.

INTRODUCTION

The textbook approach is probably the most familiar of the science curricula materials that you will study. Wherever you teach, you will almost certainly have a textbook program from which to work. Unfortunately, not all schools with textbook programs have current textbooks in use. Some may be using books that are dated, and others may be using earlier editions of current texts.

Most of the newer textbooks have integrated the strengths of the laboratory approach into their programs. Hands-on activities, process skills, and thought-provoking questions are included; however, they are not always required for completion of each unit of work. Thus, the teacher has the security of the traditional textbook plus the option of using the discovery approach for some aspects of the lesson. As you become more familiar with the ESS, SCIS, and SAPA II activities, you will find many of them or recognizable variations included as textbook activities.

This chapter covers three areas:

1. Science textbooks
2. Reviewing a textbook
3. Activities on reviewing a textbook

The first section gives you information about the textbook approach and how it is used, the second contains information about review criteria, and the third gives you the opportunity to examine some textbooks and find out for yourself what actually is in an elementary science book. A group discussion of the textbooks reviewed will allow you to share your views with others and to get their opinions of your textbook. Your instructor might want to be a part of this discussion.

You may be asked to make a presentation of some type, based on the textbooks reviewed and your group discussion. Do some serious thinking about how you can use what you are learning in this and previous chapters to help you develop and teach a sound science program for your students. Discuss your thoughts with your group. This will help you to assimilate the information that you have learned. Individual work will provide you with a certain amount of information, but interaction with the group and the instructor will broaden your perspective.

Textbooks have been around for a long time and are considered by many teachers to be the only way to teach. In this section, you will discover why they are so popular, what their weaknesses are, and how to use them most effectively.

SCIENCE TEXTBOOKS

In the past, science textbooks were usually science readers. As part of the reading program, children were given a science text and asked to read it. They read about

Children will experiment with the science they read about in their textbooks.

flowers, birds, and a trip to the zoo. Some physical science—such as the planets, magnets, and simple machines—was also included; in general, however, nature study was the extent of science in the elementary school, and it went hand in hand with the reading program. Textbooks changed somewhat to include science experiments, or at least they were called "experiments." Too often they were either read about, performed by the teacher as a demonstration, or ignored. Very little actual hands-on experimenting by the students was suggested or carried out. Reading was and still is the main learning tool. The student was the passive receptor of factual knowledge contained in the textbook.

Current learning theories—such as those by Piaget, Bruner, and Gagné—stress the need for learning experiences to include concrete involvement. Their emphasis has resulted in the formation of new hands-on programs. To compete with these programs, textbooks have had to revise their approach to include the concrete-involvement concept. Activities have become an integral part of each lesson and are used to introduce science concepts and facts, to extend lessons, and to allow students to practice skills. Optional long-term or take-home projects encourage students to become involved in science outside of the regular class time.

The need for a strong science program, separate from the reading program, was also recognized by science educators. Consequently, science textbook series have been designed to present a total science curriculum for the school. Revised philosophies, help for the teacher, provisions for exceptional children (either above or below the norm), and the availability of supplies in the classroom have contributed to the updating of modern elementary science textbooks. With other programs available, why do most schools still use traditional textbooks? This is a good question, and it has several answers.

1. Good textbooks are excellent teaching aids. They are a resource for the teacher, providing factual material, experiments, demonstrations, illustrations, and references as well as suggestions for teaching. For the students, they provide information about specific subjects or topics, suggest activities or experiments, and provide illustrations that might not be available otherwise. Textbooks are primarily designed to be sourcebooks for teachers and students, and to provide everything needed to complete a specific amount of work successfully.

2. A textbook series provides the school system with an organized science program. Most schools do not have the expertise, personnel, or financial resources to develop a K-through-six science curriculum. Commercial publishers, however, can fund development of sound programs by professionals who have experience in curricula, elementary science, and child development. The school administration knows that by adopting a particular science series it will have a balanced, sequential science curriculum that will provide a basic science education for children.

3. Textbooks provide teachers with organized units of work. Most teachers like to teach by the unit method, in which one topic is explored thoroughly over a period of time, using a variety of activities. The scope and sequence of each topic are clearly defined. The teacher knows exactly what to cover without infringing on material covered in other grade levels.

4. Textbooks are especially helpful for beginning teachers. The teacher's manual provides general suggestions for teaching the unit as well as specific suggestions, page by page, for teaching the material to be covered. The beginning teacher can find security in knowing exactly what is to be taught and having directions for teaching it.

5. Textbooks may be less expensive to purchase and use than some of the kits or kitlike materials. It depends upon the school system and the way that it purchases, uses, and supports the program that is adopted. If cost is really going to be a significant factor in the type of program that will be selected and used, a detailed cost analysis of all programs and textbooks under consideration should be made.

6. Kits are available from the publisher or outside suppliers to supplement the textbook. A school can purchase a classroom kit that contains all of the materials necessary for the students to do the activities that are suggested by the text. Teachers then have the option of doing the activities without having to resort to scrounging for materials.

7. Textbooks are popular in many schools because the teachers and administration do not know that any other programs exist. In this situation, you will probably find that textbooks are selected by the administration from a small list of publishing companies who have been supplying similar books in the past. Wherever you teach, you should try to provide information about new materials to your colleagues.

8. Textbooks are popular with some teachers because they feel insecure with any other program. This is not a good reason but, unfortunately, a valid one for selecting not just the textbook approach, but a specific textbook series. Many teachers are unsure of themselves, especially in science, and they need the security the textbook can provide. It tells the teacher exactly what to say and do, what to expect the students to do, what questions to ask, and specific answers to questions. Teachers are never put in the position of being asked questions they cannot answer or of having to decide what should be taught next. Everything is in the book.

In choosing a science program, teachers should realize that the *best program* is a relative term. What might be the best choice for one school might be the poorest choice for another. Each school must consider all possible programs and select the one that suits its particular needs. Only then can the school claim to have selected the best program available.

There are some inherent weaknesses in textbook programs that should be considered. Think about how you might be able to overcome these weaknesses if you use a textbook:

1. Too often the readability of the textbook is either below or beyond the grade level of the children using it. If children cannot, or will not, read the textbook, obviously they cannot get very much out of it. Most publishers are trying to control the reading level of their textbooks to make them more attractive to students.

2. Many teachers use the textbook as the only source of information. However, the textbook cannot include everything that any student needs or wants to know about a subject. Teachers need to supplement textbook activities just as they supplement nontextbook activities. Quite often, teachers who limit themselves to the textbook are either a little bit lazy or they are insecure and afraid to do anything not found in the textbook. Publishers can, and do, include suggestions for supplementary work, but they cannot force the teacher to use the suggestions.

3. Textbooks are generally designed to be read. They try to substitute words for hands-on experiences. This is a serious weakness if you consider the work of Piaget, Gagné, Bruner, and others who have been mentioned throughout this text. Teachers should try to involve the students as much as possible in activities that help provide hands-on opportunities to go along with reading.

Furthermore, many children cannot read or are severely limited in their reading ability. They are heavily penalized if their work is based totally on textbook material.

4. Many textbooks tell all the answers. Experiments and illustrations are shown step by step, from beginning to end. The children follow along to the end, where they are told the answer. There is no opportunity for students to question, make suggestions, or find out answers. They are passive receptors, not actively involved learners.

5. Each textbook series has developed its own scope and sequence, which creates a curriculum problem. There is always a question as to the proper grade placement of the various science concepts and principles, as well as to which ones should be taught or omitted. Since textbook series do not agree on this subject, the schools have to find the textbook that best agrees with their scope and sequence philosophies. If no textbook meets the requirements of a school, the school must modify its program to fit the text, since it cannot modify the textbook to fit the school.

6. Textbooks become outdated. This last weakness of the textbook approach is not really the fault of the textbook but of the users. Publishers revise textbooks periodically and bring out new editions for the market; however, sometimes publishers will only face-lift the programs and not update the content. This does not help teachers stay on top of what is new in elementary science. Probably more serious, though, is that too many schools do not update their textbook series. A series is adopted, and it then remains until the covers fall off. It is hard to imagine that a teacher must teach from a textbook that is over 20 years old, but it is done. Although it is hard to get rid of a book that is still in good physical shape, it must be done periodically to keep from using outdated programs.

As you can see, the textbook approach has both strengths and weaknesses. Many teachers think that the strengths far outweigh the weaknesses, especially if you know the weaknesses and can compensate for them. Is the textbook approach for you? This question can be answered only by you when you start teaching. But for now, think about what the textbook has to offer you as a teaching aid and how you can use it in your classroom.

There are several ways to use the textbook effectively. Remember that it is a teaching tool, not the entire science program. Your first task is to decide (a) whether or not you like your textbook and (b) how much you intend to use it. These two decisions go hand in hand. If you like your text and consider it suitable, you will use it much more than if you consider it to be a poor text. There are four ways for a teacher to use a textbook in the classroom.

1. Not to use it at all, except to occupy space on the bookshelf. Obviously, this is a poor use of the textbook. This situation might occur for two reasons. First, the teacher does not like science or is afraid to try it and so does not teach it. There is no excuse for this. The science program is as important as any of the other programs. Second, the text is either so obsolete or so poorly structured (in the teacher's eyes) that it offers no real help to the teacher. If this is the case, the teacher probably has developed a science program and is teaching it with supplementary materials and trade books.

2. To use the textbook occasionally as a reference. Usually this situation arises when the teacher considers the text inadequate for some reason and develops his or her own program. This is an inefficient use of the textbook, and the teacher might be just as well off without it.

3. To use the textbook as a resource, supplying ideas for discussion, demonstration, and experiments, and to refer to it for background information about the topic being studied and for verification of experimental results. This is probably the best way to use a textbook. A partnership exists between the teacher and the textbook—the textbook helps the teacher to teach.

4. To rely very heavily on the textbook, following it very closely. In extreme cases, the textbook may literally be used as a science reader. Usually though, the teacher follows the teacher's guide step by step, suggestion by suggestion, page by page from cover to cover. This overdependence severely limits the teacher and students, whether they know it or not. A majority of teachers are probably teaching this way.

How should you use the textbook? As a beginning teacher, you will probably rely on the textbook more than you should, but there are good reasons for doing so. The textbook will provide you with a course outline, teaching suggestions, content information, appropriate grade-level materials, and suggestions for evaluating the students. All of this you need to know but probably do not because of your inexperience. The textbook can give you the security you need to do a good job, because you know that if you follow the textbook, you will teach what you are expected to teach and will achieve reasonably acceptable results.

After your first few lessons, you should be confident enough to begin doing more than merely following the book. Continue to use the textbook as a guide, but also begin to use some of the other strategies you have learned as a supplement to your basic approach. Try to move toward using the textbook as a resource to help you teach, but do not be limited by it.

Try using the textbook as a source for experiments, demonstrations, or discussion topics. Read the material; then involve the students in discussions or experiments before they read the material. As a final step, students go to the textbook to see how their experiments compare with those given. This strategy keeps the textbook from giving the answers before the children ever have a chance to try to find them. You can also use the textbook to provide data or background information for your topic. The material is in the book, so have the children read it. Do not be afraid to bring in supplemental material or to modify the textbook materials to fit what you are trying to do. Remember that you are the teacher and the textbook is an aid. The text cannot teach for you, although many teachers seem to think it can.

REVIEWING A TEXTBOOK

Suppose that you have just been given a copy of the textbook you will be using next year or that you are at a book display and see a new science textbook. What are you going to do? You will probably look through the book, but do you really know what you are looking for? If you do, you are indeed a rare individual, because most teachers do not. In this section, you will be given some guidelines to help you evaluate, or review, a textbook; then you will have the opportunity to actually review a science textbook. The following material discusses 12 items to consider when reviewing or evaluating a textbook.

Author(s) and Publisher

Who wrote and published the textbook? This might seem minor, but it is not. Does the publisher have a good reputation in the textbook field? There are some good materials available from minor publishers, but most of the established programs come from the major publishers. Who are the authors and what are their credentials? Is this their first series, or have they written others? What is the date of publication? Is the text new, or is it a revision of an old text? The answers to these questions can give you clues as to what to expect when you look through the text. You may not know or recognize the names of the authors, but you should recognize the names of major publishers and be familiar with the types of materials associated with each of them.

Appearance

The book's appearance is probably the first thing you will notice, and it is important. It is very difficult to get a child interested in a dull-looking book, no matter how well written it may be. Eye appeal plays a major role in the acceptability of a textbook to the teacher and students who have to use it. Look for such characteristics as the use of color, illustrations (we will come back to this point later), format, and physical size. A book that is too large or too small is awkward to handle, and the odd size can detract from its usefulness. Look at the cover and paper. How durable will the book be? Does the book look like one that you might like to use?

Illustrations

Illustrations serve two purposes in a textbook: (a) to add to the overall appearance and (b) to illustrate the material. Good illustrations, either photographs or drawings, brighten a book by adding variety to the black-and-white plainness of the

The library provides materials to supplement the textbook.

print and paper. Are the photos current or dated? Posed or realistic? Proper placement can also make the reading material seem a little less formidable to slower readers. The primary purpose of an illustration is, of course, to clarify some specific material. Students can read the material and look at the picture. They might also "read" the picture to help them understand the material they have read. Having this opportunity is a great help for the slow reader. As you look at the illustrations and/or photos in a textbook, think about what they do for the book. Do they merely decorate, or do they also teach? Do they make you want to look further, or do they turn you away from the book? Would your students like the illustrations?

Readability

There is more to readability than proper vocabulary. First of all, look at the size of the type. Is it too small, too large, or just right to be easily read? Does the layout of the reading material allow you to find the beginning easily and then to follow the text without losing your place? Is the reading material appropriate for the children using it? Too often, authors use vocabulary and writing styles that are more appropriate for upper-level students than for elementary students. The textbook is not really of much value if your students cannot read it.

Every teacher is a reading teacher, although teaching children to read the content of a science lesson is a major task overlooked by too many teachers. You must teach your students how to read science materials as well as how to understand and use science concepts.

Content

This is material that you will be teaching; look at it closely. Is it scientifically accurate? You would assume that it would be, but sometimes errors appear either through oversight or because information is obsolete. A good textbook should contain current, accurate information. Who wants to read that people may someday go to the moon, when you know that they have already been there? If the textbook is obsolete or inaccurate, you might want to try to find a different text. Does the content fit the students using it? If it is too simple or too advanced, you will have trouble getting your students to relate to it. Are the analogies appropriate? Analogies and examples should relate to the child's world, not the teacher's; the student is the one who is trying to understand the concepts being illustrated. How is the content organized? It should be in a logical sequence that children can follow. Determine whether there is a pattern, or teaching strategy, to each lesson or unit. Can you find the central theme—the foundation of the textbook? You usually find it explained in the teacher's manual, but you may have to look for it. If no central theme exists, the book may not have much continuity. Does the textbook include any materials about, or related to, any of the various cultures of the world? Science is not a cold, impersonal field. The effect of science on culture should be included to help students understand how science can benefit or harm humanity. How does the textbook treat controversial materials? There always have been and will be differing opinions in science. Does the textbook ignore controversy or present it for discussion? Are there suggested ways of teaching controversial material?

The content of the textbook is important to you and to your students because it is the reason for the textbook's existence. Everything else (teaching strategies, experiments, illustrations, etc.) is directly related to the effective teaching of the content.

Presentation of Content

There must be a method for presenting the content material to the student. Each textbook will have its own method or teaching strategy. Can you describe the teaching strategy used in your textbook? What kinds of questions are asked of the student? Look for memory-based as well as thought-provoking questions. How are the students involved in the learning process? Are experiments and investigations conducted by the students, or are they demonstrated by the teacher? How much reading is required of the student? Find out if your textbook is a *reader* or a *guide* for the students. What does the teacher do in your program? Examine the teacher's role, and try to determine how you would teach the material. Would you have much freedom, or is the teaching procedure highly structured? As you look at a textbook, you should remember that not only do the students have to learn from it, you have to teach from it. If the material is not presented in an interesting manner or does not require much thought or effort from the students, does it really matter what content is being taught or what the pictures look like?

Materials for Activities

If you are going to do the activities suggested, you must have the necessary materials available. Does the textbook give you an easy-to-follow materials list? Material handling is a time-consuming task that discourages many teachers from using activities. A well-organized materials list with suggestions for obtaining, storing, and distributing the materials can be very valuable. Are the required materials easily obtainable? If you have to spend a lot of time, effort, and money to obtain materials, you probably will not use the activities. Some publishers provide material kits for use with their textbooks. Merrill Science has an extensive kit as a part of its science program. Independent suppliers (notably Delta Education) have developed material kits for the major textbook series. Is there a kit for your textbook?

Do the activities require special equipment? Some specialized equipment such as microscopes may be required, but look for activities that use common materials. Activities that use familiar items encourage the students to replicate the experiments and activities at home. Can students bring the needed materials from home? Can you identify supermarket items in the materials list?

You need time to gather materials for your activities. If you must start plants or order live organisms, how much lead-time do you need? Does your textbook provide advance warning in the teacher's guide?

Supplementary Materials

Supplementary materials for both teacher and students can be helpful, especially for beginning teachers who have not had the opportunity to develop their own. What is available to you?

1. Are workbooks available? Many teachers consider them very important.
2. Is there help in testing? Test items in the form of test masters and test booklets that can be duplicated help you test to the objectives of the lesson as well as save you the time and effort required to write tests.

3. Copy masters of lessons, information sheets, and activities are often available as part of a textbook program. Does your textbook have masters that you can duplicate?

4. Are pictures and/or posters available as part of the teaching materials? Correlated pictures and posters add visual impact to your lessons, but they can be difficult to obtain on your own.

5. Are references or teacher's resource materials provided? A list of supplementary reading materials for both teacher and student can be helpful.

6. Background information for the teacher is usually most welcome when starting a lesson containing unfamiliar material.

7. Does the manual suggest any films, filmstrips, recordings, or sets of pictures that might be used with the textbook? You should supplement textbooks with audiovisual material.

Remember, one weakness of textbooks is that they tend to be used as the only source of information. A good list of supplementary materials, with suggestions for using them, can help the teacher overcome this weakness.

Mathematics

You are not going to teach mathematics using your science textbook, but some science does involve the use of mathematics. Mathematics can be called the *language of science,* and children need to know the basic mathematics that will be needed to carry out the activities in the textbook. Does your textbook discuss or use mathematics? What mathematics skills are necessary to do the science activities? Do the children have these skills, or will you have to teach them? You may have to correlate your science and mathematics lessons to be successful.

Teaching Suggestions

How much help does the textbook give teachers? Look for a teacher's manual or a teacher's edition of the text. How is it organized? It should give some background information about the philosophy, goals, objectives, and teaching strategy, followed by a reproduction of the actual text with suggestions for teaching the material. Is the teacher's manual usable? If it is too large and clumsy, the print is too small, or you have trouble finding the teaching suggestions, you may need help that this teacher's edition cannot give you.

How complete are the teaching suggestions? Some manuals offer only general ideas, but others provide specific directions. Would you feel confident using the teaching suggestions provided, or would you want more?

Computers are in many classrooms for the children to use.

Computer Courseware

Computers are in many elementary school classrooms. Publishers are beginning to provide supplementary courseware (software that is designed to supplement or be an integral part of the program) for use on these machines. Does your textbook have software for simulations and activities that correlate with the textbook material? Courseware is an important new addition to the traditional textbook program. Children are able to interact with the computer in simulation exercises, making decisions and experiencing consequences related to the material in the textbook. Computer activities provide the child with simulated experiences and graphic presentations of the lessons. If your textbook does not have software for simulations and activities, does it provide a listing of appropriate commercial software as an alternative?

Some textbooks encourage teachers to use the computer for testing and record keeping. Does your textbook provide classroom management software? If so, what does it include? Does it seem easy to use? As a beginning teacher, do you think you would find this a useful feature?

The computer is a valuable teaching tool, but it does require appropriate software. Publishers are in the best position to provide correlated software to go with their textbooks.

Evaluation

Are there any suggestions for evaluating a student's work or progress? How will you know whether the child has achieved the objectives set forth in the textbook? The textbook should give suggestions that will help you follow the progress of your students and decide what must be taught next. Does evaluation consist of suggested test items or testing techniques, or does it also address informal evaluation? Evaluation is a continuous effort to determine what a child knows so that the teacher can develop an individualized plan to help the student take the next step in learning. Good suggestions for evaluation can help you better know and understand your students, their needs, and their progress.

Now you should have some information to help you judge a textbook. There are other considerations you will probably include in your review that will reflect your own concerns and prejudices. That is why people, using the same list of criteria, will rate textbooks differently. The final judgment on the appropriateness of any textbook is based on personal opinion.

ACTIVITY 3.1: REVIEWING A TEXTBOOK

The purpose of this activity is twofold. First, you will apply what you have learned by actually reviewing a textbook, and, second, you will become familiar with one or more of the textbooks available to you. Remember to think about how your knowledge of textbooks can help you become a better teacher.

Group discussions and your instructor's checks will be an integral part of this activity, and you may be asked to make a presentation to the class. Your instructor will help you decide on the appropriate type of presentation. You will share information about several textbooks or textbook series as you interact with your group, class, and instructor.

Access to several science textbook series will be necessary. Your instructor will direct you to the textbooks available for your use. Here is a list of textbook series and publishers to get you started. This is not a complete list, as it includes only current, major publications. There are other series that might be locally available.

Publisher	Title	Copyright
Addison-Wesley Publishing Co.	*Addison-Wesley Science*	1986
Coronado Publishing Co.	*Science and Technology*	1985
D. C. Heath & Co.	*Heath Science*	1985
Harcourt Brace Jovanovich	*Concepts in Science* (Nova Edition)	1989
Holt, Rinehart and Winston	*Holt Elementary Science*	1986
McGraw-Hill Co. (Webster Division) (Correlated with the ESS program and materials)	*Gateways to Science*	1985

Macmillan and Co.	*Journeys in Science*	1988
Merrill Publishing Co.	*Merrill Science*	1989
Scott, Foresman and Co.	*Discover Science*	1989
Silver Burdett & Ginn Co.	*Science: Understanding Your Environment*	1987
Steck-Vaughn Co.	*Science for You*	1987

All of these textbook programs have material kits available from the publisher and/or Delta Education.

A. Select a textbook or textbook series to evaluate. Use the teacher's edition if possible. Your instructor will work with you to help you decide which of the following suggestions to use:

  1. Select a textbook or textbook series and proceed with the textbook review in this section (see *B* below).

  2. Meet with your group and decide how to proceed. A particular series might be selected so each member of your group could review a different grade level. Or one grade level might be chosen so each group member could review a textbook for that grade from different series.

  3. Follow your instructor's directions.

B. Start your review. Think about the suggestions that were presented earlier in the chapter. You will need to refer to them as you go through the textbook review activities.

Examine the introductory material in the teacher's guide. Determine if these specifics are included in the text, and quote an example:

Title and Grade Level:

Copyright Date:

Publisher:

1. Content

   Scope and Sequence: What is taught in this textbook series and in what order?

   Process Skills: What process skills are taught? How are they identified?

   Objectives: Are objectives given? Are they presented to the student? How?

   Teaching Strategy: Is the teaching strategy clearly stated? What is it?

   Activities: Are activities provided? Are they required or optional? What kind of materials would be needed?

Vocabulary: How are new concepts taught? Are definitions given as part of the lesson or as a supplement? Are examples and nonexamples provided? Is there a glossary?

Computer Supplement: Are there suggested computer activities? What kind?

2. Classroom management

Safety: Is safety discussed? How much emphasis is put on safety? Does the text give you any help in planning for a safe classroom?

Handling and Storage of Materials: Are suggestions provided for obtaining materials? For distributing and taking them up? Any suggestions for storage?

Computer Supplement: Are there computer programs available for record keeping and class lists? For test construction?

3. Teaching Aids

   Bibliography: Are there bibliographies of

   a. Audiovisual materials?

   b. Student reading materials?

   c. Teacher references?

   d. Equipment sources?

   Bulletin Boards and Displays: Does the text provide suggestions for construction and use of bulletin boards? Any for special displays? Are materials listed? Any teaching suggestions?

   Duplicating Masters: Are ready-to-copy sheets or duplication masters available? What are the rules for using them? Are teaching suggestions included?

4. Enrichment

   Field Trips: Are field trips suggested? How well are the trips coordinated with the content materials? Are the sites practical? Easily visited? Readily available? Safe?

   Resource People: Are people listed by occupation or by generic source? Are the people correlated with the content? Are suggestions given for using the resource person? Any follow-up suggestions?

Science Fairs: Are they suggested? Is any help given for organizing and implementing one? Are any criteria provided for judging the entries?

Olympics: Are they suggested? Are any state or national programs identified? Is there any help in organizing your own? Does the teacher's edition suggest ways to include all students, or are the Olympics designed more for a specific type of student?

Projects: Does the text suggest long-term or outside projects? Are they required or optional? Are they class or individual oriented?

Learning Centers: Are they used? Does the text provide help in organizing and implementing them? Are they a part of the lesson, or are they used as enrichment?

5. Exceptional students

Mainstreaming: Does the text encourage mainstreaming? What special provisions are made for the mainstreamed child? What type of activities are provided?

Slow Learners: Are there any special programs or activities for these children? What kind? Are any suggestions given to help you identify those who might need this type of help? Are there any special instructions for teaching these children?

Gifted and Talented: Is any help given here in identifying them? Are special enrichment lessons suggested? Is working with the gifted suggested?

English as a Second Language (ESL): Are Spanish-language editions available? Are there any in other foreign languages? Are suggestions for the use of ESL texts included?

Physically Handicapped: Are any activities provided for the physically handicapped? The blind student? The wheelchair student?

6. Special Features
Are there any special features that deserve noting?

7. Specific Criteria
Rate your textbook using the following rating scale and criteria. Space is provided for the other members of your group to record the ratings of their textbooks. This should allow you to compare several textbooks. Think about your ratings; not every item will be a 5, even if you really like the text.

Rating Scale

0—Book totally lacking in the characteristic

1—Occasional evidence of the characteristic

2—Evidence of the characteristic but below average

3—Frequent evidence of the characteristic

4—Excellent evidence of the characteristic

5—Superior in all aspects of the characteristics (Sund & Trowbridge, 1973, p. 451)

Table 3.1   Rating a Textbook

Criteria for Rating Textbook	Names of Series Reviewed				
Appearance					
1. Attractive and appealing to children					
2. Margins and page arrangements contribute to readability and attractiveness					
3. Adequate spacing and appropriate type size					
4. Suitable size for easy handling					
5. Durable backings					
6. Good quality paper					
Illustrations					
1. Contribute to meaningfulness of the content					
2. Interesting and scientifically accurate					
3. Clearly produced and well placed on the page					
4. Placed near the text they illustrate					
5. Appropriate to the grade level					
6. Clear in meaning					
7. Current and attractive					
Readability					
1. Reading level appropriate for the children using the book					
2. Appropriate page layout—students can easily follow the sentences					
3. Type size and style easy to read					
Content					
1. Develops problem-solving skills					
2. Scientifically accurate and up-to-date					

Table 3.1   (continued)

Criteria for Rating Textbook	Names of Series Reviewed				
3. Appropriate for the developmental level of student					
4. Analogies and activities appropriate					
5. Follows a logical sequence					
6. Develops positive attitudes toward science					
7. Suggested lessons stimulate interest that will lead to further study					
8. Provides for various ability levels (the nonverbal child, the child with reading problems, the high achiever, etc.)					
9. Well balanced in terms of scientific content					
10. Central theme clearly defined					
11. Free from anthropomorphism, teleology, and personification (attributing human form, qualities, purpose, or will to nonhuman things)					
12. Usable index and table of contents					
13. Glossary of science terms with clearly stated explanations of meanings					
14. Free from sex bias					
15. Suggestions for treatment of controversial materials					
Presentation of Material 1. Has a clearly defined teaching strategy					
2. Uses class discussion					
3. Uses divergent as well as convergent questioning					
4. Encourages children to do experiments					
5. Material presented in an interesting manner					

Table 3.1   (continued)

Criteria for Rating Textbook	Names of Series Reviewed				
Mathematics 1. Includes mathematics in the experiments and activities					
2. Offers suggestions for using mathematics					
Teacher's Guide 1. Offers alternate activities					
2. Gives necessary background information for effective use of textbook material					
3. Suggests teaching aids, games, etc.					
4. Lists resources (printed, visual, audiovisual)					
5. Suggests remedial and/or enrichment activities					
6. Suggests a variety of evaluation techniques					
7. Offers help in planning and implementing text material					
Total points for textbook (225 possible)					

    C. By now, you should have some definite opinions about the textbook you have been reviewing.

        1. What do you consider to be the *strengths* of the textbooks?

        2. What do you consider to be a *weakness* of the textbook?

        3. Would you like to use this textbook in your classroom? Why or why not?

    D. Meet with your group and discuss the textbooks you have reviewed. Record some of your comments and discussions.

    E. Arrange for a group or class discussion. Suggestions for discussion include:

        1. One member of the group acts as a spokesperson to present a series to the class, using the criteria on the rating sheet to prepare the report, but condensing it to a usable format.

        2. Each member of the class makes a presentation to his or her group and the instructor.

3. The instructor makes suggestions or requirements for the evaluation.

4. Design your own evaluation and submit it to your instructor.

☑ **Self-Check**

For the activity:

Did you have any trouble finding the information you were looking for? If so, that difficulty might indicate a weak area in the textbook. Did you rate everything high because you liked the textbook or low because you did not like it, or did you try to overcome your biases and be honest? Sometimes this is hard to do, but you have to try.

Implications for teaching:

Do you have a clear concept of the textbook approach to teaching? You will probably use textbooks when you start teaching, so you should be especially concerned about using them. Did you find out what kinds of activities are considered appropriate for particular grade levels? Think about this, because it can be important. Textbooks can give you, the beginning teacher, information about the capabilities of students at different age levels and about the topics generally covered in specific grade levels. This information might be a source of help when you plan your own science program.

☐ **Comments**

SUMMARY

In this chapter, you have been introduced to the elementary science textbook. The textbook approach to science instruction has a number of strengths: textbook series provide school systems with organized science programs, and good textbooks provide teachers with organized units of work, are especially helpful for beginning teachers, may be less expensive than kits to purchase but can be supplemented by kits (if desired), and provide familiarity and security. The textbook approach, however, does contain several weaknesses: the reading level may not match the students' grade level; teachers may use the text as the *only* source of information; textbooks are generally designed to be read, not to promote hands-on experiences, and thus relegate the student to a role of passive receptor of information; each textbook series has its own scope and sequence, which creates a curriculum problem; and textbooks become outdated. In classroom use, the textbook may either be relied on heavily or totally ignored; probably the best way to use a textbook, however, is to use it as a resource for discussion ideas, demonstrations, experiments, background material, and verification of experimental results.

You have been given some suggestions as to what to look for when reviewing a textbook. Items to consider include the author and publisher, appearance, illustrations, readability, content and its presentation, materials for activities, supplementary materials, use of mathematics, teaching suggestions, availability of computer software, and suggestions for evaluation. You used these suggestions and the criteria offered for them when you actually reviewed a textbook.

The purpose of this chapter was to make you familiar with the most widely used of all science programs, the textbook. The objectives were that in completing this chapter you would

1. Evaluate elementary science textbooks using the criteria presented in this chapter.
2. List and explain the strengths and weaknesses of an elementary science textbook program.

Do you think you have met the objectives? If not, go back over the material and see your instructor for help. Review your textbook evaluation and the background material you have read. Meet with your small group to bring up any unanswered questions that you have and to help answer those that your classmates might have.

REFERENCES

Sund, R. B., & Trowbridge, L. W. (1973). Teaching science by inquiry in the secondary school (2nd ed.). Columbus, OH: Merrill Publishing Co.

SUGGESTED READINGS

Bruner, J. S. (1967). *Toward a theory of instruction.* Cambridge: Harvard University Press, 1967.

Eisner, E. W. (1987). Why the textbook influences curriculum [excerpt from *The educational imagination*]. *Curriculum Review, 26*(3), 11–13.

Gagné, R. M. (1965). *The conditions of learning.* New York: Holt, Rinehart and Winston.

McLeod, R. J. (1979). Selecting a textbook for good science teaching. *Science and Children, 17*(2), 14–15. Note: *Science and Children* presents a monthly "Curriculum Review" section in which new textbooks and materials are reviewed.

Straham, D. B., & Herlihy, J. G. (1985). A model for analyzing textbook content. *Journal of Reading, 28,* 430–443.

Wolfinger, D. M. (1984). *Teaching science in the elementary school* (pp. 311–324).

CHAPTER 4

The Sciencing Teacher

Goals:

After completing this chapter, you will demonstrate competence in using acquired information, ideas, and skills to develop decision-making and management skills related to active science teaching.

Objectives:

In completing this chapter, you will do the following:

1. Identify and describe the four elements that a sciencing teacher must consider in decision making.

2. Identify and explain how an existing science program can be modified to meet classroom needs.

3. Identify and describe how acquired ideas, information, and skills can be used in selecting an appropriate science program for a specific school system.

4. Describe how acquired ideas, information, and skills can be used in helping you develop your own science program.

5. Identify and describe means of controlling physical factors in order to enhance learning.

6. Identify and construct classroom arrangements that are appropriate for the large group, small group, and individual instruction.

7. Identify and explain techniques that can be used in organizing and utilizing science materials and equipment.

8. Identify potential safety hazards in a classroom situation and suggest ways to prevent injury to students.

INTRODUCTION

Teaching is both an art and a skill, both affective and cognitive. A sciencing teacher is an active decision maker, a manager, and a coordinator. A sciencing teacher develops, modifies, adapts, and implements. A sciencing teacher is never simply a recipe follower. This chapter focuses on your role as a sciencing teacher.

As a sciencing teacher, you must be aware of the essential areas into which most of your decision making will fall. These areas include

1. Students
2. Curricular materials
3. Physical environment
4. You, the teacher

It is your responsibility to serve as an active manager and coordinator in these areas so that optimal learning outcomes are increased. Each area is discussed as it relates to the role of an active teacher, decision maker, manager, and coordinator.

STUDENTS

Your students will differ in sex, race, ethnic background, intelligence, cognitive style, and social, physical, and affective characteristics. You must take these individual differences into consideration in planning appropriate science experiences for children. Chapter 1 provides you with insight into the nature of learning and the nature of the child. We know that learning does not occur in the same way for each child. As teachers, we must provide alternate avenues for children to use in reaching the same science objective. In some cases, we must even provide alternate objectives.

Piaget's research has provided us with knowledge and understanding about the stages of cognitive development that children pass through. Teachers must be able to recognize the particular stage of cognitive development of their students and provide instruction that is cognitively meaningful. You may wish to review these stages in Chapter 1.

CURRICULAR MATERIALS

Which approach and materials you use and how you use them will affect the learning outcome. Most of your decisions related to curriculum or program management will fall into one of three areas: making the most out of an existing

Teaching must consider individual differences in planning
appropriate science experiences for children.

science program, selecting a new science program, or developing your own
science program. We will explore some specific suggestions in each of these
areas.

Using an Existing Program

Most schools have a science program of some type. If you are fortunate enough
to teach in a school that has a strong science program based on one of the new
science approaches or one of the current textbook programs, you can follow the
teacher's guide and teach reasonably well. But what if you are given an obsolete
or, in your opinion, a very poor or weak textbook? Several options are open to
you. As a beginning teacher, you should talk to other teachers or the principal to
find out how you are expected to use the textbook. They can tell you whether you
are supposed to follow it closely, if you can digress somewhat, or if you are free
to develop your own program. This is important because you do have to meet
the expectations of the school system that employs you. Do remember, though,
that you can exceed the expectations by supplementing the minimum requirements. Develop a strong science program with what you have or can beg, buy,
or borrow.

Here are some suggestions to help you with your science program. Use any
of them that are appropriate to your situation. They can apply to any textbook
series, good or bad, that you may have in your classroom.

The Textbook. Use the textbook to help you decide *what* to teach. In most school systems, the adopted textbook series acts as a curriculum guide, establishing the philosophy, scope, and sequence of the science program. Your textbook can tell you what content you are expected to cover. Look at the table of contents to see what topics are listed and use this as your guide. The actual material in the text can help you decide how thoroughly, or superficially, you should treat each topic.

In short, use your textbook as a *resource*. Even the poorest textbook can serve in this capacity. It can provide you with teaching suggestions, experiments and demonstrations, suggested reading lists, teaching aids, and background information. You do not have to use every suggestion or activity. Be selective, but do not ignore this source just because it is old or you do not like the color of the cover.

Hands-on Activities.   Develop some *hands-on* experience for your students. If activities in your textbook are nonexistent or teacher-oriented, use what you have learned here to develop new, or modify existing, activities to involve the students. Look for ways to involve them in concrete experiences rather than the more traditional abstractions. Let the students do the demonstrations and experiments rather than doing them yourself.

Find a way to include *process skills* in your science program. Some textbooks include these skills, but many do not. Process skills are the tools of the scientist, and children should learn to use them automatically when presented with a problem or a learning situation.

Try to provide *something for everyone* in your classroom. Most textbooks are written for the average student. You must have activities simple enough for your slower students as well as enrichment activities for your gifted students. Every child should be able to work at a level commensurate with that child's ability. Students who cannot do the work assigned or who find no challenge to it are not receiving fair treatment from the teacher.

Supplemental Activities.   Bring in *outside speakers.* Use parents and other members of the community to present information to your students. You have access to scientists, professional people, and knowledgeable amateurs if you will look around the community for them. Let them help you teach science by bringing in expertise that you and your textbook may not be able to provide.

Use *trade books to supplement* your science program (trade books are any books other than textbooks). Science trade books can be a valuable resource for the classroom teacher. They can be used to spark interest about natural and physical phenomena. Children can use them to find out about the things around them. If possible, trade books should be part of your own classroom library so that children can use them individually or in small groups to meet specific interests. Trade books provide children with additional sources of information. They often provide more motivation for a reluctant reader than does the textbook.

Trade books deal with a great many topics. In one typical year, for instance, the books published fell into a broad spectrum of science topics. Some focused on animals, with titles such as *Ant Cities, City Geese, The Friendly Prairie Dog, Raccoons and Ripe Corn,* and *White Tail. Icebergs and Glaciers, Water and Sky,* and *Who Lives In . . . The Forest* are titles found in the area of earth science, the environment, and conservation. In the area of space and astronomy are found such titles as *They Dance in the Sky: Native American Star Myths* and *Hello, Who's Out There? The Search for Extraterrestrial Life.* The life science area contains titles such as *Dinosaurs Walked Here: And Other Stories Fossils Tell; The Human Body: How We Evolved;* and *Wheat: The Golden Harvest.* The area of medical and health sciences features titles such as *AIDS: What Does It Mean To You?* and *Crack: The New Drug Epidemic. Get Ready for Robots* and *You Won't Believe Your Eyes!* are two of the trade books published in the area of physics, technology and engineering. Biographies are also excellent sources of information; for example, *Carl Sagan: Superstar Scientist* and *Anne Morrow Lindbergh: Pilot and Poet* were published that year. Some trade books fall under the category of "other"; *Dots, Spots, Speckles and Stripes* and *I Eat Dinner* are two of the more interesting titles found there.

Teachers can keep up to date in this area by consulting the list "Outstanding Science Tradebooks" published in *Science and Children* each year. Copies of this list, which includes a brief review and appropriate grade-level notation, are available free from the National Science Teachers Association (NSTA) headquarters, if you send a self-addressed, stamped envelope. The list contains books that are suitable for Grades K–8. These books are selected by a special book

Trade books provide children with additional sources of information.

review subcommittee appointed by NSTA in cooperation with the Children's Book Council (CBC). The school library should have a good selection of these kinds of books available. In addition, a classroom library might be developed from books brought from home by the students.

You may wish to add to these suggestions. Remember, whatever happens to your classroom is directly related to what you *plan* to do there.

Selecting a Science Program

If you are employed by a school system that does not have a science program or wants to replace an existing program, you may be asked to serve on a science selection committee, or at least to give your opinion to the committee. This is your chance to contribute to the improvement of science education. Obviously, you want to recommend only the best, but which is best? Although it is often a temptation to ask your college instructors or others for an authoritative opinion, you must decide for yourself what you mean by best. Best for whom? Only then can you decide upon the program that "best" fits the needs of the user.

Many of the programs and textbooks are good. There are many school systems using each with great success. The trick is to fit the program to the school. When you select a new program, it may be easy to decide which program *you* like best. But, more importantly, you must decide which one is most appropriate for the kind of *students* you teach. The preferences of other teachers in the school must also be considered. A program must be selected that they can and will use. Remember, no program is effective unless it is used.

Several lists of criteria are available to help you select an appropriate program, or you may want to develop your own list. Here are two lists that might be of help when you consider programs for adoption.

The first one was developed and used by the Mesa County Valley School District No. 51 in Grand Junction, Colorado, and was reported in *Science and Children*. A science committee was established and given the task of developing criteria and reviewing science programs. Their list was developed in 1976, so you will want to update some of the criteria, but it does provide a helpful guide.

Selection Criteria   The primary goal of the science committee was to recommend a science program that could be taught by educators representing a variety of teaching philosophies. To meet this goal, and to give each program under consideration an equal evaluation, twelve basic criteria were established. A comparison of all elementary school science programs evaluated was possible by recording the results in chart form.

   1. *Level of Readability.* A majority of the teachers surveyed felt that reading and science were closely interrelated. The teachers requested a science textbook that was written at a grade level that was consistent with their respective reading programs. The general consensus was that reading would be reinforced.

2. *Durability of the Program.* As a cost-saving factor, the committee studied each series in terms of its physical construction. This analysis went beyond the textbook analyzed, and was applied to all instructional material within the science program. Some specifics researched were as follows: Was the text a paper or hardbound design? If a laboratory kit was included, was it sturdy, or would replacement of parts be an ongoing cost? How was the teacher's manual bound? (paperback, spiral, or hardbound?)

3. *Preparation Time.* The teachers surveyed felt that science rated well behind mathematics, reading, language arts, and other instructional areas in terms of their priorities and time expended. The preparation time devoted to science instruction was to be minimal. Any materials to be supplied for use in an experiment should be easily obtained.

4. *Text Format.* The committees desired to afford teachers a degree of flexibility in the utilization of the text. A textual program which contained that unit format was desirable. The order in which the units were to be taught would be left to the individual teacher. If district-wide uniformity were needed, a specific order for unit presentation could be established. This would help in cases of in-district transfer of children.

5. *Teacher's Manual Format.* Because preparation time devoted to science is normally minimal, the committee searched for a comprehensive teacher's manual. Were teaching suggestions included on the student pages? Were materials needed for each lesson listed? Were goals and possible outcomes of each lesson provided? Were lessons clearly outlined?

6. *Laboratory Kit.* If a program included a laboratory kit, could the kit be utilized by more than one classroom at a time? Was the kit set up so that students could maintain and inventory it? Were the components of the laboratory sturdy enough to stand up for an extended period of time? The committee felt that a kit which could be easily maintained, was durable, and would require little replacement of component parts would be readily accepted.

7. *Testing Materials.* Was a set of testing materials included with the program? Although many teacher-made evaluation materials were good, a comprehensive evaluation system would insure more valid testing results. To obtain some degree of grading uniformity across the district elementary schools, a comprehensive set of text materials should be included with the basic instructional program.

8. *Kindergarten Materials.* Although many elementary science programs do not include the kindergarten level, the committee deemed this to be desirable. The kindergarten readiness for science should be conducted in the same program that would be used in later grades. Within a single program, major concepts could be introduced in kindergarten. Some degree of program uniformity in science content and how it is presented could thus be established from the very beginning.

9. *Supplementary Books.* Are any books other than the textbooks required? If a laboratory book or a record book is included, is it necessary to the program? If another book is needed, is it reusable or consumable? Audiovisual and manipulatory materials for the program could be subjected to this test.

10. *Health.* Since science and health are frequently scheduled into the same block

of time for instructional purposes, the committee sought a science program which included some large amount of health education.

11. *Content and "Hands-on."* Since the district employs teachers who use a wide variety of instructional approaches, how can one science program meet their instructional needs? The most acceptable answer was the identification of a science program which was well balanced between content or printed information and "hands-on" or experiment oriented material.

12. *Experiments.* Because the district wanted a program which included experiments as a part of the learning process, there was the need to evaluate the kind of experiments which were included. The committee looked for purposeful experiments which require some limited amount of preparation time. The materials required should either be included in the laboratory kit, or easily and inexpensively obtained. The committee desired open-ended exploration, rather than a guided step-by-step approach. (Reeder & Adams, 1977, pp. 8–10)

The second list, presented in *The Science Teacher,* was developed by DeRose and Whittle (1976) for use by teachers as a guideline for evaluating science programs. Although oriented more toward textbook selection than toward the laboratory kits or teacher-developed science programs, the list of criteria, with a little modification, can apply to any science program.

What to Look for in Science Programs

1. What is the underlying philosophy of the program, and do you feel comfortable with it?

2. Do the materials communicate their intent to the student, and do the teacher materials communicate their message to the teacher?

3. Is the program practical in terms of its aims, teachability, application to student's everyday living, and in building a foundation of science knowledge?

4. Does the program permit flexibility in teaching styles, sequence, time, content, classroom facilities?

5. Does the program appear to be appealing to the students?

6. Is there a variety of science topics and are the topics appropriate?

7. Does the program include opportunities to apply scientific methods?

8. How are the various parts of the program organized, and do you feel comfortable with the arrangements?

9. Are tests and other assessments provided?

10. Are learning objectives for the program stated, and do you feel they are appropriate and reasonable?

11. Is the student reading material at a reasonable level, and is there a good balance between "reading" and "doing" activities?

12. To what extent are students directly involved with "things" and laboratory activities, and do you consider it sufficient?

13. Are there provisions for individual student differences?

14. Are the time requirements to teach the material on a day-to-day or week-to-week basis reasonable?

15. Does the teacher's guide provide helpful suggestions relating to teaching strategies, student activities, methods of evaluation, use of audiovisual aids, and other material?

16. Does the program provide for the needed mathematics?

17. Does the program give you a feeling that you could successfully teach science?[1]

Criteria lists are a helpful guide, but you also have to consider which of the criteria you wish to place the most, and which the least, emphasis on. You and the other members of your faculty may use the same list but have entirely different opinions of the material being evaluated. A good selection can be made only after much evaluation, discussion, and give and take among all of those teachers who are going to use the program.

One final point: look at as many programs as you can before making a selection. Too many schools limit themselves to the consideration of only a few textbooks from some of the more familiar publishers. They may not be aware that other options exist. One of the purposes of this chapter is to make you aware of the alternatives available, so that you can make intelligent choices.

These teachers are reviewing science textbooks in order to decide which program will be best for their school.

Developing Your Own Science Program

Not every school has an established science curriculum. There may be various reasons for the lack of an established program. Some schools may furnish teachers with many resources and basic curriculum guidelines. The teachers are expected to use these materials in developing an innovative science program.

Other schools may provide teachers with a good basic program and give them the freedom to use it in whole, in part, or not at all in providing science experiences for the students. In a school where a weak or outdated program exists, the teacher has the responsibility to develop supplementary experiences. In a few cases, there may be no program at all, and the teacher must start from scratch. In any case, you will face a challenging, but rewarding opportunity.

1. Textbooks as resources. In developing your own science program, you will need all the help you can get. There are several good sources. In all probability, you will go to a textbook first. This is an excellent place to start because it can provide you with a course outline, teaching suggestions, experiments and demonstrations, and factual information.

2. Other teachers as resources. Your fellow teachers are also an excellent source of help. There is nothing wrong with looking to more experienced teachers for information and helpful suggestions. It is only when you depend on others for everything that you are in trouble. Teachers who have been in the school system for a few years can help you find equipment, suggest what units might be taught, and offer teaching suggestions. If consultants or resource people are available, do not hesitate to use their services. Too often, beginning, and even experienced, teachers are reluctant to ask for help because they are afraid it will be construed as a sign of weakness or inability to do the job they were hired to do. This is nonsense. Good teachers use every tool, idea, or resource available to help improve their teaching.

3. Children as resources. A third, infrequently used resource is the children in your classroom. Find out what their interests are and what problem-solving skills they have. Look for hidden talents that might be useful. Above all, do not underestimate the contributions that your children can make or what they can teach you. Good teachers learn as they teach.

4. Parents and local residents as resources. Parents and local residents often provide a rich source of information related to the science technology and society theme.

5. Professional journals, meetings, and inservices as resources. Reading professional journals such as *Science and Children* and attending local, state, regional and national professional meetings and inservices are excellent ways to add to your knowledge base of content, process, and teaching techniques.

This teacher is looking through professional literature to gather ideas and information to use in developing his science program.

According to Penick, Yager, and Bonnstetter (1984), excellent science programs foster the development of students who are active hypothesizers, discoverers, and evaluators. These successful programs also focus on science lessons that are related to the rest of the curriculum, as science is related to the rest of life. In the concluding portion of his article based on research findings, John Penick (1986) declared that science programs should

1. Emphasize both the mental and the physical
2. Encourage models of inquiry
3. *Not* be reading based
4. Reflect the nature of science

The National Science Teachers Association offers the following criteria for use in evaluating a science program.

1. Does it offer genuine alternatives, so that real decisions can be made and real problems can be solved?
2. Does it provide problems that are based on firsthand experience?

3. Are students actively involved in gathering data?

4. Is information presented several ways—through books, films, and hands-on experience?

5. Is the information appropriate for students' age levels? Do kids learn how the information was originally developed?

6. Is science tied to other subjects?

7. Do kids use information they've gathered and values they've learned to make decisions? Do they evaluate the consequences for others?

The classroom teacher can make use of research results. They provide the data base necessary for good curricular decision making. Developing science programs that foster active teacher and student interaction and that involve the students directly in sciencing is a worthy goal.

PHYSICAL ENVIRONMENT

The classroom itself, the way it is organized, the procedures used, and the materials and equipment available must be skillfully managed. The hands-on

Teachers must be sensitive to the physical environment of the classroom.

approach to science teaching demands that teachers be skillful classroom managers. Although a teacher's knowledge of and skill in teaching science are necessary, these alone will not produce a successful learning experience.

The physical environment of the science classroom has both a direct and an indirect influence on the kind of learning that takes place. Teachers must also plan for students' safety. This involves being aware of potential hazards in any given activity or situation. Identifying potential hazards and controlling them can greatly decrease the likelihood of injury in the classroom. As a teacher, you must become increasingly sensitive to the physical environment of the classroom and be able to control and direct it so that learning is enhanced. Many an otherwise well-planned lesson has failed because of the environment. Four areas of concern that will be discussed briefly are

1. Lighting, room temperature, desk size, and distracting noises and sights
2. Classroom arrangements: physical furnishings and groupings of students
3. Organization and storage of materials and equipment
4. Safety factors

While reading and discussing the information included here, think of your own experiences in elementary school science. Think of specific examples when the physical environment enhanced or inhibited your learning experience. As you observe others in miniteaching experiences or during student teaching, or as you engage in the activities included here, begin to look for ways the physical environment can directly or indirectly affect the learning experience.

Lighting/Temperature/ Desk Size/Distracting Noises

A most important factor to consider when checking a classroom's physical environment is lighting. Improper, inappropriate lighting in a classroom can inhibit learning. Both natural lighting and artificial lighting need to be surveyed to determine possible problems. Look for glare in the room, particularly on the chalkboard. Shadows can also be a problem. Check the various work areas of the room to see that light is adequate there. Make your checks at different times of the day and during different weather conditions to account for the influence of natural light. Once the problem areas are identified, possible solutions can be generated and put into effect. These solutions may result in structural changes in the classroom itself or in changes in the type and/or arrangement of the lighting fixtures. Such solutions are usually long-range and expensive. Less expensive solutions can be utilized. Shades, blinds, curtains, cardboard, or other opaque and translucent objects and materials can be used effectively to control the amount and direction of both inside and outside light. If the specific areas within the classroom need more direct light, extra light sources, such as lamps and flashlights, can be made available. Work areas needing less light, such as

One important factor to consider in the physical environment of the classroom is desk size.

those set up for filmstrip viewing and using the overhead projector, can be located in the darker areas of the room. Bookcases or cardboard walls can be used to block out some of the unwanted light in these areas.

Room temperature is another physical factor that can affect learning. When classrooms are too warm, children become drowsy and listless. On the other hand, cold classrooms can cause the learners to become preoccupied with their need for physical comfort. Thus, physical discomfort from either extreme can cause a lack of attention and result in a poor learning experience. If the classroom temperature cannot be directly controlled by adjusting the thermostat, other measures must be taken. If the room is too warm, fresh air can be circulated by opening a window or door. A fan can also be used to help circulate the air. Shades and heavy curtains or outside awnings can be used to block some of the direct sun rays that can overheat a room. Furthermore, if the room temperature changes frequently, the children can be instructed to wear layered clothing that can be added to or taken off as the temperature fluctuates.

Desk size is another important consideration. Children are all sizes, and they need appropriate desks. Therefore, various desk sizes need to be available in the classroom. Feet should be able to rest comfortably on the floor. The desk top should be at a level that is comfortable for writing. A child's knees should not touch the writing desk. Generally, flat, table-like desks are best. They can be pushed together to form larger working areas for group projects.

Distracting background noises and sights are factors in the physical environment that can cause children's attention to be drawn away from the planned learning experience. Minimize these by having children face away from possible distraction. For example, do not let a caged animal or a window with a view of the playground be your backdrop. Sometimes quiet background music helps to minimize other distracting sounds.

As a teacher, you will need to be alert to the many factors in the physical environment that could interfere with the science experience. Some of the more common ones have been discussed here. However, as you gain experience in the classroom, you may identify others. Many times, the problem factor cannot be totally eliminated, but it can be minimized by utilizing alternative solutions. Perhaps you will want to involve your students in the process. After all, identifying problems and generating alternative solutions are important aspects of sciencing.

Classroom Arrangements

Both the arrangement of classroom furnishings and the grouping patterns of the students have an effect on the learning process. This is true for the self-contained classroom (one grade, all subjects) as well as for the departmentalized classroom (just science for one or more grades). The same general problems exist in both kinds of classrooms. First, our discussion focuses on the area of classroom furnishings.

Arrangement of Furnishings. As a teacher, you will probably have little input into the design of your classroom. Most likely, you will simply be assigned a classroom and be expected to utilize the already existing furnishings. Given this probable situation, what possibilities are open to you? Your classroom will contain both permanently placed and movable furnishings. Permanently placed furnishings—such as the sink, electrical outlets, windows, chalkboard, lighting fixtures, and perhaps a closet area—must become the core of your classroom arrangement. The movable furnishings—such as desks, tables, bookcases, plants, an aquarium, and the microcomputer—can be used to modify and enhance a core arrangement.

No one room arrangement will be appropriate for every science experience. Generally, however, there are four designated areas that should be considered in any arrangement.

1. Work Area. One area of the classroom should be arranged to accommodate the manipulative aspect of sciencing. In this area, students find the materials, equipment, and facilities necessary for firsthand data gathering.

This area has been set aside for firsthand data gathering.

2. Resource Area. Another part of the classroom should be designated as a resource center. Here, books, magazines, newspapers, cassette tapes, records, filmstrips, film loops, pictures, and models—as well as videotapes, videodisks, and computer software—should be available for students to use.

3. Conference Area. A small area that can be used for individual conferences or small group discussions needs to be located away from the center of activity. A certain amount of privacy should be provided in this area so that students who wish to talk with the teacher can do so freely. This area can also be used for individual testing and tutorial sessions.

4. Storage Area. Storage areas should also be a part of the overall room arrangement. Some areas will be needed to house the materials and equipment in use, while other areas must be found to store supplies not in immediate use. Facilities must accommodate both large and small items. Living things, such as small animals, fish, plants, and insects require special attention. More specific ideas for utilizing storage areas are explored in the next section of this chapter.

The way the furnishings in a classroom are arranged can affect learning outcome. Therefore, teachers must provide arrangements that facilitate learning. Students should have easy access to the various materials, equipment and facilities to be used in a learning experience.

Grouping Patterns.   The second area of concern in classroom arrangements is the way in which students group themselves or are grouped by the teacher. Much sciencing is done in small groups, partly to accommodate for the lack of equipment and materials in most elementary classrooms. However, even when there is an abundance of science materials, students need to have the experience of working, sharing, and communicating with their peers. The process aspect of science is enhanced at the elementary school level by increased interaction among students.

Keeping materials organized is important to a successful science program.

Various types of groupings can be used to facilitate learning. The three grouping patterns to be discussed are

1. Individual grouping
2. Small groups (two–five people)
3. Large groups (six or more people)

Some science experiences are best accomplished when each student works independently. Upper elementary students can be expected to work alone on projects much more successfully than can younger students. Highly motivated students may prefer working alone much of the time. Both the age of the student and the individual motivation should be considered in grouping students for science activities.

Each specific science experience should also be considered in order to determine the appropriate type of grouping. Some experiences can be done successfully alone; others require constant interaction among the students. Different grouping patterns may also be used during one activity. For example, during the data-gathering phase, students may work alone, but they may find it helpful to interact with others during the data processing phase.

Some science experiences are best accomplished where students work independently.

As mentioned earlier, the small group seems to work well for many types of science experiences. Three ways to organize small groups for science experiences are suggested here. Sometimes students should be allowed to determine with whom they would like to work. They may form their small group on the basis of friendship, common interest, or some other factor of their choosing.

Other times, the grouping should be done by the teacher. For example, students could be grouped to minimize behavioral problems, to take advantage of their special skills, or to encourage verbal participation and leadership.

Random assignment can also be used effectively in grouping students. Occasionally, students enjoy being placed in a group on the basis of luck. For example, numbers could be drawn from a hat to form the groupings. Often, in this manner, relationships can develop between students who otherwise might never have worked together.

Large group instruction is most successfully used for giving information and directions and for summarizing. During large group instruction, students are generally put in a passive role. Interaction becomes limited; otherwise, chaos can easily result. Large groups serve quite well for purposes such as films, some demonstrations, and lectures.

Grouping should be done purposely to facilitate learning. Teachers must determine which type of grouping is most appropriate for each activity.

Organization and Storage of Materials and Equipment

Poor organization of science materials and equipment often is the major cause of an unsuccessful science program. Most teachers would "do science" more often if materials and equipment were arranged for easy access. Some practical ideas for storing science equipment and materials, and suggestions for organizing in-use materials are explored here.

A master list of on-hand materials and equipment is invaluable. The list can be alphabetized, or items can be grouped according to identified headings. The exact location of each item should be included. This list can be organized to correlate with specific lessons or broad topic areas. Cabinets, drawers, shelves, boxes, and other storage facilities being used should have a materials list posted to identify the items that can be found there.

All items should be labeled to facilitate easy identification. Harmful chemicals and other hazardous materials must be so labeled. A designated area might be used to house "off limits" materials and equipment. These types of materials should be kept in a rather isolated area of the room in facilities that can be locked. Appropriate containers, preferably plastic, should also be provided. More detailed suggestions regarding safety in the classroom are provided in the next section of this chapter.

Teachers have used many techniques for organizing needed materials and equipment. Shoe boxes are just the right size for storing materials and small

**Science materials have been organized into plastic bins
for easy use by students.**

equipment for one or two persons. They stack well and can be acquired easily.
Plastic dishpans and buckets serve well for holding materials for small groups.
They can easily be carried from a storage shelf to a table where several students
could share the materials. You can probably think of other similar ways to make
materials easily accessible to elementary students.

Frequent inventories will help to keep the materials and equipment organized for ready use. Consumable items must be replaced as they are used, and
equipment must be kept in good repair. A teacher will want to make sure that
sufficient amounts of needed materials are always available.

An integral part of most science lessons is the distribution of materials at
the beginning of the lesson and the collection of them when the lesson is finished.
Both of these procedures can be accomplished with ease by planning appropriately. A simple routine can be established using helpers who pass out the equipment and materials. If boxes, buckets, plastic bags or dishpans containing only
the needed items are used, this task becomes simple. Children should be directed to clean all items after using them and return them to the appropriate
box, bucket, bag or dishpan. Consumable materials must be replaced, and all
boxes, buckets, bags, and dishpans returned to the storage areas.

To avoid confusion, make sure that elementary students are able to operate
any equipment to be used in a science experience. Frequently, this may mean
spending one or more days just learning how to manipulate the equipment before

actually beginning the lesson. Written directions should be provided for each student. These should be given orally as well. Generally, short steps are more easily followed than long, detailed directions. For young children, simple visual illustrations showing the procedure and the sequence in which it must be performed can be posted for easy reference.

Safety Factors

Elementary school teachers have long been responsible for the safety and well-being of students entrusted to their care. Perhaps because this concept has become so much a part of a teacher's daily responsibilities, it is sometimes taken for granted. Consequently, care and *conscientious attention to detail* are more and more frequently omitted.

Teachers must plan for students' safety. Such planning requires foresight and insight. Teachers must be aware of the potential hazards in any given activity or situation. Moreover, care must be exercised in planning lessons to anticipate or, even better, to eliminate situations in which an injury might occur.

Teachers are not born with skill in foreseeing hazards, just as they are not born with skill in planning lessons. By attempting to identify hazardous situations, teachers become more aware of such situations. Certainly every teacher would caution students who are boiling water on the stove; perhaps students would not even be allowed to do it at all. Some things are fairly obvious; we are all aware that boiling water poses a potential hazard: the student might be burned.

Not all hazards are so obvious, however. Would we all recognize the potential hazards in other simple activities such as the following: A kindergarten class has been developing observation and simple classification skills. The teacher has planned a lesson using beans, peas, marbles, and other small items. During the lesson the teacher is to give the students containers of objects to be sorted into three groups according to some criteria. The students are to put the objects into three different baby-food jars to demonstrate their skills in observing and classifying. Can you identify at least *five* potential hazards in this situation?

Did you think of these?

1. Having an allergic reaction to handling the objects.
2. Throwing the objects and perhaps injuring another student.
3. Putting the objects into ears, nose, or mouth and having them become lodged there.
4. Breaking the jars and sustaining a cut.
5. Spilling the objects and perhaps injuring someone who might step on the spilled items and fall.

Did you think of something not listed here? If so, please share it with your instructor and the class.

Students are encouraged to do activities in the newer science curricula. This hands-on approach requires that they manipulate materials and equipment frequently. Consequently, potential hazards abound in an up-to-date classroom.

To decrease the likelihood of injury, teachers could eliminate the manipulation of materials. However, that would defeat our purposes in science education. More logically, plans could be made in such a way as to identify hazards in advance. Alternative methods to accomplish the same goal, without the hazard, could be substituted. If that were impossible, at least the students could be warned, and techniques could be demonstrated for using extreme caution.

Students should be taught proper techniques in handling and caring for materials and equipment. This step is more likely to occur when expensive equipment or materials are being used (for example, the expensive microscope or rare book). However, the cost of an item does not indicate its relative potential as a hazard. Even collectables can be handled in such a way as to result in injury. Proper techniques can and should be taught.

Most teachers make rules for proper conduct in the classroom and designate specific procedures to be followed in certain situations. Likewise, rules should be made concerning the use and handling of science materials and equipment. Perhaps a specific area of the room can be designated as the science area. Rules concerning the use of selected equipment (the hot plate, for example) might specify that the equipment will be used only when the teacher is assisting the student. Reminders can be posted in the form of charts or cartoon-like posters.

In the activity example provided earlier, one danger is spilling the objects, stepping on one, and falling. The danger might be reduced somewhat by limiting the area in which the activity is conducted. Perhaps a carpeted area might reduce injury from a fall and the chance of breaking the jars if they were dropped. In planning that lesson, the teacher could plan to carry it out on a carpeted area of the room. In addition, the teacher could eliminate part of the potential danger by using nonglass containers.

Safety guides have been developed in many states and local school districts. If one is available in your state or area, obtain a copy and read it carefully. Then save it for future reference. The hints and suggestions in such guides can save a lot of time and perhaps even save a child from injury.

A technique of utmost importance in avoiding injury to students is to *give clear, complete directions* each and every time an activity is to be performed. Do not assume your students will remember even general directions or rules from one day to the next or from one manipulation to the next. Give directions and repeat rules each time. Put the basic rules on a chart, and refer to it each time.

With the growing practice in our society of people's entering a lawsuit against someone for minor, or maybe even imagined, injuries or slights, teachers need to develop an awareness of such action and protect themselves against it. Students can and do bring lawsuits against teachers for injury. The best defense is to make sure that no students sustain injury in your class. However, no one can absolutely ensure against injury. A student will occasionally become injured even with the most careful planning. In that case, a teacher's best legal defense

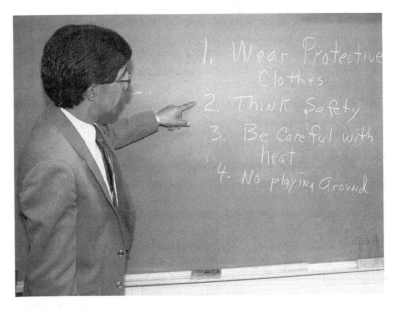

This teacher stresses safety guidelines.

is the *careful planning*. Without careful planning, a teacher could be found negligent and perhaps legally liable for the student's injury. Teachers must guard against injury and against negligence.

A standard technique for determining possible negligence is to ask, "Did the teacher do everything any reasonable person would do in a similar situation?" Teachers should keep this question in mind and ask it of themselves. At this phase of your professional development, it would be a good idea to establish the habit of asking this question as a self-check each time you write a lesson plan.

It is not the purpose of this section to scare prospective teachers, only to build awareness. Prevention is so much better than regret. Therefore, plan lessons carefully, think about safety needs, caution students, and keep hazards to a minimum. Ask yourself, "Have I done everything any reasonable teacher would do in a similar situation?" Do not become careless or be lulled into a sense of false security.

Some teachers believe that the school board or the state would be legally liable for a student's injury. True, teachers do work for the state. However, many states adhere to the doctrine of *sovereign immunity,* which means that one cannot sue the state in cases of injury resulting from the negligence of an employee. In such states, the individual teacher would face possible conviction in a *tort liability suit,* or a civil suit brought to establish liability for an injury to an individual. (Of course, in all states the individual teacher is responsible for criminal acts, or wrongs committed against society.)

The topic of tort liability is far too complex to be covered completely here. The intention here is to build an awareness to help teachers avoid situations that would leave their students exposed to possible injury and themselves vulnerable to a claim of negligence. Careful planning is the best prevention. Try at all times to keep your students safe from injury. Many safeguards are simple, common-sense precautions:

1. Make and enforce rules.
2. Label dangerous substances and store them out of the reach of children.
3. Avoid hazardous situations.
4. Remind students regularly of safety rules.
5. Supervise students at all times.

You will be able to do these things—the problem is remembering to do them consistently. You must remember, for the children's safety and for your safety.

YOU, THE TEACHER

The fourth element, and by far the most important, that you must consider as part of the decision-making process is you, the teacher. Your own strengths, weaknesses, skills, personality, background, and philosophy will have a profound effect, positive or negative, on those you teach. You must be aware of who you are.

Anne Lewis, a review panelist for the U.S. Department of Education's school recognition program, pointed out that schools chosen for recognition not only adhere "to high standards for students, but also give equal attention to making sure that everyone who influences individual children does everything possible to help them learn" (Lewis, 1986, pp. 187–188). This means that teachers must see themselves as cultivators, not weeders. You must be prepared to help students succeed. Your job will involve creating opportunities for learning to occur. Teachers who provide a warm, open, caring environment for students and challenge them to do their best do make a difference! How do you see yourself? Will you make a difference?

SUGGESTED ACTIVITIES

ACTIVITY 4.1: EXAMINING TRADE BOOKS

Examine some of the outstanding science trade books that have been published in the last several years. How could you use these trade books to enrich a science lesson for children? Find several trade books on the same subject. How could these be used to individualize your science program?

ACTIVITY 4.2: CONTROLLING PHYSICAL FACTORS

A. Using the room in which your class is held, work with a small group in identifying and suggesting ways of controlling the following physical factors in order to enhance learning:

1. Classroom lighting
2. Room temperature
3. Desk assignment
4. Distracting noises and sights

Organize and record your group's recommendations.

B. Visit an elementary classroom during a science lesson. Observe how the lighting, room temperature, desk assignment, and distracting sights and sounds affect the learning experience. Record your observations and offer suggestions for improvement. Be sure to make note of the ways in which each of the factors is used to enhance the learning experience. Share your findings with a group of your classmates.

ACTIVITY 4.3: ARRANGING CLASSROOMS

A. On a separate sheet of paper, identify some common classroom furnishings, such as desks, tables, bookcases, chalkboard, sink, and so on. Draw separate diagrams illustrating how the identified furnishings could be arranged for

1. Large group instruction

2. Small group instruction

3. Individual instruction

Remember, this is the same room with the same furnishings, but they are arranged in different ways in order to facilitate the type of specified instruction.

B. Share and discuss your arrangements with a small group of your classmates. Make note of any new ideas you get from this group sharing.

Note: This activity can be modified so that a real elementary classroom is used. The actual furnishings can be listed and the room drawn to scale; or, if arrangements can be made, you can actually move the furnishings around.

ACTIVITY 4.4: ORGANIZING EQUIPMENT AND MATERIALS

A. Work with a small group in checking the room in which your class is held in order to identify various techniques that are utilized in organizing science equipment and materials. List them.

B. Discuss your findings with your group. What recommendations can your group make that would improve the existing organization of the science materials? List your recommendations.

C. As a group, choose one of the recommendations you listed, and make plans for implementing it. Discuss your plans with your instructor for approval; then put them into action.

Note: This activity can be done using an elementary classroom if one is available. You might want to discuss this possibility with your instructor.

ACTIVITY 4.5: IDENTIFYING POTENTIAL HAZARDS

Do one of the following with a small group of your classmates:

A. From an elementary school science textbook, select two activities and identify all possible hazards. Suggest ways to prevent injury to the students involved in these activities. How could the hazard be removed or reduced? Give specific suggestions. What alternative methods could be used in the lesson?

B. Observe an elementary school class for two hours (including the science period, if possible). Identify and list all potential hazards to students' safety. How could the hazards be removed or reduced? Give specific suggestions. How could potential injury to the students involved be prevented? What alternative methods could be used in this lesson? If time permits, discuss your ideas with the classroom teacher.

ACTIVITY 4.6: RECOGNIZING SAFETY RULES

A. Ask a teacher or principal of an elementary school about the safety rules of that school or district. Is there a safety guide for the teachers? Obtain a copy of the list and/or guide. Does the list have a rule about using open flames or candles? Are goggles required? What special requirements are there for field trips? Is there a rule about washing hands? When do pupils have to wear an apron or other clothes protectors?

B. Do either of the following:

1. Make pictorial posters as reminders of safety rules for use in your classroom later. (Posters may be $8\frac{1}{2}'' \times 11''$ or larger.)

2. Make and display a bulletin board for safety. Include safety rules listed in *A* of this activity. Maybe you can try your posters or bulletin board in an elementary school classroom. The children can provide helpful feedback and creative suggestions.

ACTIVITY 4.7: LEARNING ABOUT LIABILITY

A. Write to the State Department of Education for information about O.S.H.A. (Occupational Safety and Health Act). Request any materials they provide for elementary school teachers. What are your rights under this act?

B. List at least three common-sense guidelines for science teachers to guard against liability for negligence and to prevent injury to students. Did you include careful planning in your list?

C. What is the difference between tort liability and criminal liability? What does sovereign immunity mean? Is sovereign immunity employed in your state? Find out.

SUMMARY

This chapter focused attention on your role as a sciencing teacher. Essentially, this role involves active decision making that includes coordinating, managing, modifying, and adapting. Four elements that a sciencing teacher must consider in decision making were identified and discussed: students, curricular materials, physical environment, and you, the teacher. You must manage and coordinate these elements, using your knowledge and experience about each to provide many opportunities for children to experience success in science.

As a teacher, you must use all the resources available to you in making decisions. Reading professional journals; attending professional meetings; participating in in-service workshops; consulting a variety of curricular materials; talking with other teachers, parents, people in the community, and your students; taking additional university classes; and being an active inquirer yourself—all are excellent ways to continue gathering information needed in the decision-making process.

The sciencing teacher is an active decision maker, manager, and coordinator, not just a recipe follower. Skillful management of your science program is necessary for meaningful science experiences.

ENDNOTES

1. James V. DeRose and Don P. Whittle, "Selecting Textbooks: A Plan That Worked," *The Science Teacher, 43*(46), 40. Reprinted with permission from *The Science Teacher* September 1976, published by the National Science Teachers Association.

REFERENCES

Bonnstetter, R. J., Penick, J. E., & Yager, R. E. (1983). *Teachers in exemplary programs: How do they compare?* Washington, DC: National Science Teachers Association.

DeRose, J. V., & Whittle, D. P. (1976). Selecting textbooks: A plan that worked. *The Science Teacher, 43*(46), 40.

Lewis, A. C. (1986, November). The search continues for effective schools. *Phi Delta Kappan*, pp. 187–188.

Penick, J. E. (1986). Science education research: Why don't we believe it? *Curriculum Review, 25*(3), 65–67.

Penick, J. E., Yager, R. E., & Bonnstetter, R. J. (1984). When the spotlight's on science, take your cue from the best. *Instructor, 94*(4), 43–44.

Reeder, W., & Adams, B. (1977). Selection of an elementary science program: Process and criteria. *Science and Children, 14*(8), 8–10.

SUGGESTED READINGS

Bozardt, D. A., & Righter, R. E. (1976). The supervisor and teachers in liability. In M. B. Harbeck (Ed.), *Second sourcebook for science supervisors* (pp. 171–176). Washington, DC: National Science Supervisor Association.

Brown, B. W., & Brown, W. R. (1969). *Science teaching and the law.* Washington, DC: National Science Teachers Association.

Carin, A. A., & Sund, R. B. (1989). Chapter 6. *Teaching science through discovery* (6th ed.). Columbus, OH: Merrill.

Irving, J. R. (1968). *How to provide safety in the science laboratory.* Washington, DC: National Science Teachers Association.

National Science Teachers Association. (1978). *Safety in the elementary school classroom.* Washington, DC: Author.

NSTA-CBC Joint Committee. (1988, March). Outstanding science tradebooks for children in 1987. *Science and Children, 25*(6), 50–54.

Occupational safety and health act: A responsibility for science teachers. (1974). *The Science Teacher, 41*(7), 35.

Rowe, M. B. (1978). Chapters 13 & 15. *Teaching science as continuous inquiry.* New York: McGraw-Hill.

Simon, S. (1982, March). Using science trade books in the classroom. *Science and Children,* pp. 5–6.

Classroom Methodology

Goals

After completing this chapter, you will demonstrate competence in the ability to incorporate the current ideas and learning theories presented into effective daily strategies for involving elementary children in sciencing activities.

Objectives

In completing this chapter, you will do the following:

1. Identify and explain the learning theories and ideas presented.

2. Describe the implications that the theories of Piaget and Bruner have for constructing teaching strategies.

3. Describe how the Hunter Model is integrated into the strategies presented.

4. Use the ideas presented here by selecting a science topic and constructing a teaching strategy that includes instructional objectives, behavioral indicators, appropriate teaching techniques, and methods of evaluation.

INTRODUCTION

The most effective and successful learning experiences result from systematic creative planning. This chapter provides you with some current ideas and learning theories pertaining to methods of classroom instruction. It is designed to help you construct effective daily teaching strategies.

This chapter begins with a brief overview of the *Hunter Model* of effective instruction. Madeline Hunter's name and her Essential Elements of Effective Instruction seem to be sweeping the country. One would have to search long and hard to find a teacher or principal who has not heard of Madeline Hunter. But how many really have a working knowledge of the principles and theories on which the model is based? The Hunter Model is integrated into the strategies and format for effective lesson planning presented in this chapter.

The three stages of lesson planning are examined in depth, one at a time. Activities are provided to engage you in a step-by-step process of lesson planning. The result is a teaching strategy for a science activity that includes instructional objectives, behavioral indicators, teaching techniques, and methods of evaluation.

The first stage is concerned with *developing and writing objectives*. Objectives identify the purpose of instruction. To provide elementary children with meaningful science experiences, a teacher needs to identify the purpose of the experience. What is supposed to be accomplished? How will the child benefit from the experience? Objectives should provide answers to these questions.

The second stage continues the planning process by offering guidance in *selecting and developing an instructional strategy*. After establishing the objectives of the lesson, the teacher must devise an instructional sequence that will help the learner attain the objectives. A variety of teaching techniques that can be used to plan the instructional portion of the lesson are presented.

Finally, stage three provides insight into the use of *evaluation techniques*. One of the most difficult tasks a teacher faces is assessing the learner's achievement; yet, it is an essential part of all science instruction. Evaluation can assume three functions: diagnostic, formative, and summative. Each of these functions is discussed, and examples of the main types of evaluation techniques are presented.

THE MADELINE HUNTER PHENOMENON

In the last several years, teachers have been bombarded with what has come to be known as the Hunter Model, Instructional Theory into Practice (ITIP), clinical teaching, or Essential Elements of Effective Instruction.

Actually Madeline Hunter, currently a faculty member of the UCLA's Graduate School of Education, had her elements of an effective lesson published by *Instructor* almost 20 years ago. Her model is the result of an attempt to use research-based knowledge and translate it into a common language that could be used by classroom teachers in making daily teaching decisions. This approach provides teachers with an excellent guide for designing and implementing effective learning experiences. It becomes hazardous only when teachers, administrators, or supervisors use it as a fail-safe recipe that *must* include every element each time a lesson is taught.

The first major part of the model is an introduction in which the teacher focuses the students' attention on the upcoming lesson, and makes clear the objectives, purpose, and importance of the lesson. Some time is also spent helping students connect the new lesson to things they already know. This part is sometimes referred to as the *anticipatory set* and statement of objectives.

In the body of the lesson, the new content is presented in small steps using demonstrations, redundant and detailed explanations, a variety of specific examples, models, and diagrams. Hunter includes in this part techniques for checking for understanding. Teachers are expected to get frequent feedback through students' responses in order to make appropriate adjustments in instruction. This feedback can take the form of signals: thumbs up for true statements, thumbs down for false ones. It can be verbal: say to yourself, then tell your neighbor—does your neighbor agree with you? A choral response is also suggested as a way to check for understanding. Students could also be asked to jot down their responses and be ready to share them.

By making frequent checks for understanding, the teacher is able to modify, adapt, and adjust instruction appropriately to meet the needs of the student. The teacher may decide to move ahead, reteach, regroup students, extend practice, provide different materials, or just stop for the time being. The purpose is to monitor and adjust. The teacher engages in the process of on-the-spot diagnosing of students' learning and making decisions about the next step of instruction.

In the final part of the Hunter Model, the students are given guided practice. They are usually given a task or problem that would require them to apply the information learned during the instructional part. This part is characterized by the teacher's asking a large number of questions, including the higher level questions designed to elicit application, analysis, and synthesis. The teacher responds to the students' answers, correcting errors and reinforcing correct responses. This interaction provides the students with immediate feedback and helps the teacher decide if they are ready for independent practice. Independent practice is assigned to help the students achieve mastery of the skills and concepts learned in the lesson.

The Hunter Model is very similar to many other teaching strategies that have been presented to teachers over the years. It is, after all, based on established principles of educational psychology. Therefore, most educators support the basic sequence and techniques of the Hunter Model; however, many are alarmed at the institutionalization of the model. Vast numbers of local school districts have designed teacher evaluation forms based on the model. Administrators all over the country are being trained through workshops in the Hunter Model and are using it to evaluate teachers. Unfortunately, many emerge from the training with many misconceptions that lead to the misuse and abuse of the model. A checklist with the essential elements frequently is formulated and used by administrators and supervisors to evaluate a teacher's performance in the classroom. Reacting against such use, Madeline Hunter (1985) herself says that the model was "designed to help teachers plan. In no way can a teacher be judged by the inclusion of all those elements. . . . any observer who uses a check-list to make sure a teacher is using all seven elements does not understand the model" (pp. 57–60).

The concept that some have of the Hunter Model for teaching needs to be examined: we cannot assume that there is only *one* way to teach. We can expect teachers to design lessons that incorporate sound educational and psychological principles; but, at the same time, we must allow them to put together lessons that are innovative, creative, and unique. In addition, every lesson plan needs to reflect the uniqueness of the particular discipline from which the skills and concepts are drawn. In science, this means the teacher must understand that the four science components—content, process, attitudes, and technology—that were introduced in Chapter 1 provide structure and guidance for planning ap-propriate science activities for children. One must understand and incorporate not only generic psychological learning principles, but also those associated with the nature of the specific discipline.

The remaining part of this chapter focuses your attention on the integration of the psychological principles of the Hunter Model into the model presented in this chapter, which addresses the specific techniques related to the concept of sciencing.

DEVELOPING AND WRITING OBJECTIVES

Before you attempt to teach a lesson, ask yourself the following questions:

1. What am I trying to accomplish?
2. How do I want the students to be different at the end of the lesson?

These questions can help you organize your efforts and provide children with meaningful instruction. When teachers just follow the instructions in the teacher's manual, without first asking these questions, learning can become purposeless and haphazard.

Your answers identify your goals and objectives. For example, suppose you want to teach your students about mold growth. When you make your plans, you need to identify the purpose of the lesson. To make the purpose most meaningful, you need to think about it in terms that relate to the learner; for example, ask yourself "How will the learner be different after the instruction?" Possible answers include

1. To teach students that there are many different kinds of molds.
2. To show students that molds have different colors.

3. To help students see that certain factors can retard or speed up mold growth.

4. To help students discover the factors that affect mold growth.

5. To encourage students to investigate and gather other information about molds.

These answers can serve as general objectives for a lesson. They can be used to give direction and purpose to the instruction being developed. Since these objectives relate to the instructional part of the lesson and not directly to the students' behavior, the term instructional objectives can be used to describe them.

Although these objectives may be desirable and helpful in developing instruction, they provide very little direction as to how a teacher can determine whether or not the students have met the objectives. In order for these objectives to be more useful, they must project specific outcomes of learning. Stating an objective in terms of observable student behavior not only provides direction for the instructional phase, but also for the appraisal of the effectiveness of the learning experience—the evaluation. *Behavioral objectives* offer a format for stating goals in terms of observable student behavior. A complete behavioral objective

1. Identifies the observable behavior that students will exhibit to show the objective has been fulfilled.

2. Identifies the conditions (when and where) under which students are to exhibit the behavior and/or identifies specific materials that are necessary for performing the task.

3. Describes how well students must perform.

Behavioral Objective

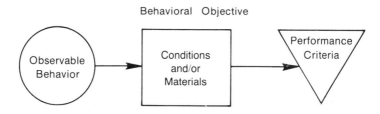

In the activity section, you will develop and write behavioral objectives. The objectives you write should contain all the information shown in the "Behavioral Objectives" chart—observable behavior, conditions, materials, and performance criteria. You should develop the behavioral objectives from the instructional objectives by asking, "What do I want the students to do when the instruction phase is finished that they couldn't do before?" Remember to state the answer in observable student behavior. Terms that are useful to denote specific observable behavior include

compare	list	differentiate
group	state	compose
create	identify	name
measure	describe	control variables
hypothesize	construct	apply
organize	explain	order
write	distinguish	demonstrate
interpret	perform alone	evaluate

To get some practice in writing behavioral objectives, rewrite the proposed instructional objectives for the lesson on molds using the terms in the list so the objectives are stated in observable student behavior. Remember that an objective identifies behavior that is learned during the instructional sequence. An objective is not necessarily the same as the activities used for appropriate practice during the instruction. The objectives are listed again for your convenience.

1. To teach students that there are many different kinds of molds.
   Behavioral Objective: The student will

2. To show students that molds have different colors.
   Behavioral Objective: The student will

3. To help students see that certain factors can retard or speed up mold growth.
   Behavioral Objective: The student will

4. To help students discover the factors that affect mold growth.
Behavioral Objective: The student will

5. To encourage students to investigate and gather other information about molds.
Behavioral Objective: The student will

You should take some time at this point to share your results with your classmates and instructor to get some immediate feedback. Once you have mastered the task of stating objectives in observable student behavior, you are ready for the next phase of developing and writing behavioral objectives—selecting *significant* objectives.

You should notice that the verbs listed earlier differ in complexity and cognitive level. Some (*name, state,* and *list,* for example) call for memory-level cognition, while others (*distinguish, apply,* and *demonstrate*) demand higher levels of cognitive functioning. Just stating objectives so that they describe specific observable learner behavior does not assure that an objective is significant and valuable. In fact, the types of behavior most easily described are often the most trivial. Significant objectives are frequently elusive and difficult to state in behavioral terms. This section will help you determine what is and what is not significant.

Science objectives can be divided into four main behavior categories.

1. Cognitive content
2. Cognitive process
3. Psychomotor
4. Affective

Cognitive

In sciencing lessons, there are two types of cognitive objectives: *cognitive content* and *cognitive process.* (You may want to refer to Chapter 1 for a review of the cognitive domain.) The cognitive domain, or area, refers to learning that involves mental ability. There are levels of mental ability, from simple recalling of facts, to applying general information in specific situations, to creative thinking, to making judgments using criteria.

Cognitive content objectives are used to identify the scientific fact(s) that you want the student to commit to memory as a result of your lesson. In daily lesson plans these must be simple facts. Such objectives are a necessary part of building a foundation for higher levels of learning. From the daily accumulation of simple facts, more complex concepts and principles will evolve. For example, a cognitive content objective appropriate for a daily lesson plan might read: "After the lesson on air, the learner will be able to state that air takes up space."

Cognitive process objectives identify inquiry skills that you want the students to develop and improve as a result of your instruction. These objectives may involve any of the basic processes of observing, classifying, measuring, using spatial relationships, communicating, predicting, inferring, and using the integrated processes of defining operationally, formulating hypotheses, interpreting data, controlling variables, and experimenting. Cognitive process objectives are more difficult to develop and write than are cognitive content objectives and usually involve a higher level of cognition. In this behavioral category, students must do more than recall some information; generally, they are involved in collecting, organizing, analyzing, and evaluating the information. Cognitive process objectives identify the mental process that a child uses in taking in and dealing with information. In a daily lesson plan, the cognitive process objective generally identifies the specific skill(s) that the child will use in the instructional portion of the lesson to discover the fact stated in the cognitive content objective.

These two objectives are closely related in a sciencing lesson. The cognitive content objective identifies *what facts the child is to recall from the lesson* and the cognitive process objective identifies the *process-inquiry skills* used in gathering and organizing information necessary for arriving at a concrete understanding of the facts. For example, an appropriate cognitive process objective for our lesson on air might read: "After the lesson on air, the learner will be able to adequately describe the observations made about the activity performed (inverted glass, with paper wad in bottom, in large, clear container filled with water) and explain (infer) that air filled the glass and kept the water out, keeping the paper wad dry." Notice the relationship between the cognitive content and cognitive process objective in the two examples given.

Psychomotor

Psychomotor objectives identify manual, manipulative skills that you want the students to develop or improve. Concern with this area of learning seems to be growing. Many early childhood programs focus on the development of movement behaviors. Curricula designed for children with learning difficulties reflect this emphasis, as do curricula for vocational education, the fine arts, and physical education. In elementary science, psychomotor objectives identify the skills involved in the proper use of science equipment and materials. Generally, these objectives are not difficult to write since, unlike the cognitive and affective areas, they deal directly with observable behaviors.

Psychomotor behaviors are important in a process-oriented science approach, where the students are involved in gathering data. The students must learn safe, correct manipulation of science equipment and materials in order for maximum learning to take place. For example, an appropriate psychomotor objective for our lesson on air might read: "After the lesson on air, the learner will be able to appropriately manipulate the given materials—a glass, a paper wad, and a large container of water—so that the paper wad remains dry when it is placed in the bottom of the glass and the glass is inverted in the large container of water." Notice how this objective relates to the cognitive content and cognitive process objectives for the lesson on air.

Affective

Affective objectives identify attitudes, feelings, emotions, and values that you want the students to develop as a result of your instruction. These objectives are frequently the most difficult to develop and write in behavioral terms. In the past, many teachers have avoided this behavioral category altogether. Leading theorists, however, such as Carl Rogers, Abraham Maslow, and Art Combs, suggest that affect plays an integral role in determining the total learning outcome. As teachers, then, we must concern ourselves with all aspects of the learning process, affective as well as cognitive and psychomotor.

The problem becomes one of identifying appropriate feelings, emotions, values, and attitudes that you think are important for children to develop as a result of your science instruction. An examination of the nature of the science discipline provides insight into the identity of many valuable science objectives that fall into the affective domain.

One of the major purposes of science is to seek rational answers and explanations to natural and physical phenomena. Helping children establish a need to seek answers in a systematic, rational way is certainly a valuable science objective. Teachers must help children develop this kind of a scientific attitude. Other characteristics that should be cultivated include curiosity, objectivity, respect for logic, persistence, critical thinking, inventiveness, questioning, and the idea that intelligent failure can be a form of success.

Children must understand that in science, a wrong answer or failure is often seen as a success because something valuable was learned. In experimenting, we may eliminate one of the variables when a hypothesis is not supported. Data are gathered and learning takes place. In science, children must be encouraged to "stick their necks out" and try things in order to gather data on what does not work as well as what does. "It's OK to be wrong" and "You don't have to know the answer ahead of time" are science attitudes that elementary children should possess.

Teachers should make sure that their science lessons provide children with many opportunities and reinforcement related to the development of positive science attitudes. Children need to see themselves as investigators and discoverers. They must assume an active role in the learning process, and the incorporation of attitudes such as those mentioned here is necessary for them to have meaningful science experiences.

Once appropriate science attitudes, feelings, values, and emotions have been identified for a particular lesson, the task becomes one of putting them into terms of observable student behavior. Because of the very nature of attitudes, values, feelings, and emotions, we can only infer their presence through outward behavior. Therefore, in developing affective objectives, you must determine what behaviors you are willing to take as evidence that a student possesses the attitude, value, feeling, or emotion you have selected. For example, an affective objective appropriate for our lesson on air might read: "After the lesson on air, the learner will demonstrate curiosity by asking questions related to the activity, repeating the activity voluntarily, and/or doing optional activities related to the lesson."

Although there is still much controversy and debate among educators as to the extent to which the school should be concerned with affective objectives, few deny that affective behaviors shape and determine the learning outcome to a great extent. It would seem that teachers cannot afford to avoid this area of learning but must examine it in order to determine what is desirable and necessary.

Summary of Developing and Writing Objectives

This part of Chapter 5 has provided you with background information related to developing and writing objectives. Objectives are used to give purpose and direction to instruction. To be most useful, they should be stated in terms of observable student behavior. Certain words, such as *state, explain, demonstrate, compare,* and *hypothesize,* have proven useful in writing behavioral objectives. However, just stating objectives so that they describe observable learner behavior does not assure that an objective is significant and valuable.

There are four main behavior categories into which objectives can be grouped: cognitive content, cognitive process, psychomotor, and affective. Effective science instruction involves all four of these categories. Even in most 30- to 45-minute sciencing lessons, learning should occur in each of the categories identified in the objectives. Including all four categories ensures that the lesson involves a child in acquiring science facts, process-inquiry skills, motor or manual manipulative skills, and in developing appropriate attitudes. These four categories are complementary, and the objectives should all be closely related with the specific objective in each category. Activity 5.1 is designed to help you assimilate the information presented thus far; you will want to refer to this section while doing it.

ACTIVITY 5.1: WRITING OBJECTIVES

A. Identify an appropriate topic for a 30- to 45-minute science experience for children in one of the following categories:

1. Kindergarten–Grade 1
2. Grades 2–4
3. Grades 5–6
4. Grades 7–8

   Review the materials presented in Chapters 2 and 3 for helpful ideas. Make sure you have enough background information about the selected topic to deal effectively and knowledgeably with the content presented. See your instructor if you need more guidance in selecting an appropriate science topic. You may wish to work with a small group in completing this activity.

B. Using the ideas and information gathered by examining the various resources available, you will formulate appropriate behavioral objectives in each of the four behavior categories—cognitive content, cognitive process, psychomotor, and affective.

   First, however, you might find it helpful to think in terms of instructional objectives—what you are trying to accomplish in each of the behavior categories. Once you have identified your instructional purposes, it is usually not too difficult to use behavioral terms. If you feel ready, you may skip this part and go directly to the behavioral objectives in Part C.

   Use the following format to organize your instructional objectives:

1. *Cognitive content:* I want the students to know that
2. *Cognitive process:* I want the students to develop or improve their ability to
3. *Psychomotor:* I want the students to develop or improve their ability to
4. *Affective:* I want the students to

C. Using the instructional objectives that you have just written, convert them to observable student behavior. Ask yourself, "What do the students have to do to show me they have met my objectives?" Behavioral objectives should be specific. They should describe learning that can be expected to occur as the result of a planned 30- to 45-minute science lesson. Use the following format to organize your behavioral objectives:

1. *Cognitive content:* The students will

2. *Cognitive process:* The students will

3. *Psychomotor:* The students will

4. *Affective:* The students will demonstrate _____ by

☑ Self-Check

D. Look over each of your instructional objectives to see if you selected valuable, worthwhile goals that provide direction and purpose for instruction. Can you give some rationale for each of your choices? Discuss the rationale with your small group so that you can share this information with your instructor.

E. Examine your behavioral objectives.

1. Do they project specific outcomes of learning in terms of observable student behavior?

2. Is it clear what the students must do to let you know they have met each objective?

3. Do the behavioral objectives relate directly to the instructional objectives?

4. Do all four objectives relate to each other?

5. Can these objectives realistically be expected to be accomplished in a 30- to 45-minute science experience?

6. Are they written as targets, or ends to be accomplished, and not as means?

These objectives should provide the purpose, or direction, for the planned science activity in the next phase of lesson planning, selecting and developing an appropriate instructional strategy. Jot down any comments or questions you want to share with your instructor.

☐ Comments

SELECTING AND DEVELOPING
AN APPROPRIATE INSTRUCTIONAL STRATEGY

This section continues the planning process by offering some guidelines in selecting appropriate instructional strategies. Instructional strategy identifies the teaching techniques or methods used to aid the learner in attaining the specified objectives.

The ideas of both Jean Piaget and Jerome Bruner provide insight for the elementary teacher. Piaget's research suggests that certain factors are involved in promoting learning:

1. *Physical experience:* Manipulation of real materials
2. *Social experience:* Interaction with others, confronting views and ideas of others
3. *Logical-mathematical experience:* Activities involving bringing together, taking apart, grouping, counting
4. *Maturation:* The passage of time
5. *Equilibration:* A mental state of balance (Furth, 1970)

The fifth factor listed is considered by Piaget to be the most essential. He asserts that the human organism strives for equilibration. When something occurs that upsets the existing mental structure, there is a basic tendency to restore it. Our mental structure is built over the years through the different experiences we have in which data are collected and incorporated into the existing framework. When new data are encountered that fit into the existing framework, according to Piaget, assimilation takes place. On the other hand, if data are encountered that do not fit into the existing mental structure, modification must be made in the existing structure to accommodate the new data. Thus, the mechanisms of assimilation and accommodation become essential in building a mental structure.

It is important to note that Piaget's five factors are considered necessary but not sufficient—meaning that just providing a child with these factors will not automatically result in learning, but without them learning cannot take place. Essentially, it is the interaction, or active involvement of the child with the environment, that causes learning to take place.

These five factors can be used to guide teachers in developing appropriate teaching strategies, methods, and techniques. Children should be exposed to a physical and social learning environment that provides them with opportunities to manipulate objects and ideas in active interaction with others. Freedom of movement, individual and personal instruction, internal motivation, flexible curriculum, a variety of relevant concrete experiences, and direct involvement are important elements to consider in developing teaching strategies.

In addition, the element of time needs to be put into proper perspective. Piaget sees the passage of time as necessary for assimilation and accommo-

This teacher is using physical experience as one teaching technique.

dation to take place. Teachers often try to speed up the learning process, but frequently this results in false or verbal accommodation and not true internalization of the concept or process. Thus, a child may seem to have grasped an idea, but he or she may have grasped it only at a memorization level. The teacher must allow time for the students to interact directly with objects, ideas, and other people.

Bruner (1967) thinks that students learn best by discovery. He suggests that allowing the learner to discover information and organize what is encountered is a necessary condition for learning the techniques of problem solving. This philosophy is consistent with Piaget's emphasis on active learner involvement.

Bruner offers guidance in developing instructional strategy by suggesting that there are three modes of presentation: action, imagery, and language. The *action mode* provides actual contact with real objects. Children are presented with objects to manipulate in order to acquire the desired learning outcome. This mode of presentation is considered most appropriate for learners in Piaget's preoperational and concrete operational stages of mental development. It is also a useful mode for learners in any stage who are encountering a new concept for which they have little background.

The *imagery mode* uses pictures, models, diagrams, and other such representations of actual objects to foster a desired learning outcome. Learners who are making the transition from concrete to formal thinking are able to use the imagery mode of presentation in acquiring desired learning outcomes. This mode is not generally as effective with learners at earlier stages of mental development.

Upon reaching what Piaget terms the formal stage of mental development, a learner can use the *language mode* of instruction to produce a desired learning outcome. Words, abstractions, and other symbols characterize this mode of instruction. Experiences involving use of the other two modes serve as necessary prerequisites for the language mode.

It can be inferred, then, that in planning for instruction the different modes of presentation need to be considered. The stage of development at which a child is operating needs to be known and plans made accordingly. Since the stage of development is not wholly dependent on age but is influenced also by past experiences, the task of selecting appropriate instructional methods or techniques is not simple. A teacher needs to provide several paths by which learners can reach the desired outcome.

Bruner's three modes of presentation are action, imagery, and language.

The work of Piaget and Bruner offers the classroom teacher valuable insight and guidance in planning for science instruction. Two types of planning are necessary: daily and long-range.

Long-range planning includes organizing the scope (the content, process skills, and attitudes you will teach) and sequence (in what order you will teach these) for the entire school year. There are many resources available to help you with long-range planning. Most schools have basic curriculum guides, textbooks, or other science program materials that provide a basic framework for teachers to use in developing long-range plans. Successful teachers use these resources along with ideas from other teachers, the interests of the students in the class, local environmental concerns, expertise provided by parents and other local residents, and their own specific interests and knowledge to make long-range planning meaningful.

Long-range plans frequently are organized into *teaching units.* Teaching units are usually from 2 to 6 weeks long and are organized around broad topics such as magnets and electricity, plants, and the human body. The teacher then selects and organizes instructional materials and activities that will help the students develop the major ideas, concepts, skills, and attitudes that relate to the selected topic. Often science teaching units integrate music, art, math, and other subject area activities into the unit to provide students with more opportunities to assimilate and accommodate the new information. Daily planning is a necessary part of long-range planning, and long-range planning provides the structure for daily planning.

This section continues the lesson plan that you began in Activity 5.1 on writing objectives. Those objectives identify what you hope to accomplish with your lesson. In this section you will develop an instructional strategy (a 30- to 45-minute science lesson plan) designed to help the child accomplish these objectives.

Four vital elements that should be a part of your instructional strategy are

1. Attention-getting and motivating techniques
2. Data-gathering techniques
3. Data-processing techniques
4. Closure techniques

These four elements represent a planned sequence of instruction. First you get the child's attention, then involve her in experiences that enable her to gather the appropriate information. This information is then processed—organized, analyzed, and conclusions reached—in phase three of this instructional sequence. In the final phase, the teacher helps the child to reach closure, to pull the lesson together and see all the related parts. Each phase in this instructional strategy will be discussed separately; and specific techniques for each, suggested. When your strategy is completed, it should provide the appropriate practice children need to accomplish the objectives.

Attention-Getting and Motivating Techniques

To begin a lesson, you must, of course, first get the students' attention and then motivate them so they feel a need to continue with the instruction. Four techniques that can be used to get students' attention and motivate them are

1. Discrepant events
2. Verbal discussion
3. Problem presentation
4. Conflicts of opinion

Discrepant Events. Piaget's theory on equilibrium relates to the first technique. Discrepant events, or inconsistencies, are valuable instructional techniques that cause the learner to become disequilibrated. This means that information is presented that does not fit the learner's existing mental structure. As a result, the learner becomes uncomfortable or frustrated. Usually this produces a desire on the part of the learner to resolve the inconsistency.

A discrepant event can be an effective technique only if it relates to the learner's past experiences. That is, a learner must have some background to enable him to perceive the event as discrepant or inconsistent. Because of previous experiences, the learner has acquired a set of expectations that prove unreliable when the new event occurs. To use Piaget's terms again, the learner is not able to assimilate the new information and must modify his existing mental structure to accommodate it. By using this instructional technique to begin a lesson, a teacher is able to capitalize on the learner's natural curiosity and need to resolve the inconsistency. The remainder of the instructional sequence would be used to provide the learner with necessary materials and guidance to resolve the inconsistency.

There are many ways to present a discrepant event. George, Dietz, Abraham, and Nelson (1974) have suggested the following:

1. *Silence:* Use exaggerated movements and conduct the entire presentation of the discrepant event in silence.
2. *In progress:* Have the event already in progress when student enters the teaching area.
3. *Pictures* and *film loops:* Use visual aids that show inconsistent observations or present information that is inconsistent with past experiences of the learner.[1]

If you select a discrepant event to use for the attention-getting and motivating portion of the instructional sequence, it is important to keep a few things in mind. Make sure that the event is directly related to the rest of the instruction. The data-gathering and data-processing portions of the instruction should involve the child with appropriate materials and guidance in resolving the inconsistency created.

This student is motivated by his desire to resolve a discrepancy presented by the experiment.

A second consideration is that, for best results, you should limit the usage of the discrepant event technique. Children sometimes begin to expect an entertainer instead of a teacher if the technique is used too frequently. Or they begin to expect the unexpected, and the technique loses its effectiveness.

A third- or fourth-grade teacher using this technique to begin a sciencing lesson might say, "I have brought with me today an ordinary empty drink-mix can." (The teacher holds up and shows the can, but keeps the plastic lid on.)

"Using a couple of books and a short board, I have set up an inclined plane. If I place this can near the top of the inclined plane and release it, what will happen?"

Most children will say, somewhat uninterestedly, that it will roll down. The teacher then says, "Watch closely; you may be surprised."

The can is then carefully placed on its side about three-fourths of the way up the inclined plane and released. To the amazement of all, it rolls *up*! The teacher then repeats the demonstration with all eyes glued on the can. During the science lesson that follows, the children will find out why the can rolled up instead of down. (In this example, four large nails are taped close together to the inside of the can. When the can is placed on the inclined plane so that the nails are positioned near the top of the can but slightly to the "up" side of the inclined plane, the pull of gravity is greater on that side than on the side where there are no weights. Thus, the can rolls up.)

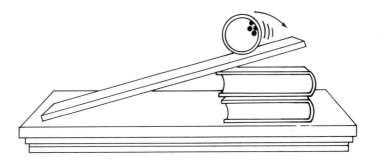

Discrepant events do provide an excellent beginning for a lesson, but a teacher must use a variety of techniques to be most effective.

Verbal Discussion.   One of the most used beginning techniques is verbal discussion. The teacher begins the lesson by establishing background information through a lecture or question-answer session to discover the students' past experiences. This information is then related to the present instruction planned for that day's lesson. The students are prepared during this portion for what is to come in the data-collecting and data-processing portions of the lesson. This technique is not as exciting as a discrepant event, but it does serve to get the students' attention and induce some motivation. For example, to begin a lesson on magnets, the teacher might hold up a horseshoe magnet and ask the children to identify it. Further discussion would continue, and opportunities would be given for students to express their personal experiences with and knowledge of magnets. The teacher would guide the discussion so that the students could establish connections with past experiences that would be helpful in relating to the new information. The purpose and focus of the lesson would be established. This technique is related to the anticipatory set and statement of objectives in the Hunter Model.

Problem Presentation.   The verbal discussion technique can be expanded to include a problem presentation. For example, in the previous discussion about magnets, the teacher could say, "Do you think a magnet can attract any object? Let's find out." Of course, the kind of problem created must depend on the stage of mental development of the students and their past experiences with the topic area. The problem presented must also be one that can be solved by the students.

Conflicts of Opinion.   Sometimes the teacher can effectively use conflicts of opinion that arise during the verbal discussion. It is best if these conflicts have more than one correct solution. Hence, you should avoid having students engage in competition with one another if the end result is a winner and a loser. But you can create a situation during the verbal discussion that fosters competition that will result in alternative means and solutions.

One example of using conflicts of opinion to begin a lesson is to say to the children, "We have been doing many activities related to floating and sinking. We have learned that some things float and some things sink. We have established that certain properties of an object, such as shape and material, affect an object's ability to float. Today we are going to continue to investigate factors that affect floating and sinking. I have brought in some raisins and a mystery liquid to use in our investigations. Before we begin, though, I want you to think about what will happen when I drop several raisins into a clear cup of this liquid. Will they float or will they sink? How many of you think they will sink?"

There will probably be a conflict of opinion. The teacher can then pass out the materials and direct the children to find out if they were right or wrong. Motivation and interest will be high. They will find that the raisins both float and sink. This truly is an amazing discovery for most children. The liquid is a clear carbonated soda drink. The bubbles attach themselves to the raisins, which float to the top of the container. There the bubbles burst, and the raisins sink to the bottom again. The sinking-floating-sinking cycle will continue for 15 minutes or longer. This phenomenon can also be used as a discrepant event.

Summary of Attention-Getting and Motivating Techniques

Combinations or adaptations of any of the techniques presented here can be used in the beginning portion of a lesson to get the students' attention and motivate them to continue with the rest of the instructional sequence. This portion should be short and to the point, no more than 3 to 5 minutes in length. The main purpose is to get the children's attention, focus it on the upcoming lesson, and help them relate the new ideas to be explored to knowledge and experiences that they already have. You want to leave them with some unanswered questions so that they will experience the disequilabration that Piaget speaks of. This natural need and curiosity that you have helped create within the children will serve as excellent motivation for the children to attend to and participate in the remaining parts of the lesson.

Data-Gathering Techniques

Once you have the students' attention and they are motivated, you are ready to move into the next portion of the lesson—involving them in gathering data. You are now ready to provide eager students with some experiences that focus on collecting information. The information collected should directly relate to specific situations created by using the attention-getting and motivating techniques. You can use Bruner's three modes of presentation—action, imagery, and language— separately or, probably more effectively, in combination to provide a format for data-collecting activities. The three modes were introduced earlier in this chapter. Each mode is discussed briefly here as it relates to data gathering.

Action Mode. The action mode calls for firsthand experiences in which the students manipulate the objects in order to gather data. Engaging the students in a variety of laboratory activities is an excellent way to accomplish this. Laboratory activities can involve the students in simple teacher-directed tasks or can provide an outlet for creative problem solving. Sophisticated equipment is not

Field trips provide an excellent opportunity to involve students in data-gathering activities.

needed for purposeful learning to take place. Simple everyday items can be used effectively to provide learners with personal experiences in data collecting. Furthermore, laboratory activities can take place outside the classroom as well as inside. Field trips on the school grounds can provide an excellent opportunity for students to be involved in firsthand experiences. Chapter 2, "Laboratory Approach to Elementary Science," involves a variety of action-mode activities. You can refer to it for ideas during the activity section.

Imagery Mode.   Data-gathering techniques using the imagery mode of presentation involve the students with representations of real objects. Models, pictures, films, charts, or other visual aids are typical examples. As stated earlier, however, the student needs previous concrete experiences to profit from the imagery mode of presentation. Generally, children who are in the transitional stage between concrete operations and formal operations can benefit from this mode of presentation more than can those at the lower levels of cognitive development. The imagery mode of presentation is useful in providing students with the opportunity to examine data not ordinarily available to them. Plastic models of body organs and the solar system are examples.

Language Mode.   The language mode of presentation is the most abstract of the three modes and is most appropriately used with students who have reached the formal stage of cognitive development. Lectures and reading assignments are typical examples of data-gathering techniques in this mode. Information obtained in this manner is considered to come from a secondary source. Secondary sources are legitimate sources of scientific information, but they differ from firsthand manipulations of equipment and materials. Overuse of language-mode activities results in a product-oriented science approach. Remember that prior experience in the action and imagery modes is a necessary prerequisite for effective functioning in the language mode.

In this data-gathering portion of the lesson, children frequently work in pairs or small groups. These small groups are actively engaged in observing and recording data. It is wise to assign children special roles within each small group. One child could be in charge of getting, setting up, and returning the materials and equipment needed for the activity. Another could be in charge of carrying out the task at hand, while the third records the observations and reports the results to the class. While the children are engaged in data collecting, the teacher is able to walk around the room, interact with the small groups, and give help and guidance where needed. From time to time, she may also interact with the class as a whole.

The Hunter Model suggests that content be presented in small steps, using demonstrations, redundant and detailed explanations, a variety of specific examples, models, and diagrams. These suggestions correspond to Bruner's modes of instruction—action, imagery, and language. The Hunter Model also includes techniques for checking understanding. In data gathering, the teacher can have the children respond by signaling (e.g., thumbs up if you observed that the paper wad in the bottom of the beaker remained dry when the beaker was inverted in the large container of water; thumbs down if this was not observed). Or the teacher could check for understanding by saying aloud to the children, "What do you think will happen when the beaker with the paper wad in the bottom is inverted in the large container filled with water? Jot down your response, and then share it with the others in your group before doing the activity. Do the activity and jot down your observations. Be prepared to discuss these with me when I come to your group."

As the teacher circulates, decisions can be made as to how well the students understand what they are doing. The teacher can decide if additional directions or information is needed, if more time or materials are desirable, or if other adjustments and modifications to the teaching plan are necessary at this time.

During this portion of the lesson, the focus is on gathering data, but many children will engage in data processing also. In fact, it is not unusual for children to go back and forth between data gathering and data processing during science activities. The important thing for teachers to remember is that as a class, the focus is on the data-gathering aspects during this portion of the lesson. Once the data are gathered and recorded by the children and the teacher has determined that this portion of the lesson was successful, the class moves into the data-processing portion of the lesson.

Data-Processing Techniques

Data-processing techniques are used to involve learners in organizing and analyzing the data gathered. In data gathering, learners quite often work alone or in small groups. In data processing, the learners should interact. A class discussion, which involves sharing and comparing information gathered, is a good data-processing technique. The teacher should bring the class back together for the data-processing portion of the lesson. Each group can report its findings and hear the results from the other groups. Some questions that lead students to analyze information are these: "What patterns do you see developing?" "Why do you think this happened?" "Can you support that statement?" "Why do you say that?" Other questions can be used to help promote peer interaction: "Brenda, do you agree with Glen's interpretation?" "Bob, can you add anything to Lynn's explanation?"

Organizing the data gathered into chart or graph form is a good data-processing activity. Making predictions, formulating hypotheses, making inferences, and classifying are other examples of data-processing skills. In all of these examples, learners are involved in doing something with the data gathered. It may involve physical manipulations of the data, as in constructing charts and graphs, or mental manipulations, as in predicting or formulating hypotheses. Providing opportunities for learners to engage in data processing is an essential part of all science instruction. Effective data-processing techniques promote assimilation and accommodation.

The teacher will check for understanding in this portion of the lesson also. Children can signal their responses to statements; choral responses might also

**Organizing the data gathered into a chart or graph form
is a good data-processing technique.**

be appropriate. The teacher constantly monitors and adjusts the instruction
based on feedback from the students.

In this portion of the lesson, the children are often given an additional task
designed to help them fully accommodate the information learned. The task is
closely related to what was done during the data-gathering portion. Many times,
it is an extension of the same task. The focus is, of course, on helping children
apply the new information just learned. They may do more hands-on activities or
they may "think about" what was learned by responding to questions designed
to elicit higher level thinking such as analysis, synthesis, and evaluation. Typical
questions are "Why do you think this happened?" "Could we show this idea in
another way?" and "Which way do you think is best?"

In the Hunter Model, this portion is referred to as *guided practice.* Hunter suggests that higher level questions be asked so that children engage in application, analysis, and synthesis. The teacher is to respond to the children's answers, correcting errors and reinforcing correct responses. By doing this, the teacher provides immediate feedback to the children and can use the information gathered to decide if the children are ready for independent practice.

The data-processing portion of the lesson usually takes from 10 to 20 minutes. Older children will spend more time processing information than will younger children.

To begin the lesson, you aroused the students' interest with attention-getting and motivating techniques. Next, you provided experiences that involved them in collecting data. Once the data were collected, you guided the students in organizing and analyzing it, which led to assimilation and accommodation. You are now ready for the final phase, closure.

Closure Techniques

Helping the learner reach closure is an important part of any lesson. Teachers must help the learners view the total learning experience. They must help bring into focus the various parts of the instruction and establish relationships.

A summarizing discussion is quite valuable in reviewing the tasks completed and pulling everything together into proper perspective. Using a question-and-answer format for this discussion involves the learners directly, but for parts of the closure, a teacher monologue is more appropriate. Any generalization made and conclusion reached should be related to the beginning sequence of the lesson. If the attention-getting and motivating technique created an inconsistency or a problem, make sure that the situation is clear for the learner.

During this final portion of the lesson, be sure to make a special effort to involve the children who may not be able to contribute during the data-processing portion when higher level thinking is needed. The same questions asked then can be asked now in a slightly different way to allow those children to respond. At this point the responses will be at the recall level, not at the higher process levels. But children need to hear and practice the responses in order to incorporate them into long-term memory.

The Hunter Model suggests ending the lesson by assigning independent practice to help children achieve mastery of the skills and concepts learned. Certainly, this is an excellent way to extend the lesson and help children incorporate the new learning into their own cognitive framework. It provides an opportunity for children to become comfortable with the new knowledge and skills and to feel cognitively in balance again.

Children need help in reaching closure. They need to feel cognitively in balance again. They should feel comfortable with the new information that was discovered and investigated. This portion of the lesson usually takes no more than five minutes; yet, it can mean the difference between success and failure.

Summary of Instructional Strategy

Teaching techniques are the methods of instruction used by teachers to aid the students in attaining specified objectives. Research indicates that children should be exposed to a physical and social learning environment that provides them with opportunities to manipulate objects and ideas in active interaction with others. Teaching strategies that provide this kind of learning environment demand that students be given time to assimilate and accommodate the new experience.

According to Bruner, instructional strategy can be categorized as action, imagery, and language modes. These three modes of presentation can be used separately; however, they would probably be more effective in combination in providing a format for science activities.

All daily science instruction should involve four elements: (a) attention-getting and motivating techniques, (b) data-gathering techniques, (c) data-processing techniques, and (d) closure techniques. To begin a lesson, you must first get the students' attention, and then motivate them so they feel a need to continue with the instruction. There are various techniques that can be used to accomplish this task. Discrepant events can be an excellent beginning for a lesson, provided that this method is not overused. A verbal discussion that prepares the students for instruction by giving a preview of what is to come is also a useful technique. Problem solving or conflicts of opinion are two other effective introductions. They both tend to create situations that result in students' using alternative means to find solutions.

The next portion of the lesson involves the learner in data gathering. Laboratory activities provide an excellent means of involving students with firsthand experience in data gathering. These activities can take place inside the classroom or outside as part of a field trip. The use of models, pictures, films, charts, or other visual aids provides the students with the opportunity to examine data they cannot experience directly. Secondary sources (such as reading and lectures) can also provide information, but overuse of these sources can result in a content- or product-oriented science approach.

Once the data are collected, the teacher uses data-processing techniques to involve the students in organizing and analyzing the information. Guided discussion can promote and encourage interaction among the learners. Engaging the students in both physical manipulation of the data (making charts, graphs, etc.) and mental manipulation of the data (formulating hypotheses, making inferences, making predictions) is essential to all science instruction.

Developing techniques that help students reach closure is the final phase of instruction. A teacher monologue that summarizes the lesson or a question-and-answer format in which students participate can help learners put the lesson into proper perspective.

Throughout this discussion of instructional strategy, corresponding techniques from the Hunter Model were identified and integrated where appropriate. Activity 5.2 has been designed to help you put to use the ideas presented here.

You will select and develop appropriate teaching techniques that you could use to aid the learner in attaining the objectives formulated in the preceding section. You will probably want to refer to portions of this chapter for guidance in developing your instructional strategy. Be sure to talk with your instructor if you need more clarification and guidance in understanding the material or in completing the activity.

ACTIVITY 5.2: INSTRUCTIONAL STRATEGY

A. Using the objectives you developed in Activity 5.1, select the appropriate teaching techniques and develop an instructional sequence that could be used to help students attain the specific objectives. Review your responses and comments from Activity 5.1. Record the grade level selected and the behavioral objectives written earlier. Remember, your instructional sequence should be planned for a period of 30 to 45 minutes. As you begin making decisions about the techniques you will use, you may find it necessary to modify your original objectives in order to develop more effective instructional strategy.

Grade Level:

Behavioral Objectives:

1. *Cognitive content:* The student will

2. *Cognitive process:* The student will

3. *Psychomotor:* The student will

4. *Affective:* The student will demonstrate _____ by

B. Using the ideas and information presented in the chapter, develop an instructional sequence to aid the learner in obtaining your specified objectives. Use a variety of resource materials to put together your instructional strategy. Use the following format to organize and describe your strategy.

Instructional Strategy:

1. Attention-getting and motivating techniques:

2. Data-gathering techniques:

3. Data-processing techniques:

4. Closure techniques:

✓ **Self-Check**

Examine your instructional strategy to see if it provides the learners with enough appropriate practice to enable them to attain the specified objectives. Evaluate your instruction using the following criteria:

1. The instruction will enable the learners to perform the behavioral tasks specified in the behavioral objectives.

2. The instruction provides appropriate practice in each of the four behavior categories—cognitive content, cognitive process, psychomotor, and affective.

3. The instruction incorporates the ideas of Piaget and Bruner by providing for (a) manipulation of real objects, (b) interaction with others, (c) guided discovery, and (d) alternate learning paths.

4. The attention-getting and motivating technique relates to the learners' past experience and provides a reason for participating in the learning experience.

5. The data-gathering technique involves the learners with experiences that focus on collecting information to be used in dealing with the specific situations created in the attention-getting and motivating portion of the instruction.

6. The data-processing technique involves the learners in
    a. Organizing and analyzing the information gathered
    b. Interacting with classmates
    c. Assimilating and accommodating information

7. The closure technique helps the learners to pull it all together. All parts of the instruction are related and seen as a whole. A state of equilibrium is achieved by the learners.

Share your plan with others in the class, and ask for comments and suggestions. Arrange to discuss your plan with your instructor.

Now you are ready for the final phase of lesson planning—utilizing evaluation techniques.

☐ **Comments**

USING EVALUATION TECHNIQUES

Evaluation refers to the difficult task of assessing the extent to which the students were able to attain specified objectives. The task of assessment is easier if you

(a) state the objectives in terms of observable student behavior, (b) include the conditions and the performance criteria, and (c) use the objectives to provide the framework for developing appropriate instruction.

Three types of evaluation are appropriate for science instruction. *Diagnostic evaluation* occurs before instruction to assess students' needs. Often a teacher pretests students to determine how much the students know before beginning instruction. The teacher uses this kind of information to match instruction to the needs of students. *Formative evaluation* usually takes place during the instruction. The teacher observes students while they are involved in the planned science experience and offers on-the-spot help in the form of feedback and reinforcement. Formative evaluation is an essential part of effective instruction. It provides immediate individual feedback that is used to guide the learner in completing the task at hand. *Summative evaluation,* perhaps the most familiar and most often used, takes place after the instruction has ended and is used primarily as a basis for assigning grades (Doran, 1980).

These types of evaluation can take various forms, but there are three broad categories that encompass them.

1. A paper-and-pencil test is probably the most widely used form of science assessment. It is particularly suitable for summative evaluation, but it can be used equally well for diagnostic evaluation.

2. Projects and written reports are other frequently used forms of evaluation, particularly in the upper elementary grades. They work well when the objectives are application-oriented.

3. The performance task is relatively new as an evaluation technique but offers much promise in assessing science learning. Essentially, the teacher provides the learner with the necessary materials and observes the performance of the specified task. This form of evaluation lends itself to the process-inquiry approach of sciencing.

Paper-and-Pencil Test

There are several different types of paper-and-pencil tests. No one type has proven more successful than any other, but matching the test format with the learning objectives to be assessed has proven critical. Before selecting any instrument to assess a student's achievement, you must be able to identify what it was that the student was supposed to accomplish. This brings us back to objectives. Objectives become the binding thread that holds together and integrates an entire lesson. The objectives must be examined and used as a guide in the selection of an assessment instrument.

There are six popular types of paper-and-pencil tests: multiple choice, fill-in-the-blank, true-false, matching, short answer, and essay. All of these types involve recalling information and identifying a correct response. In some types—such as multiple choice, true-false, and matching—very little writing is required.

The correct choice is indicated by circling, marking, drawing a line, or perhaps writing a letter or number. These tests are usually considered to be objective, meaning that there is one correct answer and they can be scored using a key that contains all the correct answers.

The following are some examples of objective tests:

Multiple Choice. Circle the correct response.
1. All matter is composed of tiny particles called
   a. elements
   b. molecules
   c. compounds
   d. gases
2. The pressure of liquids or gases will be low if they are moving fast and will be high if they are moving slowly. This principle is called

   a. Newton's principle
   b. Galileo's principle
   c. Bernoulli's principle
   d. Jenner's principle

True-False.   Circle the correct response.

   T F   1. Limestone and marble are chemically the same.

   T F   2. The point where the earth's crust cracks and moves is called a geyser.

Matching. Draw a line to connect the word on the left with the appropriate example on the right.

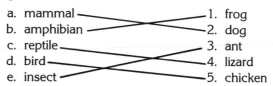

    a. mammal   1. frog
    b. amphibian   2. dog
    c. reptile   3. ant
    d. bird   4. lizard
    e. insect   5. chicken

The other paper-and-pencil tests mentioned—short answer, fill-in-the-blank, and essay—require more grading time, frequently have a variety of acceptable responses, and tend to be more subjective in nature. Students must generally do more recalling and organizing of stored information in these types of tests. The simplest of these three is the fill-in-the-blank. Sometimes there is only one word missing, but the student must recall it without benefit of being presented with multiple choices. More often, several words are omitted, and the student must supply the missing thought. Communicating the general idea, not the exact wording, is the issue.

The short answer and essay forms of evaluation expand on the fill-in-the-blank-type. Generally, a question is asked or a term given, and the learner must define, describe, explain, and give examples in answering the question. This type of evaluation is most appropriate for children who are toward the end of the concrete stage of mental development or already operating at the formal level.

Children at lower levels of cognitive development have not sufficiently developed the skills necessary to organize and express their thoughts through writing.

Following are some examples of subjective tests:

Fill-in-the-Blank

1. Most plants have four parts: ____(root)____ , ____(stems)____ , ____(leaves)____ , and ___(flowers)___ .

2. One of the main purposes of the stem of a plant is (to carry water from the roots to the leaves).

Short Answer

1. How does a rock differ from a plant?
2. What causes food to spoil?

Essay

1. Describe and compare two ways in which a plant can reproduce.
2. How does the environment affect living things?

Paper-and-pencil tests provide an effective means of assessing learners' achievement. A variety of forms allows the teacher a choice as to which form or combination of forms would be best for evaluating the learning process. Paper-and-pencil tests should not limit learners to low-level memory responses. The recall of facts and information is certainly a necessary part of all learning, but it must not be all that is required. Higher levels of cognitive functioning should be elicited also.

Although most paper-and-pencil tests are used as summative evaluation to provide a basis for grading, they can be used effectively as diagnostic evaluation. The format of the test remains the same, but in summative evaluation the results are not used to plan for further instruction, as is the case with diagnostic evaluation. Thus, the main difference between the two forms of evaluation is in the use of the test results. In diagnostic evaluation, the results become a part of the instructional process and students are able to use them. In summative evaluation, the test results are not used because the learning process is essentially over, a grade is given, and the class proceeds to another area of learning.

Projects and Written Reports

A project or written report is appropriate for assessing students' achievement if the objectives are more application oriented. This type of evaluation usually involves students in long-term preparation and final presentation. The instructor measures students' achievement by comparing the project results or the written report with the established criteria. If the students and teacher are in constant communication throughout the project, this type of evaluation can be formative as well as summative.

Many science teachers find this type of evaluation more appropriate than paper-and-pencil tests. It allows for assessment of the skills of process-inquiry-oriented science and is not limited to mental manipulation of the concepts.

Performance Tasks

The performance task is closely related to the project and written report. Generally, it does not require as much time as does a project or written report. The students receive the necessary materials and equipment and demonstrate achievement of the specified objectives by performing an appropriate task. The teacher observes and evaluates using criteria based upon the specified objectives.

This type of evaluation is particularly appropriate for assessing attainment of cognitive process, psychomotor, and affective objectives. A checklist or other method for recording observations is helpful in using this type of evaluation.

The performance task provides an excellent means of formative evaluation. The students become involved in both the means and end of instruction. As the instruction is taking place, the students are involved in appropriate practice activities and receive feedback and guidance from the teacher. This appropriate practice also becomes the end product of instruction as the students perform the task and the teacher observes them to make a final assessment of the performance.

Summary of Evaluation

Evaluation is an essential part of all science instruction. It has three functions:

1. *Diagnostic:* Providing information about students' needs before instruction.
2. *Formative:* Providing feedback during instruction and offering guidance for continued learning in the same area.
3. *Summative:* Providing a basis for assigning a grade after instruction is completed.

Assessing the extent to which the students have attained the specified objectives of instruction is a difficult task. A variety of techniques are needed, which a teacher can select, adapt, and modify to fit the requirements of a specific situation.

Paper-and-pencil tests, projects and written reports, and performance tasks form three broad categories of evaluative techniques into which specific types of evaluation can be grouped. The selection of an evaluation instrument involves matching the instrument to what is being assessed. In order to make an appropriate match, the teacher must use the stated objectives and the instructional procedure as guides.

Activity 5.3 is designed to help you use the ideas presented here.

ACTIVITY 5.3: EVALUATION

A. This activity will involve you in the total planning process. In Activity 5.1, you developed and wrote instructional and behavioral objectives. In Activity 5.2, you used those objectives to develop an instructional sequence that included attention-getting and motivating techniques, data-gathering techniques, data-processing techniques, and closure techniques. In this final phase of planning, you are to develop appropriate evaluation techniques that can be used to assess the extent to which the learner has attained the specified objectives you developed previously. The evaluation for your 30- to 45-minute lesson plan will focus on what the teacher will do during and perhaps toward the end of the instruction to determine if each objective has been met. Formative evaluation strategies are most appropriate for specific day-by-day assessment of objectives. Summative evaluation is more frequently used at the end of a week or at the end of a unit of instruction. Therefore, for the lesson that you have been asked to prepare here, *formative* evaluation techniques such as observations, immediate feedback, and checklists would be most appropriate.

B. Examine the first two phases of the planning sequence. You may find that you wish to alter or modify the original objectives or instructional strategy now that you can view the entire planning process from an integrated point of view; in fact, you may decide to discard your original efforts altogether and begin anew. Before making the decision, take time to review all three sections of this chapter, both the reading sections and the corresponding activities. When you have made a decision, record your plan on separate sheets to hand in to your instructor. Use the following outline to describe your entire lesson plan. Remember this is a 30- to 45-minute lesson plan.

Title of Lesson:

Grade Level:

Behavioral Objectives:

1. *Cognitive content:* The learner will
2. *Cognitive process:* The learner will
3. *Psychomotor:* The learner will
4. *Affective:* The learner will demonstrate _____ by

Instructional Strategy:

1. Attention-getting and motivating techniques:
2. Data-gathering techniques:
3. Data-processing techniques
4. Closure techniques:

Evaluation: Describe what the teacher will do to determine if the students have met the objectives for this lesson.

1. *Cognitive content objective:* The teacher will
2. *Cognitive process objective:* The teacher will
3. *Psychomotor objective:* The teacher will
4. *Affective objective:* The teacher will

☑ Self-Check

A. When your lesson plan is completed, use the following questions to guide you in evaluating your understanding of the ideas and information presented in this chapter.

1. What were the main learning theories and ideas of Piaget and Bruner that were presented in the chapter?
2. What implications do these theories have for constructing teaching strategies?
3. How are the ideas of Piaget and Bruner reflected in your lesson plan?
4. How is the Hunter Model integrated into the strategies presented?

B. Turn back to pages 179–180 and use the criteria presented there to evaluate the objectives developed for your final lesson plan. Make any adjustments you feel are necessary.

C. Use the criteria on pages 196–197 to evaluate your instructional strategy. Make the necessary modifications that result from this evaluation or that result from changes in the objectives.

D. Use the following questions to judge the effectiveness of the evaluation portion of your lesson plan.

1. Are all the objectives—cognitive content, cognitive process, psychomotor, and affective—evaluated?

2. Does your evaluation describe what the teacher will do to determine if the objectives of the lesson are met?

3. Does your evaluation provide for both a formative (during instruction) and a summative (after instruction) function?

4. How could diagnostic evaluation be used in your lesson?

☐ **Comments**

SUMMARY

This chapter involved you in a step-by-step process of developing a teaching strategy for daily lesson planning that included behavioral objectives, instructional strategy, and evaluation. Each of these three stages of lesson planning was examined, and techniques were identified that could be used in each stage to engage children in successful sciencing experiences. A brief overview of the Madeline Hunter Model of effective instruction was also included. The Hunter Model was integrated into the strategies and format of the lesson plan model presented in this chapter. The learning theories of Piaget and Bruner were presented and form the basis for the teaching strategies that were included.

There is no doubt that effective, successful learning experiences result from systematic, creative planning. Good teachers recognize the value of objectives that identify the purpose of instruction and specify what the child is to do to meet the objectives. They also realize that they must devise a good instructional strategy to help the child attain the objectives. A variety of teaching techniques is needed for this phase of the lesson. Those included in this chapter were divided into attention-getting and motivating techniques, data-gathering techniques, data-processing techniques, and closure techniques. In the final phase of lesson planning, the teacher must assess the learners' achievement. Three types of evaluation were identified and discussed: diagnostic, formative, and summative.

Long-range planning provides the structure for daily planning; therefore, teachers must organize the science curriculum into a logical sequence. This is usually accomplished by developing teaching units that focus on broad science topics and extend from 2 to 6 weeks. Daily lesson planning is a necessary part of long-range planning, and the three-phase lesson model presented here should provide you with a flexible guide for developing and constructing effective daily sciencing experiences for children that emphasize active, hands-on involvement with concepts and materials.

ENDNOTES

1. Reprinted by permission of the publisher, from George/Dietz et al.: *Elementary School Science: Why and How* (Lexington, Mass.: D.C. Heath, 1974).

REFERENCES

Bruner, J. S. (1967). *Toward a theory of instruction.* Cambridge, MA: Harvard University Press.

Doran, R. L. (1980). *Basic measurement and evaluation of instruction.* Washington, DC: National Science Teachers Association.

Furth, H. G. (1970). *Piaget for teachers.* Englewood Cliffs, NJ: Prentice-Hall.

George, K., Dietz, M., Abraham, E., & Nelson, M. (1974). *Elementary school science: Why and how.* Lexington, MA: D.C. Heath.

Hunter, M. (1985, February). What's wrong with Madeline Hunter? *Educational Leadership,* pp. 57–60.

SUGGESTED READINGS

Alney, M., Chittenden, E. A., & Miller, P. (1966). *Young children's thinking: Studies of some aspects of Piaget's theory.* New York: Teachers College Press.

Bloom, B. S., Hastings, J. T., & Madaus, G. F. (1971). *Handbook on formative and summative evaluation of student learning.* New York: McGraw-Hill.

Bruner, J. S., Goodnow, J. J., & Austin, G. A. (1956). *A study of thinking.* New York: John Wiley and Sons.

Carin, A., & Sund, R. (1989). Chapter 3. *Teaching science through discovery* (6th ed.). Columbus, OH: Merrill Publishing.

Combs, A. W., Blume, R. A., Newman, A. J., & Wass, H. L. (1974). *The professional education of teachers: A humanistic approach to teacher preparation* (2nd ed.). Boston: Allyn and Bacon.

Garman, N. B., & Hazi, H. M. (1988, May). Teachers ask: Is there life after Madeline Hunter? *Phi Delta Kappan,* pp. 669–672.

Mager, R. F. (1986). *Developing attitudes toward learning.* Belmont, CA: Rearon Publishers.

———. (1972). *Goal analysis,* Belmont, CA: Fearon Publishers.

Maslow, A. H. (1954). *Toward a psychology of being.* New York: Van Nostrand Reinhold.

Piltz, A., & Sund, R. (1974). *Creative teaching of science in the elementary school* (2nd ed.). Boston, MA: Allyn and Bacon.

Rogers, C. R. (1969). *Freedom to learn.* Columbus, OH: Merrill Publishing.

Slavin, R. (1987, April). The Hunterization of America's schools. *Instructor,* pp. 56–59.

CHAPTER 6

Questioning Techniques

Goals

After completing this chapter, you will demonstrate competence in the following:

1. The ability to formulate effective questions that foster more than rote-memory responses.

2. The ability to apply appropriate questioning strategies in formulating questions to be used as part of a planned science activity for elementary students.

Objectives

In completing this chapter, you will do the following:

1. Identify and describe the questioning strategies presented.

2. Write science questions designed to elicit more than rote-memory responses from elementary students.

3. Use the ideas presented in this chapter by selecting a science topic and constructing an appropriate questioning strategy as part of a planned science activity for elementary students.

INTRODUCTION

The ability to formulate and ask questions fostering creative, thoughtful, high-level responses is an integral part of the instructional strategy. Unfortunately, most classroom teachers ask questions that require only low-level, memory responses. Questions that encourage and solicit responses indicating more than rote memory need to be included in the instructional process if high-level thinking is desired.

There are various questioning strategies that offer guidance to elementary teachers in planning and integrating effective questions into the instructional strategy. In this chapter, the themes and ideas of two of the more well-known questioning strategies are presented. Information about the purpose and kinds of questions is also included. Factors to consider in designing your own questioning strategy for use with sciencing activities are also discussed.

Planning for effective questioning may involve a change in teacher-student relationships. This occurs because questions that require more than rote-memory responses often stimulate students to respond with different answers from different points of view. The teacher must adjust to the new role of discussion facilitator. Furthermore, different kinds of questions demand different kinds of responses. A single "Yes, Lynn, that's right," or "No, Bob, that's wrong" is not an appropriate response for higher level questions. This chapter will provide some guidance in the area of responding to students' replies to higher level questions. Activities designed to involve you in formulating questions that foster creative, thoughtful, high-level responses are also included.

EFFECTIVE QUESTIONING

Effective questioning is an art. Unfortunately, few teachers make use of well-developed questioning techniques or strategies. Too often they limit themselves to questions arising spontaneously during instruction. Carefully planned questions can offer direction and guidance for instruction. However, such effective questioning involves the use of specific skills, techniques, and strategies. Often a change in attitude toward the learning process itself is necessary.

In order to help you acquire the skills involved in effective questioning, it is necessary to examine the role of questioning in the learning process. Questions are most often used by teachers to see if the learner can remember information that was presented. This use of questioning is limiting, in that students are merely required to recall previously memorized information. Memory-level knowledge is considered to be the lowest level of cognition.

Questions can serve a more useful purpose than testing students' abilities to recall information. They can stimulate students' involvement and interaction. Chapter 5 presents a sequenced format composed of four elements—attention-getting and motivating techniques, data-gathering techniques, data-processing techniques, and closure techniques—for making plans for instruction. You can use effective questioning in each of these phases to involve the students both mentally and physically in the learning process.

Stimulating Involvement

Questions designed to get students' attention and motivate them might focus on discrepancies, create a problem situation, result in conflicts of opinion, or aid the students in relating past experiences to new information. The following are examples of such questions:

1. How can it be that the water doesn't come out of the glass when it is turned upside down?
2. Does the length of the string affect the pendulum's period of oscillation?
3. How can we find out which magnet is stronger?
4. Have you ever used a thermometer before? Where? What did you find out by using a thermometer? Is this thermometer like the one you have seen or used before? What could we find out by using a thermometer?

Data Gathering

Questions can also be structured to aid students in data collecting. In firsthand experiences, questions or statements such as "What does it feel like?" "Describe the sound it makes" and "Describe the odor" guide the students in using their senses to make observations. Others focus the students' attention on quantitative measurements: "How heavy is it?" or "How long is it?" Still others suggest actions the students might take in gathering information: "Do you think it will float?" or "How high will it bounce?"

When data are collected using pictures, models, charts, and graphs, questions such as the following can be asked: "How would you describe the animal in this picture?" "According to the graph, what can you tell about the rainfall in Michigan last year?" "After observing an operating model of our solar system, how would you describe the relationship in space of the planets to each other ard to the sun?"

Questions that are designed to guide learners in gathering information from secondary sources, such as lectures and reading assignments, are often quite difficult to structure. Too often questions merely involve the students in recalling information. Consider the following examples: "In reviewing the reading assignment, how would you describe the process of oxidation?" or "After listening to the lecture on heat energy, how would you describe the ways in which heat energy travels?" Questions such as these can guide learners in gathering specific information that is presented in the language mode. Their purpose is *not* to have the

This teacher is using questions to help students gather data about the solar system.

learners recall from memory specific information but to have them use the source material in gathering the appropriate information. This same emphasis is reflected in the questions presented earlier, which guide the students in using action and imagery sources in gathering data. By asking questions with this emphasis, you encourage learners to assume a more active role in the data-collecting process.

Data Processing

Following the data-gathering phase of instruction, you will guide the students in organizing and analyzing the data. This phase of instruction is referred to as data processing. Questions asked during this portion of instruction should require the learners to engage in one or more of the following process-inquiry skills: classifying, measuring, using space relationships, communicating, predicting, inferring, defining operationally, formulating hypotheses, interpreting data, controlling variables, and experimenting. All of these skills involve the learners in organizing and analyzing the data. Review the following sample questions and notice how they are designed to engage the learners in organizing and analyzing data:

1. How could you separate these objects into two different groups?
2. How can you present the data you gathered so that others can understand them?
3. Based on the observations you made about the object concealed inside the opaque container, can you identify it?
4. After examining the three closed, identical circuits, what reasons can you give for the bulb on only one of the circuits *not* lighting?
5. How would you determine the effect of the length of the pendulum on its period of oscillation?

Closure

You can effectively pose questions in the final phase of the lesson to help the learners reach closure. Questions that require the learners to relate the various parts of the lesson, cause them to focus on the main points, or help them "put it all together" are most appropriate here. The following are some examples:

1. Kim, how do the kind, size, and length of materials used affect the flow of electricity?
2. Trey, our lesson today focused on making complete circuits. Look at this sample circuit and explain why it isn't complete.
3. Cory, what did we find out about the effect of the length of the pendulum on its period of oscillation?

You should now be familiar with the ways in which questioning can be used in each of the four phases of the lesson in order to involve the students both mentally and physically. The important thing to remember is the *purpose* of the question. Questions should be carefully chosen and worded so they contribute to the learning process in the way intended. Furthermore, careful planning can give a teacher the security needed to include spontaneous questions also.

Convergent and Divergent Questions

Another role that questioning plays in the learning process is that of stimulating convergent or divergent thinking. *Convergent questions* involve the learners in centering. Such questions have a limited number of acceptable or appropriate answers. In contrast, *divergent questions* have many acceptable responses. The students are encouraged to offer alternative solutions. Divergent questions also encourage creativity and require more than rote-memory responses.

You need to plan for both convergent and divergent questions. The trick is to know when to use each type of question. Generally, divergent questions work best with the first three phases of a science lesson. In these phases—attention getting and motivating, data gathering, and data processing—divergent questions allow for maximum input from students and foster interactions among them.

Convergent questions are most appropriate to use during the final phase of the lesson. In formulating a response to a convergent question, the students focus on specific bits of information. Their thinking is drawn toward a common point. However, there may also be times when convergent questions are appropriate in the earlier parts of the lesson. Careful planning will help you to use the appropriate kind of question. Read over the following questions and see if you can distinguish the ones designed to encourage convergent thinking from those designed to elicit divergent thought:

1. Do your hands feel warm when you rub them together very rapidly?
2. What causes the molecules of a liquid to move?
3. How can we find out if heat affects the time it takes for a substance to dissolve in water?
4. How do you know air is around you?
5. Do you think the sugar cube will dissolve faster in the cold water than in the hot water?
6. What do you think will happen when the sugar is heated?

Did you have any difficulty deciding which questions were the most divergent and which were the most convergent? Did you try to answer these questions yourself? You might want to compare your answers with those of your classmates. (Answers are on page 219.)

Questions for Evaluating

Another role of questioning in the learning process pertains to evaluation. *Diagnostic* evaluation occurs *before* instruction to assess student needs. *Formative* evaluation occurs *during* the learning process and is aimed at providing feedback and reinforcement. *Summative* evaluation occurs *after* the instructional process and is used as a basis for assigning a grade. Refer to Chapter 5 for more information on the three functions of evaluation.

Teachers most frequently ask questions to obtain a summative evaluation. Generally, these questions tend to be content oriented, but this does not have to be the case, as you will see when you are introduced to the various questioning strategies. Summative evaluation questions are designed to find out how well the students have learned, and they are asked after the instruction is complete.

Formative evaluation questions, on the other hand, are asked at intervals during the instruction. They serve to keep the teacher informed of the students' progress. They also provide the students with immediate feedback. Adjustments in the instruction may result, or individual learner prescriptions may be given. There is no real structural difference between formative and summative evaluation questions. The difference is in the use or purpose of the questions.

QUESTIONING STRATEGIES

There are several well-known questioning strategies that offer guidance to teachers in planning and integrating effective questioning into the instructional sequence. Probably the most popular system used in classifying classroom questions is Bloom's (1956) *Taxomony,* or systematic classification principles. The six levels of thinking identified by Bloom are knowledge, comprehension, application, analysis, synthesis, and evaluation.

The six sequential levels provide the teacher with a framework in formulating questions that will encourage students to engage in a specific level of thinking in responding. The following outline presents each of the six levels of thinking as identified by Bloom. The intended student behavior for each level and some examples of questions that could elicit that intellectual behavior are also included.

Level 1: Memory. The student is asked to recall information. For example:

1. To which group of animals do frogs belong?
2. What are the four developmental stages of a moth?
3. What is the young undeveloped baby plant in a seed called?

Level 2: Comprehension. The student is asked to show understanding of the information. For example:

1. In your own words, how would you describe the four developmental stages of a moth?
2. Explain how fish are able to breathe under water.
3. We have been involved in gathering data concerning the amount of time a candle continues to burn when a beaker is inverted and placed over it. We have used three of four beakers and found that under beaker one (100 ml), the candle continued to burn for 11 seconds, under beaker two (200 ml), the candle burned for 22 seconds, and under beaker three (300 ml), it burned for 33 seconds. How long do you think it will burn under beaker four (400 ml)?

Level 3: Application. The student is asked to use abstract ideas and apply them to a specific concrete situation. For example:

1. What would happen if you placed a fish in a covered container of cooled, boiled water?

2. How would you prepare an environment to grow frogs?

3. How would you use a balloon to demonstrate how our lungs work?

Level 4: Analysis. The student is asked to examine information by separating it into its parts. For example:

1. Why do you think people are not more concerned about pollution problems?

2. Tim, can you explain how Rob's conclusion is consistent with yours?

3. Brent, why is Courtney's approach sound?

Level 5: Synthesis. The student is asked to engage in creative thinking. For example:

1. What could you do to find out how much water the bucket of snow would make?

2. How would you improve the pencil?

3. How would you describe life on earth in the year 2090?

Level 6: Evaluation. The student is asked to make a judgment. For example:

1. What is the best way to find out if water is a good conductor of heat?

2. Do you think that there should be a law to limit the number of children a person could have? Why? Why not?

3. What do you see as the best solution to the energy problem?

Bloom's six levels represent a hierarchy. The knowledge level is considered to be the lowest (simplest) level of thinking and the evaluation level is considered to be the highest (most complex) level. Each higher level includes any lower level(s). Beware that asking a question designed to elicit thinking at a specific level does not mean the learner will automatically respond at that level. Careful planning is necessary. Quite often it is necessary to guide the learner to higher level thinking by developing a series of questions that gradually move from the knowledge level to the comprehension level and on up to the higher levels. Learners cannot be expected to respond with evaluation-level thinking until they have had many experiences involving the lower levels.

You must consider the students' background experiences and developmental levels when you plan effective questioning. As a teacher, you must provide many opportunities for students to gather, organize, analyze, and evaluate information. These experiences provide the necessary background that students need to draw upon when responding to questions. Without these kinds of experiences, students are unable to operate at the higher level of thinking.

Furthermore, a student's developmental level is a determining factor of the level of thinking at which he is capable of responding. Generally, young children before age seven or eight are unable to operate above the first three levels of thinking on Bloom's hierarchy. But that does *not* mean a teacher should never ask a higher level question to children below the age of eight. It does mean, however, that these children need many more concrete experiences and that questions should relate directly to these concrete experiences.

TABA'S QUESTIONING STRATEGY

Hilda Taba (1971) has devised a questioning strategy that involves learners in a step-by-step process aimed at encouraging effective thinking. In the first step, the teacher uses an *opening question* that requires only low-level cognitive responses, thus allowing most learners to enter the discussion. To be effective, an opening question should involve general knowledge but permit a wide range of responses within specific parameters. A question such as "What are the four basic parts that most plants have?" is considered a closed question and would be inappropriate as an opening question. It has a "right" answer and does not encourage other meaningful responses once the right answer has been given. Using the same general theme, a teacher might ask, "How do the roots from a carrot, turnip, and beet differ?" This question allows more students to enter the discussion at a relatively low level since there are several possible responses.

The second criterion of an effective opening question involves establishing a focus for the discussion. The teacher must decide beforehand what the discussion's purpose is to be and guide the students in that direction. Consequently, the opening question should set the general direction for the discussion. This does not mean the teacher should attempt to control the content of the students' responses. It does mean, however, that he guides the students to engage in certain thought processes. For example, if the purpose of the discussion is to compare and contrast the roots from different types of plants, the teacher must guide the students in that direction. The question that opens the discussion must be worded so that it relates to the initial purpose of eliciting low-level, factual responses as well as to the overall purpose of using this needed data in the higher level cognitive processes of inferring and generalizing.

In the second step of Taba's scheme, the teacher attempts to raise the students' thinking from that of low-level memory or factual knowledge to a higher level in which they are required to look for relationships among data. Such questions are known as *lifting questions* and should be designed to encourage students to respond with tentative opinions rather than more qualified ones. Questions that include phrases such as "what seems to be," "what might be," and "what do you think," are suggested in promoting open, tentative responses. The following are examples of lifting questions:

1. Ashley, what factors might account for the difference in the size of your bean plant and Patrick's bean plant?
2. Adrian, what seems to be the best environment for growing bread mold, based on your own findings?

3. Carmen, what do you think will happen when we drop the raisins into the liquid in this beaker?

Not all students will be able to initiate a response at this level, so the teacher must attempt to involve as many students as possible by asking for other examples. In this way, a student who cannot raise the level of the discussion with an original response can participate once the level has been established by offering responses and examples similar to the initial response or with a thought that is correct but incomplete. When this happens, the teacher should continue with that student in order to permit him to develop the idea, provided the rest of the class can be kept mentally involved also.

The third step of Taba's strategy requires the students to combine relationships and make generalizations about them. During this phase of the discussion, the teacher guides the students into thinking and speaking in abstract terms. *Supporting questions* that require the learners to clarify, extend, and synthesize are used during this phase. These questions should encourage the learners to (a) build on the ideas already presented, (b) use gathered data as the basis for statements, and (c) establish a rationale for their opinions. Such questions— such as "Cherí, what evidence have we gathered that would support our hypothesis that gases expand when heated?" or "Chandler, explain why the balloon in the ice-cold water changed shape," or "What is the purpose of leaving one of the three balloons at room temperature?"—permit learners to infer and generalize, thus operating at a higher cognitive level.

Taba also suggests that the teacher may find it helpful to let the students in on this step-by-step process of becoming more effective thinkers. The students can then be more directly involved in assessing their ability and their classmates' ability to respond at a higher level to different questions. Once the students become skilled at identifying the levels of thinking that different types of questions require, they are ready to assume more responsibility in the role of questioner. In the beginning, you, as teacher, must assume the responsibility for designing and asking questions that require the students to respond at the different levels. As time passes, the students, we hope, will incorporate the process inherent in this strategy and begin to use it on their own in questioning the teacher, each other, and their textbooks.

The Taba strategy uses questions to direct the students' thinking step by step, from low-level, specific concrete ideas toward more abstract, generalized concepts. It suggests that the nature of the class as well as the purpose of the discussion are both important factors and must be considered when planning questioning sequences. There will be times when the teacher must supply needed information or use examples to clarify the situation so that the students can deal effectively with it. As the students gain more experience, however, the teacher's role should become more indirect.

It is important for the teacher and the students to work together in creating a classroom climate that allows for differences of opinion. The teacher should take the lead in offering support to students whose ideas are rejected or proven

This teacher is effectively using Taba's questioning strategy.

incorrect, because it is important that these learners feel comfortable and secure enough to reenter the discussion. The students themselves must also assume this supportive role.

The questioning strategies of both Taba and Bloom provide the classroom teacher with helpful guidelines in formulating a workable plan for effective questioning. No one series of questions will work every time or with all learners. It is up to the teacher to determine the specific purpose of a dialogue and survey the students who will be participating in order to devise effective questioning strategies. In addition, there are several other factors to consider. These include wait-time, verbal and nonverbal congruence, and the avoidance of teleological and anthropomorphic questions.

OTHER FACTORS IN QUESTIONING STRATEGIES

Importance of Wait-Time

Mary Budd Rowe (1973) has concluded that there is probably a relationship between the quality of inquiry and the wait-time a teacher allows for a learner to begin a response to a question. This also holds true for the time the teacher allows before replying to a student's statement. Many small groups of students and their teachers were involved in a study that explored the effects of increased wait-time. Before the study, the average wait-time allowed by the teachers was between 1 and 2 seconds for beginning a response and less than 1 second before replying to a student's statement. In the study, the teachers increased the wait-time in both instances and found that several changes occurred that led to increased quality in the dialogue.

Not only were the students' responses longer than before, but there also were more of them. More learners were able to answer more of the questions. Relationships between evidence and inferences were better established, and more alternative explanations were offered by the students. Increased wait-time on the part of the teacher can lead to a more effective discussion and, therefore, should be part of the overall questioning strategy.

Congruence of Verbal and Nonverbal Cues

Another factor to consider in implementing a questioning strategy is that of verbal and nonverbal congruence. In facilitating a dialogue, the teacher should pay particular attention to the nonverbal cues that the learners are receiving. The learners need to feel that the teacher is interested and is listening to what they are saying. Facing the child who is speaking and maintaining eye contact is one way to let the child know that you are interested. Nodding appropriately, making facial gestures such as smiling, and making other gestures with the hands and body to indicate involvement with the discussion also demonstrate interest.

When the teacher is talking, the nonverbal and verbal cues need to be coordinated so that students are not confused by words that indicate an involvement in the dialogue and body language that clearly indicates detachment. When conflicts between verbal and nonverbal cues occur, the nonverbal action tends to be taken by students as the more reliable of the two. Therefore, in order to facilitate an effective dialogue, the teacher must demonstrate both verbal and nonverbal involvement in the dialogue.

Avoidance of Teleological and Anthropomorphic Questions

The teacher should avoid science questions that attribute purpose or will to nonhuman things and those that imply that natural phenomena have human characteristics. These teleological and anthropomorphic questions are not consistent with scientific attitudes. When asking questions about natural phenomena, do not suggest or imply that nonhuman things think or feel in the same way that humans do. Questions that do so—such as "How do you think a plant feels when it doesn't get enough water?" or "Why do some animals like to hibernate in the winter?"—are misleading and do not help students understand natural phenomena.

Appropriate Response Schemes

As the facilitator of a dialogue, the teacher not only assumes the responsibility for designing and implementing the questioning sequence, but also must be aware of an appropriate response scheme. The purpose of a discussion should be to promote continued interaction among the participants. The teacher's response to a student's reply can impede the discussion or can serve to stimulate further thought.

The most common teacher responses are those that accept or reject the student's reply. These responses do nothing to stimulate further thought unless combined with a response that asks the learner to extend, clarify, support, or supply evidence. Continually giving accepting and rejecting kinds of responses is usually indicative of low-level questioning. Questions that require the learner to engage in high-level thinking call for teacher's responses that encourage continued dialogue. Some examples follow of responses that could be used to stimulate dialogue:

1. Explain that further, using your own words.
2. Give another example.
3. What evidence do you have to support your conclusions?
4. Adrian, can you add anything to Jeff's explanation?
5. Yes, Gladys, one function of the roots of a plant is the absorption of food materials. Tell us another, Glen.

The activities that follow will help you use the ideas presented in this chapter. You will probably want to refer to parts of this chapter for guidance in completing the activities.

(*Answers* to page 212: 1. Convergent, 2. Convergent, 3. Divergent, 4. Divergent, 5. Convergent, 6. Divergent)

SUGGESTED ACTIVITIES

As you complete these activities, keep in mind that they have been designed to help you assimilate and accommodate the information in the chapter. You should try to analyze the purpose of each activity to relate it to the information presented. It might be helpful to reread the goals and objectives listed at the beginning of this chapter. Use them as a guide to what direction you should take and what you are to achieve.

ACTIVITY 6.1: FORMULATING SCIENCE QUESTIONS

In this activity, you are to formulate several science questions designed to elicit higher than rote-memory responses from elementary students. You may select a central theme, or concept, and relate all your questions to it, or you may choose to formulate questions from a variety of science topics. The important thing to remember is to design the questions so that the learners are encouraged to reply at a higher than rote-memory level.

Samples of science questions:

1.

2.

3.

4.

5.

6.

☑ **Self-Check**

A. If you did this activity alone, get together with several others and share your questions.

B. Use the following questions to analyze and evaluate your efforts:

1. Do all your questions require more than a rote-memory reply from the learners? Rewrite those that do not meet this criterion.

2. Do you or does anyone in your group have any questions that could be used effectively to (a) begin a lesson, (b) aid students in data collecting, (c) encourage students to process the data, or (d) help students reach closure? Think of other examples of questions that could be used for any of these purposes and discuss the possibilities with your group.

3. Do you or does anyone in your group have any questions that are designed to stimulate convergent thinking? Divergent thinking? For what purpose would each kind be used? Refer to the questions on page 212 and discuss these with your group. Can you agree on which are most divergent and which are most convergent? Discuss any problems that occur. What other examples of divergent and convergent questions can your group think of?

4. Do you or does anyone in your group have any questions that could be used in evaluating or assessing a student's ability? Could they be used just as effectively for formative as well as summative evaluation? What other examples can you give of evaluative questions?

5. Do you or does anyone in your group have questions that imply or suggest that nonliving things think or feel in the same way as humans? If so, change these so that the students will not be misled.

☐ **Comments**

ACTIVITY 6.2: FORMULATING TEACHER RESPONSES

In this activity, you are to formulate appropriate teacher's responses to possible students' replies. Select several of the questions from Activity 6.1 or formulate some new ones. Think about the possible students' replies to each of the selected questions, and formulate an appropriate teacher's response. Record your responses so they can be discussed.

1. Question:

    Possible learners' replies:

    Appropriate teacher's responses:

2. Question:

    Possible learners' replies:

    Appropriate teacher's responses:

3. Question:

Possible learners' replies:

Appropriate teacher's responses:

✓ **Self-Check**

    A. Do your questions generate several possible meaningful learners' replies? If not, they probably encourage only low-level memory answers. Rewrite them, if necessary, so that they stimulate several higher than memory-level responses.

    B. Do your responses tend to stimulate further thought on the part of the students by encouraging them to to extend, clarify, support, or supply evidence? If not, how could they be altered to accomplish this purpose?

☐ **Comments**

ACTIVITY 6.3: CONSTRUCTING A QUESTIONING STRATEGY

    A. In this activity, you will select a science topic and construct an appropriate questioning strategy as part of a planned science activity for elementary students. You may want to use the ideas and information presented in Chapters 2 and 3 in selecting your topic. You may use the lesson, or portions of it, that you developed in Chapter 5, or you may develop another one. Your questioning strategy should incorporate the ideas presented in this chapter. Use either of the two strategies presented, combinations of both, or formulate one of your own based on the information presented. Outline your strategy on a separate sheet of paper using the guide that follows. Give examples of questions that could be used. Limit your selected topic or content area so that it can be dealt with effectively in 30 to 45 minutes.

Outline of Questioning Strategy

    Science topic:

    Grade level:

    Brief description of lesson (purpose, content or concepts to be explored, and teaching strategy):

    Description of question strategy (include examples of questions):

B. Submit your questioning strategy to your instructor for feedback.

SUMMARY

Questions are important teaching tools. To be effective and integral to the instructional strategy, questioning sequences need to be carefully planned. Teachers must be aware of the various instructional purposes for which they can use questions. A teacher can successfully use questions in any of the four phases of a lesson. Attention-getting and motivating questions can begin a lesson. Questions can be structured to aid students in both the data-collecting and data-processing portions of the lesson. They can also help students reach closure in the final phase of the lesson.

Moreover, questions can stimulate convergent or divergent thinking. Both kinds of thinking are necessary in most learning situations. The teacher must be able to determine which is most appropriate in a particular learning situation.

Information gathered by using evaluative questions can serve two functions—providing a basis for a grade and providing the teacher with information to be used in diagnosing and prescribing. If the purpose of the evaluation question is to elicit information to be used as a basis for assigning a grade, it is asked at the *end* of the instructional sequence. Evaluative questions asked *during* the instructional sequence can keep the teacher informed of the learners' progress. If warranted, adjustments can be made in the instruction or individual learner prescriptions.

Two well-known questioning strategies by Bloom and Taba offer guidance to teachers in planning and integrating effective questioning into the instructional sequence. Bloom has identified six sequential levels of thinking. He asserts that questions can be designed to elicit responses that involve the learner at each of the identified levels. These levels along with the intended student behavior and some examples of questions that could elicit that intellectual behavior were outlined in this section.

Hilda Taba's questioning strategy begins with a broad opening question that encourages many learners to enter the discussion at a low cognitive level. It continues with a lifting question aimed at raising the learners' level of thinking. During this phase of the discussion, the teacher poses additional questions that call for an extension of the original response in order to allow as many students as possible to continue in the discussion. In the final questioning phase, the students are guided into thinking and speaking in abstract terms by questions that require the learners to clarify, synthesize, infer, and generalize. Taba's strategy also includes the goal of preparing the students to incorporate the process of the strategy and use it on their own when questioning the teacher, their classmates, and their textbooks.

Three other factors lead to effective questioning. The wait-time a teacher allows for a learner to begin a response and also the time allowed before replying to a student's statement have been found to affect the quality of inquiry in discussion. A teacher must coordinate verbal and nonverbal cues to the students during a discussion so that learners are not receiving conflicting signals. Many times, a teacher will be verbally involved in the dialogue, but nonverbal cues, such as eye contact and facial gestures, indicate a detachment. Avoid teleological and anthropomorphic questions, which tend to imply or suggest that nonhuman things think and feel in the same way humans do. These types of questions are not consistent with a scientific attitude, are misleading, and do not help the children understand natural phenomena.

In addition to designing and implementing the questioning sequence, the teacher must also be aware of appropriate response schemes. In responding to a learner's reply, the teacher should try to stimulate further thought by asking the learners to extend, clarify, support, or supply evidence.

REFERENCES

Bloom, B. S. (1956). *Taxonomy of educational objectives: The classification of educational goals. Handbook I: Cognitive Domain.* New York: Longman.

Rowe, M. B. (1973). Chapter 8. *Teaching science as continuous inquiry.* New York: McGraw-Hill.

Taba, H., Durkin, M., Fraenkel, J., & McNaughton, A. (1971). Chapter 6. *A teacher's handbook to elementary social studies* (2nd ed.). Reading, MA: Addison-Wesley Publishing.

SUGGESTED READINGS

Bozardt, D. A. (1973). Development of systematic questioning skills in an elementary science methods course (Doctoral dissertation, University of Georgia).

Carin, A., & Sund, R. (1989). Chapter 8. *Teaching science through discovery* (6th ed.). Columbus, OH: Merrill Publishing.

George, K. (1974). Chapter 4. *Elementary school science: Why and how.* Lexington, MA: D.C. Heath.

Hunkins, F. P. (1972). *Questioning strategies and techniques.* Boston, MA: Allyn & Bacon.

Riegel, R. (1976). Classifying classroom questions. *Journal of Teacher Education, 27* (2), 156–61.

CHAPTER 7

Sciencing and Children with Special Educational Needs

Goals

After completing this chapter, you will demonstrate competence in the following:

1. Recognizing the role of the elementary school science teacher in working with special-needs students.

2. Recognizing and providing for the special needs of students.

Objectives

In completing this chapter, you will do the following:

1. Identify and describe the special educational needs of students.

2. Use the ideas presented here by selecting a science topic and listing a variety of activities and instructional objectives for specific educational needs.

Chapter contributed by Susan B. Brown, Ph.D.

INTRODUCTION

Until the 1960s, children with special educational needs were segregated from the mainstream of public education. They were placed in special classes, special schools, or institutions, or they were excluded entirely from public education. A series of court cases on behalf of a number of these children challenged the constitutionality of such treatment. Litigation was followed by legislative action to guarantee equal rights, which culminated in 1975 with the passage of Public Law (PL) 94–142, The Education for All Handicapped Children Act. The stated purpose of PL 94–142 was

> to assure that all handicapped children have available to them . . . a free appropriate public education which emphasizes special education and related services designed to meet their unique needs. (PL 94–142, 1975)

Implementation of PL 94–142 resulted in many special needs students being mainstreamed into regular education programs, including science classes.

Not all special needs students were included in PL 94–142, the Education of All Handicapped Children Act. Gifted children also have special educational needs that require modification of regular classroom programs. Some students may exhibit characteristics related to handicapping conditions covered by PL 94–142, but their needs may not be severe enough to make them eligible for special education or related services as determined by the Individual Education Placement Committee (IEPC). Students from different cultural and language backgrounds may be eligible for services under other programs such as chapter or bilingual education programs. The purpose of this chapter is

1. To introduce PL 94–142 and its requirements.
2. To list and define the types of special-needs students and their educational needs.
3. To present activity and learning-objective modifications for special-needs students in science classes.

PL 94–142:
THE EDUCATION FOR ALL HANDICAPPED CHILDREN ACT

Special education is defined as specially designed programs to meet unique needs, and it is to take place in the least restrictive environment. The least restrictive environment must be determined individually for each child by an Individual Education Program Committee (IEPC). It is the educational setting that best meets the child's educational needs and that is as close to normal as possible. The alternatives are presented in Figure 7–1, The Cascade Model of Special Education Service.

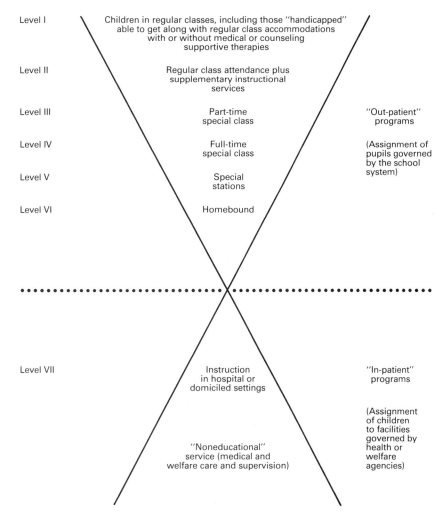

Figure 7–1. Cascade Model of Special Education Service.

From: Special education as development capital by Evelyn Deno,
Exceptional Children 37 (1970): 229–237. Copyright 1970 by The
Council for Exceptional Children. Reprinted with permission.

As a teacher, you will be expected to participate in the achievement of the
goals of least restrictive environment. Appropriate placement is determined at
an Individual Education Program Committee (IEPC) meeting. The regular classroom teacher attends the meeting to participate in the educational planning
process and to help determine the extent of integration into the regular
classroom.

When regular classroom placement is recommended by the IEPC, Reynolds
and Birch (1984) suggest that integration of handicapped children into the regular classrooms may take three forms:

Classroom teachers, parents, special educators, and other school personnel work together to plan individual education programs.

1. Physical integration
2. Social integration
3. Instructional integration

Physical integration is the inclusion of handicapped students in regular classrooms for a certain amount of time specified in the Individual Education Program (IEP). The purpose of physical integration is to allow handicapped students contact with normal peers, even though they do not have sufficient academic skills for participation in the academic program. These students will generally be scheduled in regular classes during nonacademic periods such as lunch rather than science classes. *Social integration* is the inclusion of handicapped students in a regular classroom so they might benefit from the social contact and models of age-appropriate behavior of peers. Although these students may be primarily scheduled in regular classrooms during nonacademic activities, they may be included in science classes if they can benefit from the cooperative learning groups, hands-on experiences, and opportunities to develop problem-solving skills. Clarification of responsibility in the IEP is essential since the regular classroom teacher may not be responsible for evaluating and reporting grades for students who are unable to meet academic objectives. Handicapped students scheduled in science classrooms for *instructional integration* should be capable of participating in science classes with minimal modifications. These modifications—such as differences in content, methods, or evaluation techniques—should be included in the IEP.

As a science teacher participating in the IEPC meeting, you will be expected to explain the science program and work with other committee members to determine how the student may be helped to succeed in science class. You may need to modify instructional objectives or activities in the science class, or you may work with the special education teacher to best meet the student's educational needs. In addition to PL 94–142, each state has regulations concerning services for handicapped children, and teachers should familiarize themselves with the requirements in their area.

WHO ARE EXCEPTIONAL STUDENTS?

Exceptional students are defined as those students who deviate from the norm (a) physically, (b) socially, or (c) intellectually to the extent that special education is necessary. The labels used to identify these differences vary from state to state. Regular education teachers need to be alert to student characteristics that indicate special educational needs and follow through on referral for special education services. There are also many other children in a typical classroom who have not been labeled and may not be eligible for special education services, but who have similar educational needs. As a teacher, you will find that the educational modifications suggested here will aid in meeting their needs as well.

Physical Differences

Physical and sensory limitations can take many forms, all of which can interfere to varying degrees with learning. Children who have limited or impaired vision or hearing may need special assistance or provisions to participate successfully in science activities. Visually impaired students include students who are blind (Braille readers) and students who are partially sighted (large-print readers). Deaf students, both with and without use of speech, and hard-of-hearing students fall within the category of hearing impaired. Students with speech and language or communication disabilities may present problems ranging from minor speech articulation disorders to the inability to use speech for communication. Some health impairments, such as allergies, may require special modifications of class requirements to ensure protection of students' health and safety. Children with physical impairments represent a heterogeneous group, including those with limited mobility (e.g., wheelchair bound), limited coordination (e.g., cerebral palsy causing inability to voluntarily control movement), or seizure disorders (e.g., epilepsy). Many physically or sensorially impaired students have had limited experiences, and teachers will need to plan for concrete experiences with basic science materials and concepts. They may also require modifications in materials, methods, or evaluation for full participation in science classes. The science teacher must consult with the student's parents, physicians, or special education teacher as to specific educational needs.

Social Differences

Some students experience difficulty in the affective domain. Special attention must be paid to helping the student who has difficulty with social interactions to learn to work cooperatively with others on science projects. These students are referred to as children with behavior disorders, emotional disturbances, or emotional impairments. Students with difficulty attending also may be included. The teacher may need to structure the classroom environment and assignment to increase such a student's on-task behavior and prevent disturbing behaviors. Behavioral methods are usually very effective with these students. Developing positive attitudes, interests, and feelings about classroom science are essential for the success of a science program.

Other students who are socially different, but who are not considered handicapped under PL 94–142, are culturally different children. Lewis and Doorlog (1987) define multicultural students as "those whose home culture is of variance with that of the school" (p. 326). Social and cultural differences can inhibit a child's learning. Some children from culturally different backgrounds may also be considered as Limited English Proficiency (LEP) students. While not all culturally different students have special learning needs, some culturally different children may have limited experiences with materials and concepts in science classes. This is particularly true if a child's home environment or language is vastly different from the one at school.

Teachers must provide instruction that will help bridge the gap between the two cultures. Science activities can be modified so that a child's immediate environment and past experiences or language are used in spanning the gap. This allows the child to relate more directly to a science concept or process, thus resulting in a more meaningful science experience. Once a link between a science concept or process and the child's world has been established, it is possible to build upon this link and the child's experiences. The science teacher may need to plan field trips and other concrete activities to provide more meaningful science experiences.

Intellectual Differences

Children with intellectual or cognitive differences include those labeled mentally retarded, slow learners, learning disabled, and gifted. *Mentally retarded* children can learn, but they develop at a much slower rate than normal children. They appear immature compared to their chronological age mates. They need concrete experiences and a great deal of repetition to enable them to acquire new concepts. Their ability to transfer information from one setting to another is limited. *Slow learners* are students with intellectual ability that is slightly below normal, but not low enough to qualify them for special education services. For these students, concrete experiences with more repetition are also important.

Learning disabled children have normal intelligence, but they learn differently than do normal children. As a result, they are often low achievers in one or more areas of learning. They represent a very heterogeneous group, and the science teacher should work closely with the special education teacher to determine how to modify activities for a particular student. Activities that address different learning styles are helpful.

Gifted students represent a great challenge to the science teacher. Services for gifted students are not provided under PL 94–142, although some school districts do have special programs. Academically gifted students may easily become bored in an elementary science class, and the science teacher should try to plan work for them on more advanced concepts or more in-depth investigation of concepts being covered by other students. The science teacher will need to help creatively gifted students focus their creative energies appropriately. To ensure safety at all times, the gifted student should be aware of rules governing individual experimentation. The teacher may help gifted students explore sources outside the regular science program for answers to the many *why* and *how* questions they have. Students gifted in psychomotor skills such as athletics or dance may need motivation to work on science activities, because they often concentrate most of their energy on developing their special talents. Students who are gifted in social or leadership skills may be a great help in a project-oriented science program if the teacher helps channel these skills.

WHY TEACH SCIENCE TO THE HANDICAPPED?

Science has not usually been included in the curriculum for special education students in segregated special programs, and few handicapped children were previously in regular education science programs. The content and methodology of science were not considered appropriate for the handicapped. Although PL 94–142 increased the integration of handicapped children in regular classrooms, many of these students have still not been able to participate fully in science programs. Part-time special education programs and many other remedial programs in school require students to be released from the regular classroom to receive services. They are most frequently pulled out of science and social studies programs because of the belief that they cannot benefit from instruction in these areas.

As is discussed in Chapter 1, educators who accept Piaget's developmental theory of learning understand that children progress through the four stages of mental development at different rates. It is the role of the science teacher to provide appropriate activities to develop the skills at each stage of development. Mentally retarded students and slow learners will be functioning at a lower developmental level than their chronological age peers, while gifted students will be functioning at a higher level. Limitations of prerequisite experiences may cause physically or sensorially impaired students, culturally different students, and children with behavior disorders also to be functioning at a lower level than expected. The science teacher should determine the stage at which the child is learning and then provide opportunities to develop skills required for success at the next stage.

The hands-on nature of science classes can be a motivating force for students with special education needs. Active involvement in the learning process is an important method for teaching exceptional students, and it is also an important element in the sciencing approach. Handicapped students need materials and activities that are familiar, relevant, and concrete. The concrete nature of sciencing activities may provide success for handicapped students that they cannot experience in traditional programs that emphasize learning from reading or lectures. These successful experiences may lead to improved communication and social skills as well as better motor and cognitive skills.

Sciencing also involves a process-oriented approach. The emphasis on development of problem-solving skills through a variety of activities helps special-needs students to generalize concepts learned in one setting and apply them to other settings. Careful sequencing of activities to help the student discover science concepts is also essential. The problem-solving skills obtained in a sciencing program will be of great benefit to handicapped students in improving their adaptive behavior, or ability to cope with the everyday problems of life.

HOW TO TEACH SCIENCE TO THE HANDICAPPED

Good teachers have always been responsive to the individual needs of the children they teach. With the advent of PL 94–142 and with more special-needs students entering regular classrooms, the task of meeting individual needs has become much more of a challenge. Teachers need to develop means of providing appropriate learning experiences for these students within the framework of the regular classroom. The science curriculum for mainstreamed students should be the same as the curriculum for students in the rest of the class. Use of separate programs can lead to social isolation. As a teacher, you may need to modify the environment, materials, methods, concepts or evaluation for mainstreamed students, or you may have to provide alternate activities. In some cases, students can work together, each using their own special abilities in completing an activity. You must take individualization a step further to include *all* children.

Slavin (1988) reports on the effectiveness of cooperative learning groups in promoting social integration and acceptance of handicapped and culturally different students. The use of mixed-ability groups also facilitates learning and contributes to self-esteem.

Mastery learning is another approach that aids in meeting the needs of a variety of students. Corrective instruction techniques are provided for students who did not master concepts after initial instruction before moving on to new concepts.

Social Environment Modifications

To enhance the social integration and acceptance of special-needs students, teachers may provide information about handicaps or differences, promote co-operation, and model acceptance. There are many information sources available to acquaint regular classroom students with the needs of their handicapped peers. Teachers may use books, stories, films, videotapes, cassettes, filmstrips, puppets, handicapped adults, and simulations to promote acceptance through understanding. (For more information, see Schulz & Turnbull, 1983; Lewis & Doorlag, 1987; and Reynolds & Birch, 1988.) Cooperative learning activities may be used to promote cooperation. Cooperative learning groups involve a hetero-geneous group of students working towards a common goal for a group grade. The teacher's model of acceptance is important in helping the regular-class students accept a handicapped classmate and in helping the handicapped student develop a better self-concept.

Physical-Environment Modifications

There are three major areas of concern that the elementary teacher must address for enhanced learning:

1. Physical factors
2. Classroom arrangements
3. Organization and storage of materials and equipment

Physical Factors. Proper lighting is essential for students with visual impair-ments. Glare, shadows, and inadequate contrast may cause both difficulty in discriminating essential materials and eye strain. Take care to provide visually impaired students with well-lighted work areas and priority seating so that they are close to the board or activity.

Removal of possible aggravations to a child's health conditions (such as an allergy to plant pollen, animals, etc.) will allow that child's participation in science activities when these objects are not essential elements for the science lesson.

Distracting background noises are a problem for hearing-impaired stu-dents; they have difficulty screening out irrelevant sounds. Hearing aids increase the volume of all sounds in the environment, particularly those that are closest. It is important, therefore, that these students sit near the teacher or relevant sound source for any activity. Priority seating is also important so that hearing-impaired students may lip read to get as much relevant information as possible to supplement what they can hear. Distracting noises also are a problem for some learning-disabled, behavior-disordered, or mentally retarded children. Take care to avoid seating students who are easily distracted near any noise source, such as an animal's cage, that could draw attention away from the science lesson.

Desk size is a problem for some students with physical differences. Students in wheelchairs require either special desks that will accommodate the wheelchair

Wheelchairs need not interfere with a child's full participation in classroom activities.

or a lap-tray work area. You may need to adjust laboratory work areas and tables. Proper height of the work surface and an open area under the work surface for the wheelchair allow the students to read and work with materials easily. Some students with limited control of their physical movements, missing limbs, or differences in size (little people) may also require special adaptations of desk and work areas.

Classroom Arrangements. Easily accessible work areas are important for physically handicapped and visually impaired students. Seat students in wheelchairs near the exit door as a safety precaution. Aisles and access to work areas must be wide enough to accommodate a wheelchair (30 to 32 inches) and to allow room to turn the wheelchair (60 by 78 inches). Students with limited physical mobility also need barrier-free access to all areas to ensure independence in the regular classroom. Maintain a predictable classroom arrangement so that visually impaired students may develop independence in moving around the science classroom for various learning activities. When changes are necessary, you should take the time to explain the changes. Then, either guide the student around so that the student may become familiar with the new arrangements, or provide a peer as a sighted guide.

Organization and Storage of Materials and Equipment. Consistent arrangement of materials is helpful to visually impaired students. As just discussed, such students may become more independent when they have learned where things are kept. They may then participate in helping prepare for and clean up after science activities. Make sure that materials are easily accessible to students in wheelchairs or with other physical differences to help promote their independence and participation.

Materials Modifications

The most common modification necessary in teaching science to mainstreamed handicapped students is adaptation of reading materials. Mentally retarded children, slow learners, and some learning-disabled students cannot read well. They require reading material on the content being covered in science class that is at a lower reading level, when available, or that has been taped so they can listen to the material. More advanced reading materials, however, benefit gifted students. The school media specialist and special education teacher can suggest materials for specific needs.

Taped lessons, Braille, or large-print copies of science textbooks are necessary for students with visual impairments. These are available at no cost from the State Library for the Blind or the American Printing House for the Blind when orders are placed far enough in advance. "Talking Books" are also available through the National Library Service for the Blind and Physically Handicapped.[1] *Science Curriculum Improvement Study* (SCIS) has Braille versions of the student manuals and special teacher aids that offer suggestions for working with visually impaired children. Regular classroom teachers must be aware of the special problems caused by impaired vision and hearing and must provide ways of obtaining information that use a child's other senses. Teachers using written directions or worksheets for activities may assign peer tutors to help students with visual or reading difficulties to participate. Audiovisual instructional aids may require modifications for some students; examples include using captioned films or filmstrips[2] and substituting visual texts for audio tapes for children with hearing impairments. An emphasis on learning by doing rather than by reading will minimize the need for major modifications.

Training special-needs children to use equipment enhances the effectiveness of learning activities that require equipment. The training session allows the teacher to observe any special difficulties that physically handicapped or visually impaired students have and to make adjustments before instruction begins. Extra training time may be necessary for mentally retarded and slow learners, since they require more repetition than the average learner. Such experience with equipment before actual use of the equipment for instruction also prevents behavioral problems by encouraging appropriate respect for and proper treatment of equipment. Some special equipment may be necessary, such as Braille-writer, slate and stylus, Braille typewriter or large-print typewriter for visually impaired students, or adaptive equipment for physically impaired students.

The use of hands-on materials is an essential element in the sciencing approach. Visually impaired students may require a sighted guide to tell them where materials are placed in the work area, to physically guide their movements, or to describe visible results of experiments. A student with a hearing impairment may require that a nonhandicapped student model actions to translate verbal directions or repeat the directions when necessary. Peer aids can help physically handicapped students who experience difficulty in manipulation of materials. The teacher may want to consult the special education teacher for help in obtaining special mechanical aids to help these students participate more independently. Concrete, relevant materials should be included for mentally retarded students, learning-disabled students, and culturally different students.

Multisensory instruction with a variety of activities provides the experiential background necessary for concept formation for all students. It also allows students with sensory limitations to profit from more activities. This approach was used with a group of blind, deaf, and emotionally disturbed children who were mainstreamed into regular classrooms at the Horace Mann School in the District of Columbia (Walsh, 1977). In order to accommodate the blind and deaf children in the regular classroom, the science teacher used both visual cues and language in conveying information to the students. In some activities, additional equipment was provided for the special students. For example, in an experiment involving the factors affecting the swinging of a pendulum, a light sensor that emits a beeping sound was used to help a blind student detect the rate of the swinging pendulum. As the pendulum swung, it cut through the light wave, causing a change in the volume and pitch of the beeping. By listening for this change, the blind student could gather the needed information.

Hands-on activities require minimal modification for special needs students.

Students with learning disabilities may also benefit from multisensory instruction. These children usually have perceptual, memory, or expressive deficits in particular areas, which prevent their getting maximum benefit from instruction that emphasizes a deficit area.

Methods Modifications

Chapter 5 addresses the issue of planning for teaching. Bruner recommended developing instructional strategies using different modes of presentation (action, imagery, and language) to promote learning by discovery. You must consider these same variables in planning for special-needs students. The action mode, which includes contact with real objects, is helpful for learners in Piaget's pre-operational and concrete operational stages of mental development, including mentally retarded and slow learning students. They need active involvement to acquire concepts. Active involvement can also provide experiential backgrounds for children from culturally different backgrounds or with limited experiences because of physical or sensory impairments.

You should employ the imagery mode—using representations of actual objects—with caution. Some visually impaired students may have difficulty discriminating pictures or diagrams unless they are enlarged, and others need a three-dimensional representation of the object so they can explore it. More verbal descriptions and use of the sense of touch are helpful. Mentally retarded children, slow learners, and some learning-disabled students need experience with both the concrete object and its representation before the representation alone has meaning.

Use of the language mode, including discussion and reading, requires action-mode and imagery-mode experiences as prerequisites. Hearing-impaired students will have difficulty with verbal discussion; seat these children near the teacher. Further, maintain eye contact during discussions, repeat comments made by students throughout the room, write key vocabulary words on the board, and speak clearly but do *not* exaggerate your speech. Exaggerated speech distorts lip movements and interferes with lip reading. Hearing-impaired students may also benefit from more hands-on experiences to develop concepts discussed. Distractable students—such as some learning-disabled students, students with behavior problems, mentally retarded students, and slow learners—may benefit from the same methods. When using reading materials, consider the adaptations discussed under the materials modification section in this chapter.

Attention-getting and motivating techniques, which are discussed in Chapter 5 as a vital element in daily instruction, are especially important when working with many special-needs students. Mentally retarded children, some learning-disabled students, some students with behavior problems, and slow learners have short attention spans. Careful planning, such as several short activities rather than one long one, will enable the teacher to maintain the students' attention throughout an entire science lesson. Many of these students also have difficulty attending to the relevant details of a task. Because they are easily distracted by irrelevant or outside stimuli, the science teacher should plan ways to draw their attention to the relevant details—perhaps by color coding important elements.

Many students with behavior disorders need extra motivation to attend to a task. Social praise is important to these students. Immediate reinforcement for accomplishing each step in a task provides extra motivation for the student with behavior problems and also helps keep the student with a short attention span on task for a longer period of time. Self-correcting materials are an excellent way to do this. This behavioral approach of stimulus, response, and reinforcement (introduced in Chapter 1) works well with students with special needs.

Questioning techniques as an instructional strategy, discussed in Chapter 6, allow great flexibility for working with special-needs students. The science teacher should use Bloom's (1956) *Taxonomy of Educational Objectives* to individualize questions and evaluate whether students are comprehending the cognitive content and process of the science lesson. Memory-level questions, especially those requiring the student to recognize or choose the correct response, are most appropriate for allowing mentally retarded and slow learning students to participate successfully in class discussions. Some learning-disabled students can participate in class discussions effectively, but others will be more successful when asked to show (application level) rather than tell about a concept. Gifted students should be challenged with questions on the synthesis and evaluation levels. During class discussion teachers should state the question, pause, allow all students time to develop an answer, and then call on a particular student. In this way, all students are actively participating, but the teacher may select which students should be checked at each level.

Mentally retarded students and slow learners will need more repetition to acquire concepts, while such repetition will bore gifted students, who quickly grasp concepts. Mastery learning approaches with corrective instruction opportunities will be beneficial. Gifted students may be offered more challenging tasks such as developing their own model or experiment, while slower learners are given the opportunity to review basic concepts. Practice in a variety of settings will enable the mentally retarded students and slow learners to acquire generalization and application of concepts and processes in other settings. The Biological Sciences Curriculum Study (1980) developed a science education program specifically for use with mentally retarded students, students with learning disabilities, and those with behavior disorders. It relates more abstract science concepts to relevant problems of students. Elementary Science Study (ESS) has assembled the *Special Education Teacher's Guide* (Ball, 1978), designed to help special education teachers use the regular ESS materials with special-needs children. Its suggestions and ideas can also be used effectively by regular classroom teachers. Even though the guide is specifically for use with the ESS program, it contains many general ideas and suggestions that are applicable to any science program. Children with special needs can and will have successful science learning experiences. Teachers must be aware of the nature of the limitations imposed by a particular handicap and must provide appropriate instruction.

Content Modifications

Bloom's (1956) *Taxonomy of Educational Objectives* also provides a way of individualizing content objectives for students with intellectual differences. Slow learners and mentally retarded students do best with cognitive content objectives requiring knowledge of specifics (e.g., definitions of terms), while gifted students should be challenged to discover knowledge of universals and abstractions in a field. The slow learners and mentally retarded students need exposure to cognitive process objectives through the application level (conducting experiments). Concrete and relevant experiences aid in development of problem-solving skills. Gifted students should be challenged by cognitive process objectives at the synthesis and evaluation level.

GRADING AND EVALUATING SPECIAL-NEEDS STUDENTS

Evaluation, the task of determining the extent to which students attain specified objectives, is discussed in Chapter 5. It provides essential information concerning the effectiveness of instruction in meeting individual needs (formative evaluation) and for assignment of grades (summative evaluation).

Different methods of evaluation may be necessary.

Evaluation of Content Mastery

Paper-and-pencil tests, the most widely used form of science assessment, may be presented as oral tests for students with reading or visual difficulties. Special education consultants may assist with individual administration of tests when the science teacher does not have time. They may assist in providing Braille or large-print copies of a test for visually impaired students, in transcribing Braille responses, and in writing responses for children with physical disabilities that interfere with writing skills and for learning-disabled students with written-expression difficulties. Teachers may also assign peers or aides to read tests or write responses for these students. The more objectively evaluated format of paper-and-pencil tests (multiple choice, true-false, and matching) involves recalling information by recognizing a correct response. These formats are easiest for mentally retarded students and slow learners, although reading level may be a concern. The teacher should challenge gifted students with essay questions requiring organization and application of information.

Evaluation of Process Mastery

Performance tasks, projects, and written reports are application-oriented methods of evaluation and allow for assessment of the skills of process-oriented science. Children with physical disabilities or visual impairments may need some assistance with manipulation of materials. This should be the same type of assistance given during instruction. With adequate instruction, children with intellectual or social differences should be able to succeed on performance tasks. Projects and written reports, however, may require more modification. Special-needs students may need modifications similar to those used during instruction. Any time reading or written expression is a required part of the assignment, students may need adapted reading materials (Braille or large print for students with visual impairments and lower reading level for mentally retarded students, slow learners, and learning-disabled students) and assistance in writing (Braille writer or Braille typewriter for blind students, typewriter for students with motor coordination problems, or peers to write notes). Long-term projects require adequate structure and more frequent progress checks by the science teacher for mentally retarded students, slow learners, students with learning-disabilities, and children with behavior disorders.

Assigning Grades

All good teachers individualize formative evaluation techniques. Individualization of summative evaluation, or final grading, raises ethical questions regarding grading criteria in mainstream classrooms. Such issues should be addressed in the Individual Education Program (IEP) for each child. Some common options include establishing appropriate objectives and criteria in the IEP; contracting specific objectives and activities for a particular grade; grading on effort as well as achievement; giving points for activities, with activities having different values based on the student's abilities; grading based on rate of progress; and shared grading by the elementary science teacher and special education teacher (Kinnison, Hayes, & Acord, 1981).

Adaptations for Special-Needs Children

Although each student is an individual, and students with special needs are more like normal students than they are different, some guidelines for adaptations may

Table 7.1   Adaptations for Children with Physical Differences

Disability	Physical Environment	Materials Modification	Methods Modification	Content Modification	Evaluation
Visual Impairment	Materials kept in predictable place Students seated near activity Sighted guide to aid in giving directions Well-lighted work area	Large-print or Braille reading materials Taped lessons Sighted tutor to read directions or guide movements Training with equipment prior to use Braille writer, slate & stylus, Braille typewriter, or large-print typewriter	Hands-on activities—use of other senses to observe More verbal description and use of touch Contact with real objects	None	More verbal evaluation, or Braille or large-print materials Aid in writing responses Assistance with manipulation of materials
Hearing Impairment	Students seated near activity so they can hear better and lip read if necessary Students seated away from distracting noises	Captioned films, filmstrips Visual text to accompany tapes Model or repetition of directions	Hands-on experience to develop concept Visual aids to accompany lectures List of new vocabulary before verbal presentation Eye contact before speaking Clear enunciation	None	None

be helpful in planning for unique needs. Tables 7.1, 7.2, and 7.3 offer suggestions for physical environment, materials modifications, methods modifications, content modifications, and evaluation for children with physical, intellectual, and social differences.

Table 7.1 *continued*

Disability	Physical Environment	Materials Modification	Methods Modification	Content Modification	Evaluation
Hearing Impairment			Contact with real objects Repetition of instructions and verbal presentation as necessary		
Health Impairment	Removal of things that could aggravate health condition (e.g., no sugar for diabetics; no plant pollen or animals for allergic child)	None	None	None	None
Physical Impairment	Adequate space for movement Desk and table height adjusted for wheelchairs Seats near exits whenever possible for safety Barrier free access	Training with equipment prior to use Peer to help with manipulation of materials Mechanical aids for manipulation of materials as necessary	Contact with real objects	None	Assistance with manipulation of materials Aid in writing responses

Contributed by: Susan Brown, Ph.D.

Table 7.2 Adaptations for Children with Intellectual Differences

Disability	Physical Environment	Materials Modification	Methods Modification	Content Modification	Evaluation
Gifted	None	More advanced reading material	Less repetition More emphasis on problem solving	More advanced concepts, such as universals & abstractions Emphasis on processes and synthesis & evaluation levels	More emphasis on organization and application of information
Learning Disabilities	Students seated away from distracting noises	Concrete, relevant materials	Immediate feedback Short activities Cueing of relevant details Social praise Pairing of an object and its symbol Eye contact and priority seating for discussion Multisensory activities	None	Oral tests or modified reading level Aid in writing responses Structure and frequent progress checks on projects
Mental Retardation (and slow learners)	Students seated away from distracting noises	Low-reading-level materials Training with equipment prior to use Concrete, relevant, tangible materials	Social praise Eye contact and priority seating for discussions Short activities Repetition Active involvement Practice in a variety of settings Contact with real objects Immediate feedback Pairing of an object with its symbol Adaptations of reading material Cueing of relevant details Mastery learning Cooperative learning	Emphasis on knowledge of specifics Emphasis on concrete & relevant experiences	Structure and frequent progress checks on projects Oral tests or modified reading-level materials Aid in writing responses More objective format

Contributed by: Susan Brown, Ph.D.

Table 7.3   Adaptations for Children with Social Differences

Disability	Physical Environment	Materials Modification	Methods Modification	Content Modification	Evaluation
Behavior Disorders	Students seated away from distracting noises	Training with equipment prior to use	Motivation Immediate reinforcement Cueing of relevant details Short activities Eye contact and priority seating for discussions Social praise	None	None
Cultural Differences	None	Concrete, relevant materials	Contact with real objects Cooperative learning	None	None
Limited English Proficiency	None	Modified reading material	Cooperative learning Concrete activities	None	Oral tests or modified for language

Contributed by: Susan Brown, Ph.D.

The following activities have been designed to help you (a) become more familiar with PL 94–142 and its requirements, (b) identify the special educational needs of exceptional students, and (c) develop skills in modifying instructional activities for special-needs students.

ACTIVITY 7.1: INDIVIDUAL EDUCATION PROGRAMS (IEPs)

A. In this activity, you will read the IEP on Tom in Appendix B.

1. List the information from "Summary of Present Levels of Performance" that would help you, as an elementary science teacher, to plan for this student.

2. List the questions you have about this student that are not addressed in the IEP.

B. Work with a small group and act out an IEP meeting. Assign group members to play the roles of parents, regular class teacher, school psychologist, special class teacher, and administrator. Discuss an appropriate special education category and placement, and regular class placement.

1. Discuss the feelings of the various members of the group in playing their roles. What recommendations can you make for encouraging all committee members to participate?

2. What variables did you discuss (such as size of class, materials available) that would affect your decisions about placement?

ACTIVITY 7.2: SPECIAL-NEEDS STUDENTS

A. Arrange to visit an elementary classroom. List the individual differences observed during your visit.

B. Meet with the teacher of the elementary classroom that you visited. Ask the teacher to tell you the number of different special-needs students in the classroom. Were you able to identify all of them? Which ones were easiest to identify? Most difficult to identify?

C. Review several of the recent educational journals for information and ideas regarding instruction for special-needs students. The "Suggested Readings" at the end of this chapter include some possible sources. List the modification ideas presented.

ACTIVITY 7.3:
MODIFICATIONS FOR SPECIAL-NEEDS STUDENTS

A. Form a small group and select a science activity designed for the regular classroom from a textbook of science programs. Working with your group, select one type of special-needs student, and modify the activity so that a student with these special needs could participate. Write up your ideas on a separate sheet of paper and submit them to your instructor for feedback.

B. Working with your small group and using the lesson plan you developed for Activities 5.1 and 5.2, modify your objectives and instructional techniques for (1) a mentally retarded child, (2) a blind child, (3) a child with motor-coordination difficulties, and (4) a child with limited English proficiency.

C. Working with your small group and using a lesson from a science textbook, develop one question for each level of Bloom's taxonomy (see Chapter 6 to review Bloom's six levels).

D. Examine science materials available. List those materials that have suggestions for adaptations for special-needs students.

SUMMARY

Areas of concern related to sciencing and special-needs students were explored in this chapter. Students with physical, social, and intellectual differences were identified as special-needs students requiring modifications for success in mainstream science classrooms.

The importance of science instruction for children with special needs was discussed. The developmental specificity, the hands-on nature, and the process-oriented approach of science instruction were all shown to be beneficial to special-needs students.

Physical-environment, materials, methods, and content modifications were suggested for various individual differences. Consultation with the special education teacher was recommended for information about the special needs of individual students and for assistance in obtaining any special materials required. The final area of concern was grading and evaluation of exceptional students. Techniques for individualization of both formative and summative evaluation were discussed. Options for determining a grade for a science class were presented.

ENDNOTES

1. For more information, write the American Printing House for the Blind, 1839 Frankfort Ave., P.O. Box 6085, Louisville, KY 40206; or Library of Congress, National Library Service for the Blind and Physically Handicapped, 1291 Taylor St. NW, Washington, DC 20542.
2. For more information, write Captioned Films for the Deaf, Special Office for Materials Distribution, Indiana University, Audio-Visual Center, Bloomington, IN 47401.

REFERENCES

Ball, D. W. (1978). *ESS/Special education teacher's guide.* St. Louis: Webster/McGraw-Hill.

Biological Sciences Curriculum Study. (1980). *Me in the future.* Boulder, CO: Author.

Bloom, B. S. (1956). *Taxonomy of educational objectives: The classification of educational goals. Handbook I: Cognitive domain.* New York: Longman.

Deno, E. (1970). Special education as development capital. *Exceptional Children, 37,* 229–237.

Lewis, R. B., & Doorlog, D. H. (1987). *Teaching special students in the mainstream.* Columbus, OH: Merrill Publishing.

Reynolds, M. C., & Birch, J. W. (1988). *Adaptive mainstreaming* (2nd ed.). New York: Longman.

Schulz, J. B., & Turnbull, A. P. (1983). *Mainstreaming handicapped students.* Boston: Allyn & Bacon.

Slavin, R. E. (1988). *Educational psychology: Theory into practice.* Englewood Cliffs, NJ: Prentice-Hall.

Walsh, E. (1977). Lab classroom: Breaking the communication barrier. *Science, 196,* 1425–1426.

SUGGESTED READINGS

Affleck, J., Lowenbraum, S., & Archer, A. (1980). *Teaching the mildly handicapped in the regular classroom.* Columbus, OH: Merrill Publishing.

Charles, C. M., & Malian, I. M. (1980). *The special student: Practical help for the classroom teacher.* St. Louis: Mosby.

Coble, C. R., Mattheis, F. E., & Vizzini, C. T. (1982). A project to promote science for the handicapped. *School Science and Mathematics, 82,* 692–701.

Cooper, K. E., & Thier, H. D. (1974). Do you have to see it? Laboratory science for visually impaired children. *Learning,* pp. 44–45.

Corrick, M. E. (Ed.). (1981). *Teaching handicapped students science.* Washington, DC: National Education Association.

Follis, H. D., & Krockover, G. H. (1982). Selecting activities in science and mathematics for gifted young children. *School Science and Mathematics, 82,* 57–64.

Gearheart, B. R., & Weishahn, M. W. (1984). *The handicapped student in the regular classroom* (3rd ed.). Columbus, OH: Merrill Publishing.

Glazzard, P. (1980). Adaptations for mainstreaming. *Teaching Exceptional Children, 13,* 26–43.

Hardman, M. L., Egan, M. W., & Landau, E. D. (1981). *What will we do in the morning?* Dubuque, IA: W. C. Brown.

Hart, V. (1981). *Mainstreaming children with special needs.* New York: Longman.

Johns, F. (1981). *Mainstreaming science students in elementary and secondary schools.* Cleveland: Cleveland State University Dean's Grant Project.

————. *Selected readings to accompany mainstreaming students in elementary and secondary schools.* Cleveland: Cleveland State University Dean's Grant Project.

Keller, W. D. (1981). Science for the handicapped. *Focus on Exceptional Children, 13,* 1–11.

Kelly, L. J., & Vergason, G. A. (1978). *Dictionary of special education and rehabilitation.* Denver: Love.

Kinnison, L. R., Hayes, C., & Acord, J. (1981). Evaluating student progress in mainstream classes. *Teaching Exceptional Children, 14,* 97–99.

Lang, H. G. (1983). Preparing science teachers to deal with handicapped students. *Science Education, 67,* 541–547.

Larsen, S. C., & Poplin, M. S. (1980). *Methods for educating the handicapped: An individualized education program approach.* Boston: Allyn and Bacon.

Meyen, E. L., Vergason, G. A., & Whelan, R. J. (1979). *Instructional planning for exceptional children.* Denver: Love.

Ochoa, A. S., & Shuster, S. K. (1980). *Social studies in the mainstreamed classroom, K–6.* Boulder, CO: Social Science Education Consortium and ERIC Clearinghouse.

Payne, J. S., Kauffman, J. M., Patton, J. R., Brown, G. B., & DeMott, R. M. (1979). *Exceptional children in focus.* Columbus, OH: Merrill Publishing.

Sheinker, A., & Coble, C. R., (1981). Science for the handicapped: Can we justify it? In M. E. Corrick (Ed.), *Teaching handicapped students science.* Washington, DC: National Education Association.

Turnbull, A. P., & Schulz, J. B. (1979). *Mainstreaming handicapped students: A guide for the classroom teacher.* Boston: Allyn and Bacon.

Turnbull, H. R., & Turnbull, A. (1978). *Free appropriate public education law and implementation*. Denver: Love.

Wielert, J. S., and Retish, P. (1983). Mainstreaming and the Science Teacher. *School Science and Mathematics,* 83, 552–559.

For Further Information:

Educational Resources Information Center (ERIC)
Science, Mathematics and Environmental Education (SE)
Ohio State University
1200 Chambers Road, Room 310
Columbus, OH 43212
(614) 422-6717

CHAPTER 8

Microcomputers in the Science Classroom

Goals

After completing this chapter, you will demonstrate competence in identifying and using microcomputers and appropriate software that can be used to improve science instruction in the elementary school classroom.

Objectives

In completing this chapter, you will do the following:

1. Identify and describe appropriate uses of the microcomputer in the science classroom.

2. Identify and describe classroom procedures for using microcomputers.

3. Define and give examples of common computer terms such as hardware, software, input, output, peripherals, memory, monitor, disk, and language.

4. Identify and describe procedures for selecting appropriate software for the science classroom.

INTRODUCTION

The microcomputer is everywhere—at home, in the workplace, and at school. It would be difficult to find any other piece of equipment that has developed so rapidly and has found its way into so many facets of our lives. Microcomputers have evolved from a hobbyist's toy with very limited capabilities in the mid-1970s into a powerful tool used by professionals and laymen in every conceivable capacity. Growth and development have been phenomenal, as has acceptance by the general public. A few years ago, computers were big, expensive, and used by only scientists, engineers, and mathematicians. Today, they are small, powerful, relatively inexpensive, and used even by children. The same machine that a businessperson uses to control inventory and keep sales records is used by children to play games, by homemakers to keep household financial records, by professionals to bill clients, and by teachers to facilitate teaching and learning. Moreover, almost everyone who owns a computer seems to find new and unique ways to use his or her machine.

Current computer technology has opened an entirely new dimension in the classroom. It is now possible for every classroom to have access to a computer. This capability, considered to be in the realm of science fiction only a few years ago, gives the teacher a powerful teaching tool. The microcomputer can be a calculator, drill master, record keeper, game master, or opponent. It can create word searches, puzzles, or problems to be solved. The uses of the microcomputer are limited only by the imagination of the user. But there is an important point to remember: the computer is a *tool* of the teacher, a teaching aid. It will help you do a better job of teaching, but it will not do your job for you!

The development of the computer is an excellent example of how fast modern technology is progressing. The first computer capable of storing instructions in its own memory and then following them was the UNIVAC (Universal Automatic Computer) developed in 1951. IBM had developed the MARK 1 in the early 1940s to compute ballistics for the army, and in 1947 built ENIAC (Electronic Number Integrator and Calculator) to forecast weather, design bridges and tunnels, and compute ballistics for the military. These two early machines were powerful calculators, but programmable only in a very limited sense. They were large, expensive, complex, and limited in use. They were fast, however, accomplishing in minutes and seconds what would take people days and even months to do. For example, UNIVAC could add a string of 237,000 five-digit numbers in 1 minute.

In 1947, the *transistor* was developed. This major breakthrough allowed the replacement of large, power-consuming, heat-producing vacuum tubes by small, reliable, low-power transistors. The invention of the integrated circuit in the late 1950s and its subsequent development in the 1960s and early 1970s allowed the computer to become the miniature marvel that it is today. The silicon chip, containing thousands of transistors and all of the related circuitry, has become the ultimate in miniaturization.

This future teacher has taken the first step in learning to use a microcomputer: hands-on experience.

Current computer development can be characterized by two words: faster and smaller. Japanese and American firms are in competition to produce the fastest machine possible, and size is a major factor. At present, computers are limited by the speed at which electricity can travel. We now think in terms of *nanoseconds* (one billionth of a second). To visualize a nanosecond, think of the speed of light. In a nanosecond, light would travel approximately eleven inches. Some of the newer supercomputers cannot have wires more than fourteen inches long because an electrical current traveling any further than that would slow down the operation of the computer.

The microcomputer came into existence in the late 1970s. Suitcase-sized units that compute in millionths of a second are now available at very reasonable cost. (Check with local merchants for current prices.) Who uses this new technology? Scientists and engineers still use computers, just as they did earlier, but now computers are available for use in both large and small businesses, in the home, and, most important for our purposes, in the classroom.

This unit is designed for you, the nontechnical, "I-don't-know-very-much-about-computers-so-what-do-I-do-now?" future classroom teacher. This situation is typical but must change. All teachers must become computer literate. It is important that you go beyond the introduction to microcomputers found in this chapter. There are many good books available, some of which are listed in the ''Suggested Readings'' at the end of this chapter. For the most current information, visit your library. You might also consider enrolling in a computer course as part of your professional training.

MICROCOMPUTERS

Computers are classified into three groups: mainframes, minicomputers, and microcomputers. The *mainframe* computer is the giant of the group, capable of storing and processing billions of pieces of information and serving many users

Today's microcomputers are powerful despite their compact size.

at the same time. Most universities have one of these machines. It may surprise you to find that you may be able to access some of these giants using a micro-computer and a telephone connection from your elementary classroom.

The *minicomputer* is an intermediate-sized computer generally found in offices, businesses, and industrial settings. It also may have several terminals and process millions of pieces of information. Minicomputers can be found in supermarkets that use automatic checkout. The bar-code reader and the cash register act as a terminal, sending information on all purchases to a central computer that records the data for inventory control and pricing. It then sends the name of the item and the price to the terminal printer on the cash register to produce a record of your purchases.

The *microcomputer* is the smallest version of the computer, but it has become so powerful that it has replaced the minicomputer in many applications. In the early 1980s, a 64K microcomputer was considered to be a very advanced and powerful machine. (Note: 64K, or kilobytes, refers to the ability to store 64,000 characters of information. This equates roughly to 25 typed pages of single-spaced text.) Information was processed at a speed of about one million operations per second. At the end of the eighties, more powerful microcompu-ters—capable of storing several megabytes (one million characters) in internal memory and operating at speeds of 10 to 12 million operations per second—are common.

Of the three types of computers available, the microcomputer is the most adaptable. It is relatively inexpensive, yet capable of meeting the computer needs of a classroom. Low cost and high power have caught the imagination of edu-cators as well as business people and hobbyists. Many of your students will have microcomputers at home and use them regularly to play games, to practice educational programs, and to run simulation programs. Today it is not uncom-mon for some students to come to school with more computer background, programming experience, and computer literacy than their teacher.

Applications

What can you do with a computer in your classroom? Charles Kinzer, Robert Sherwood, and John Bransford (1986) have developed a list of five general roles of the computer in the classroom.

1. **Learning about computers,** where the focus is instruction on the operation, use, and programming of computers in class settings.
2. **Learning with computers,** where the computer takes the role of a partner with the student. Computer software used with this role is usually of the simulation and game type, where direct instruction is not emphasized in the program, but the student has an opportunity to work in alternate environments to those of regular classroom settings. The use of computers as tools to gather and analyze laboratory data also fits under this area.

3. **Learning from computers,** where the computer takes the role of a dispenser of information or a tester of student ability. Types of software used with this role include tutorial and drill-and-practice programs.

4. **Learning about thinking with computers,** which involves attempts to assist in developing thinking and problem-solving skills in students through the use of computers. Computer languages such as LOGO and problem-solving programs are used in this role.

5. **Managing learning with computers,** where the focus is on the use of computers to assist teachers and administrators in the management of instruction. A variety of computer programs such as word processors, school schedulers, and similar programs is available for use in this role. (pp. 253–254)

Some of these roles will be more applicable than others to your science class. This chapter modifies these categories slightly by exploring

1. Teaching about computers
2. Teaching science using computers
3. Special projects using computers
4. Software for science

TEACHING ABOUT COMPUTERS

Literacy has been the goal of educators ever since schools began. To be literate is to be able to read and write. A further definition is to be educated. After the Soviet Union launched Sputnik in 1957, inaugurating the "space age," our nation, as well as others, pressed for *scientific literacy.* We saw the need to better educate our children in science. We are now in the "computer age," and *computer literacy* is a necessity. As we competed with the Soviet Union in the space race, we are now competing with Japan in a computer-technology race to develop faster, cheaper, and more powerful computers. The prize is the world economic market. Children must learn about computers because the computer has become a production tool in the workplace. It is estimated that at present 85 percent of the jobs available are in some way computer related. We are seeing this in our daily lives. We encounter computer records of our charge accounts, computerized banking, and computerized cash registers in department stores and supermarkets. Schools use computer registration, test scoring, and record keeping. They also teach classes in computer science and data processing. Many new automobiles now have computer-controlled ignition and fuel systems, seat belts, and various other devices that compute mileage and fuel consumption and that even talk to tell the driver that the lights are on or the door is not closed. When you take your automobile in for service, it is hooked up to a computer that checks all the systems, gives a diagnosis of current problems, and even predicts future ones. If you want to be a mechanic, you must know something about computers.

To begin your, and your students', journey toward computer literacy, you need to do three things. First, develop an understanding of computer vocabulary; second, understand, in an elementary manner, how a computer works; and third, use a computer. The person who is not computer literate will suffer the same limitations and frustrations in the workplace as those who cannot read and write.

Teaching children about computers can easily fit into the science curriculum, as they are a product of science and technology. In teaching science, we should spend a certain amount of time teaching about scientific and technological developments so that our students can see how science has affected their lives. The history and development of computers certainly fit into this category.

History of Computers

Few inventions have made as much impact in such a short time as the computer. The idea of a machine that could rapidly calculate or do a repetitive operation has been around for a long time, but without the technology to carry it out. Once the technology was perfected, development was very rapid.

We can teach about the visionaries of the past and their ideas and inventions that laid the foundations. The list might include

1. **John Napier**—Invented Napier's Rods (1617).
2. **Blaise Pascal**—Built the first mechanical calculating machine (1642).
3. **Joseph Piccard**—Invented the punch card-controlled loom (1801).
4. **Charles Babbage**—Invented the analytical engine (1835).
5. **Ada Augusta Lovelace**—Worked with Babbage and is considered the world's first programmer
6. **Herman Hollerith**—Invented the tabulating machine and card sorter for census data. Founded International Business Machines Company (IBM) (1890).
7. **Vannevar Bush**—Built the first analog computer and called it a differential analyzer (1930).
8. **John von Neumann**—Developed the idea of storing the computer program in the machine's memory (1940s).

Follow this study with an examination of the "breakthrough" inventions (and the people who made them) that have allowed the computer to reach present-day capabilities. Start with the electrical relay, transistor, and integrated circuit. Then look at the development of the computer, from the very large and slow Mark I (1944), ENIAC (1946) and UNIVAC (1951) to the very small, powerful, and inexpensive computers of today. Culminate your exploration of the history of computers by speculating on the future. What does the future hold? What will computers be used for? How will each of us be affected by computers?

Vocabulary

The people who work with computers have developed a descriptive language called *computerese*. They have taken many familiar words and given them new meanings. They have also created new words. Computerese has become a part of our normal vocabulary. You use words such as compute, data base, hard copy, and user-friendly in normal conversations. Your students will know a lot of computer terms, but you will have to teach them others. Look at this list of computer terms. How many do you know? How many do you use without thinking of their being computer terms?

artificial intelligence	cursor	integrated circuit
authoring	daisy wheel	joystick
BASIC	data processing	kilobyte (K)
binary	debug	modem
bit	disk drive	monitor
bulletin board	floppy (disk)	output
byte	flow chart	program
chip	hard copy	software
coding	hardware	user-friendly
	input	word processing

This is only a short list of some of the more common terms. There are many more that you will need to teach your students. In order to communicate, you must know the language.

How Computers Work

All students should have a general understanding of how a computer works so that they are not afraid to use them. It is not necessary that everyone knows all about the internal workings of a computer. A person can drive an automobile without knowing how the engine works, and someone can use a computer without being able to explain how the microprocessor functions. Nevertheless, if you (and your students) have a basic knowledge of the computer and its components, you can become better users.

You should know

1. How the computer gets data and instructions.
2. How and where information is stored.
3. How information is processed.

Many children start to learn about computers at home.

4. What the parts of a computer system are and what each part does—keyboard, floppy disks, hard disks, monitor, printer, central processing unit (CPU), microprocessor, memory.

Languages and Programs

Computers are not intelligent. They can count to only one, but they can do it very fast. The computer operator must tell the machine exactly what to do, in zeros and ones. This is complicated, but computer languages have been devised to allow the machine and the operator to understand each other and carry out a set of instructions called a *program.*

Programs are a series of instructions to tell the computer what to do. Programs are written (coded) in a specific language with a specific syntax, and they provide step-by-step instructions for the computer to follow. A computer must have a program installed or it cannot operate.

You can buy commercial programs, write your own, or have someone write them for you. If you write your own, you must know and use one of the computer languages. Programs tend to be long and complex. It is easier, and most often better, to purchase programs from commercial vendors.

You may type in a program on the keyboard (a long and tedious task) or load a program from a disk (a quick and easy task). If you write your own program and then type it into the computer, you will want to save it on a disk so that you can use it again without having to retype it every time you want to use it. Programs are generally referred to as *software* because they are not a part of the computer and do not remain in the computer's memory when the power is turned off. Software must be loaded each time it is used.

There are several *computer languages* in use today. The two most common languages for the elementary classroom are BASIC and LOGO. BASIC is not as powerful as other languages such as Pascal or PL1, but it is easier to learn and use. It was devised as a beginner's language. LOGO is a very simple language used to teach thinking and programming. You do not purchase programs written in LOGO. You write them as you learn how to control the computer. It is a learning language rather than a programming language.

TEACHING SCIENCE USING COMPUTERS

The computer is useful in all subject areas, but especially in the science class. It is a product of science as well as a teaching aid, and as such we can use it both to teach about science and technology and to use it as an instructional tool. In this section, you will learn ways to use the computer in your science class.

Learning with Computers

The teacher presents a lesson; then students use the computer to reinforce learning. The computer is well-suited to this role, and most of the classroom applications have developed along this line. The microcomputer becomes a teaching aid that can perform all of the following tasks:

1. Tirelessly drill students on facts and problems, spelling words, science vocabulary, and much more.
2. Act as a gamemaster in simulation games involving one student, several students, or the entire class.
3. Be an opponent in a game of logic and/or skill.
4. Present new materials on an individualized basis.

5. Be an integral part of a textbook curriculum.

6. Collect, store, sort, and analyze data.

Drill and Practice.   The first use of the computer in the classroom was for drill and practice. The computer is excellent at this as it can tirelessly repeat material. Can you imagine how long you would last if you had to repeat the same vocabulary list, listening for correct spelling and definitions, for all 25 of your students, not to mention the time wasted? The computer can do this on an individualized basis, keep score, and repeat questions that are missed.

Many programs are available for drill and practice through public domain software sources such as MECC (Minnesota Educational Computer Consortium). Some textbook companies are now providing software to go with their textbooks.

This teacher is supervising a science lesson.

You may prefer one of several authoring programs that allow you to provide questions and answers, word lists, or problems for the computer to use.

The basic format for a drill-and-practice session is

1. Presentation of the question or item by the computer.

2. A response by the student.

3. Reinforcement, either positive or negative, by the computer.

Drill-and-practice programs make limited use of the computer's capabilities, but they can be helpful. Slower students can work at their own pace and level. Students who are weak in certain areas can work on what needs strengthening. The computer can even help them determine what these areas are. Many programs are available for drill and practice, and it is not too difficult for teachers to write their own.

Simulation. Simulations are very effective in the science classroom. They provide information, an opportunity to think and make decisions, and consequences resulting from the decisions. They can be carried out by the entire class, small groups, or individual students. There are two types of simulations commonly used in the science classroom: decision-making and process simulations. *Decision-making simulations* provide a scenario. Students consider alternatives and then make a decision. The computer provides the consequences of the decision. *Odell Lake* (Minnesota Educational Computing Corporation, St. Paul, MN) is a good example of an ecological simulation. The student takes the role of a fish. He must decide when to feed, retreat, attack, or hide. If he makes a good decision, he goes on living, but a bad decision can terminate his fish. Not all simulations have a win-lose type of consequence. Some have a ''what if'' structure that allows the student to change variables and show what would occur under different conditions. The student can try different strategies or variables just to see how they affect the outcome, without a win-lose penalty attached.

Process simulations, which show how a process occurs, are becoming more available for science, especially in the upper grades. These simulations are especially useful when the process would be impossible to carry out in class for reasons of safety, expense, or equipment. Simulations can also slow down or speed up the process, making it more observable. In addition, they can also be easily repeated.

Collecting and Analyzing Data. The computer can be useful in helping students make sense out of the data they collect in their classroom experiments. Computers can be connected to sensors that register such information as temperature or a count of repetitious operations, thus collecting data for the students. As these devices become less expensive and more available, they will find their way into the elementary science classroom. One example of such a kit is *The Science Tool Kit* by Broderbund Software (San Rafael, CA). Data processing programs are readily available. They can take students' data and turn them into graphs, charts, or statistics. Lower elementary children may not yet have the skills to make a graph or a chart of their data, but they can interpret the graphs and charts produced by the computer.

Learning from Computers

Computers can be used to teach subject matter content. The computer can present new material to students on an individualized basis. Graphics and step-by-step presentations make this a powerful innovation, especially when remedial branches are built in. The computer can present material, ask for responses, diagnose trouble spots, refer the student to remedial experiences, monitor the remedial work, and return the student to the main program. All the while, the computer can keep a record of the student's activities and progress for later use by the teacher. Some textbook series are beginning to incorporate computer lessons as a part of their learning package, but this is not yet widespread.

Learning from the computer has several advantages over the more traditional information sources such as the textbook or reference books. It can provide

Students work independently on a learning activity.

still and moving pictures or graphics to go with the written material and an interactive learning situation for every user. It is good for individual instruction, as it can match the pace of the user. On the other hand, there are some limitations. First, there is a limited amount of software available, and it is usually quite subject-specific and may not fit what you are trying to teach. Second, the level of difficulty of the content and the vocabulary may not be appropriate. And, third, reading is required, putting the low or nonreader at a disadvantage.

Special Uses

The computer is more than a teaching machine. It is a tool that allows increased production in the classroom as well as in the workplace. Application software can be used by students in much the same way as it is used in business.

Word Processing.   Writing reports can be a chore for children of all ages. They write slowly and laboriously, thinking more of how they form each character than what they are trying to say. Editing and recopying a report or experiment is a time-consuming task and is usually not done. For most students, the first draft is also the final draft. The word processing capabilities of the computer make the task of writing and editing much easier for students. They can write, correct spelling and grammar, add new details, make changes, and then print a final revised version. This may seem more like language arts than science, but good communication skills are as important as any other skill in science.

Data Base and Data Processing.   Learning requires information. The more information (data) available to a student, the better his chances for knowledge and understanding. Data-base programs are used to store information in an easily accessible form that can be retrieved and processed in some manner. You may want to build a data base of information on different topics. For instance, as students gather information about scientists and inventors, they can store biographical information, sources, and accomplishments in a data file. This file can be added to by others, increasing the amount of available information. It can also be processed. The computer will sort the information by characteristics such as alphabetically by name of person, by accomplishment, chronologically, topically, or any other way you desire. Numerical data from experiments or activities can also be collected and stored, such as daily temperature or a record of plant growth. Any data you can collect, you can store, sort, and retrieve for further study.

Graphs, Charts, and Statistics.   Data is useful only if something is done with it. Students may count buttons in the first grade and then put them in rows by color. The children can see how many of each there are by physically forming a bar graph. They have processed data into a usable form. Children may have trouble seeing relationships in the data they collect, but if they are in a visual form, such as a pie chart or bar graph, they can interpret them. There are programs available that will process data into usable forms such as graphs, charts, and numbers.

Statistics need not be elaborate, but simple statistics such as average or frequency of occurrence can be easily understood by upper and many lower elementary students. The computer can do calculations that the students may not yet know or understand, or it can accurately do the mathematics (addition, subtraction, multiplication, and division) of a long series of numbers that might otherwise be a time-consuming, nonproductive task. Adding a column of 365 numbers and then dividing by 365 to get an average doesn't really add to your science lesson, does it? Your data processing program can do this quickly or, if you wish, do variations such as averaging every third number.

Using the computer to enhance production in the classroom is just as important as production in the home or office. If the computer can relieve some of the drudgery of learning, you will have more time to teach the joy of learning.

SPECIAL PROJECTS USING COMPUTERS

A lot of science is taught using special projects. A single student, a team, or the entire class may work on the project. Data gathering and processing, construction, role playing, decision making, evaluation, and reporting are all part of the process. The computer can be a useful tool in several of these areas. Here are a few examples of special projects and ways to use the computer. They are by no means complete, as you and your students will find variations of these applications and new uses not given here.

Space Shuttle

NASA has an excellent simulation project built around a space shuttle mission. Students plan the mission, assume various roles, and then carry out the simulated mission. The NASA video tape *Launching a Dream* (NASA Lewis Research Center, Teacher Resource Center) describes the efforts of two elementary schools and provides guidelines for a similar project. The computer can be used to store data, keep a time schedule, and simulate a launch. A program such as *Rendezvous: A Space Shuttle Flight Simulation* (1982; Edu-Ware Services, San Francisco, CA) can simulate the launch and necessary maneuvering to put the shuttle into orbit.

Model Rocketry

Rocket design, propulsion, and flight are components of a model rocketry project. Estes Industries (Penrose, CO) provides information and teaching guides for a unit on model rocketry. Suggestions for design, construction, and launching of model rockets are also included. Compatible computer software is available. You can also collect flight data such as altitude, time of flight, and type of engine to make performance graphs.

Astronomy

Special events such as the passing of Halley's Comet or the appearance of a new comet, an upcoming eclipse of the sun or moon, or a general interest in astronomy can be the basis of an astronomy project. There are several software programs such as *The Observatory* (Lightspeed Software, Berkeley, CA), *Planet Hopping* (Bergwall), and *All About the Solar System* (Ventura) that teach stellar movement and star location. Other programs show how interstellar distances are calculated. The computer can easily calculate the large numbers required. Data such as a daily record of the location of the sun and/or moon can be graphed to show the revolution of the earth and moon.

Weather

The weather and how to forecast it is always interesting. Students can set up a weather station, collect daily information, and make predictions while they learn about the various elements of weather. Activities such as (a) predicting weather, (b) types of measurements used in forecasting, (c) keeping a daily weather log, (d) weather in other parts of the country, and (e) storm tracking can be done on the computer. Students can build their own data base from measurements they take and then graph the information.

SOFTWARE FOR SCIENCE

Software might be described as anything that can be fed into a computer. This is an oversimplification but basically true. The computer and peripherals are machines (hardware) that must be given instructions, or *programmed,* for what they are to do. The programs that are loaded by disk or typed in on the keyboard are software. The importance of software is clear: the computer cannot function without it.

As we mentioned earlier, software can be programs written by you or someone else. Most of the software that you use will be developed by someone else. This may include programs found in books or magazines that you can type into the computer, professionally written programs from publishers or distributors, or public-domain material written by users and distributed free of charge. Only a short time ago, software was scarce, but today there is a constant stream of new material flooding the market and overwhelming the user. You will probably find that about 80 percent of this material is useless. This is not to say that most of it is of poor quality or inadequate design, just that it is not appropriate for your use.

How do you select good software? There are checklists available in computer magazines, specialty books on the selection of software, and software reviews in various educational journals (look in *Science and Children*). Each will have its own criteria, and at present there is much variation as to what constitutes good software. We have gleaned the following criteria from lists, readings, conversations, and workshops:

1. Is the program appropriate to your class and the lesson that you are teaching? Much of the available software was written for a specific group of children or to teach a specific concept. Such narrowness is probably the single most significant factor that can make a program useless. If the program does not teach the concepts that you consider important, or drills in a manner contrary to your teaching, you cannot expect much help from the computer.

2. Is the subject appropriate for computer use? Purists claim that all subjects are appropriate to computer instruction, but many topics can be taught more efficiently using traditional methods. The computer and a software program are not economically justifiable if a workbook or class game can achieve the same objective.

3. How much help does the program give? A good program should be well-documented, giving objectives, teaching instructions, and evaluation procedures. Once the program is loaded, it should give clear, concise instructions to the students and should provide a way for the student to reaccess these instructions during the program if necessary. Programs with no documentation are generally a waste of time, unless you accidentally stumble upon one that you can adapt to your own purposes.

4. Is the program pedagogically sound? Sloppy programs produce sloppy results. We know a lot about how children learn, and we must apply this knowledge to computer instruction as well as to the regular classroom instruction. The program should be free of spelling, grammatical, and content errors. Instructional objectives should be clear and appropriate to the lesson, and be presented at a level appropriate to the students using it. The treatment of right and wrong answers should emphasize reinforcement of correct responses. Finally, you and your students should like the program and enjoy using it.

5. Will the program work on your computer? This may sound funny, but not all programs work as they should on the machines they are designed for, and they certainly will not operate on any other machine. If loading a particular program is a problem for you and your students, either edit the program to remedy the problem, or junk it. You cannot teach if you spend all of your time trying to make a problem program run.

6. For whom is the program designed? Remember what you have been told, time and time again, in your methods courses: Each child is unique and should have instruction appropriate to that child's particular needs and abilities. This is as true for Computer Assisted Instruction (CAI) as for any other form of instruction. Select software based on the needs of particular groups of children, and avoid the temptation of trying to make all students fit one program.

7. General considerations. Here are a few final things to think about:

a. How long is the program?
b. Do the graphics and sound add to or distract from the program?
c. How much does it cost?
d. In case of accidental erasure or destruction, can it be readily replaced?

Two students start a new program.

e. Is the program crash-proof—can the students accidentally, or purposefully, ruin the whole program? This consideration is last, but by no means least.

The selection of software is a difficult task at best, considering the funds you have (or do not have) available, the large number of programs to choose from, and the constant change in the state of the art. Do not hesitate to read product reviews in current magazines or to ask fellow teachers for recommendations.

The alternative to selecting commercial software is to write your own. More teachers are doing this as they become more familiar with the computers in their classrooms. Program writing requires some degree of skill and a knowledge of computer languages (usually BASIC), but it is not beyond the ability of most teachers who care to spend the time it requires. By writing your own programs, you can be sure that they are appropriate in content and to your students. A large number of the commercial programs offered to you originated as a classroom teacher's attempt to produce something better than was available. You, in turn, might produce the next "best seller."

SUMMARY

In this chapter, you have been introduced to computers, computer literacy, and the use of the microcomputer in the science classroom. The activities that follow will help you develop a basic computer vocabulary as well as a minimal understanding of how computers work. Selection and use of software presented to show you how to use the microcomputer in the classroom. In a small group, or as a class, discuss your experiences with the microcomputer and your ideas and concerns about software that you have seen or used. Do not hesitate to use your new-found computer vocabulary to show competence in this area. If you need more information, ask your instructor for help.

By now, you should have had some experience with a computer. You should know how to turn it on, boot it up, load a program, and make it operate. If you don't, you will need to work with someone to learn these basic skills before you proceed with these three activities.

Activity 8.1 does not require the use of a computer, but it will require that you do some outside research. Some of the books listed under "Suggested Readings" might be a good place to start. This activity will give you a basic computer vocabulary and an awareness of the parts of the computer system that are important to you, the user. It is nontechnical, so don't be afraid to try it. Your instructor may choose to give you a list of vocabulary terms, a current bibliography, and/or a diagram of the parts of a computer system. If not, you will have to go to your library for information.

ACTIVITY 8.1: LEARNING ABOUT COMPUTERS

A. Computer Vocabulary

Define the following terms as they apply to computers. Try to keep your definitions clear and usable so that you know what they mean and how they are used. Also, as you look through your sources for these definitions, you will encounter other terms that are not listed here. Space has been provided for you to add some of these terms to your list.

Authoring system	Hardware
ASCII	Input
BASIC	Keyboard
Binary	Language
Bit	Load
Buffer	LOGO

Bug	Mainframe
Bulletin board	Memory
Byte	Modem
Chip	Monitor
Cursor	Output
Daisy wheel printer	Peripheral device
	Program
Debug	Soft copy
Dot matrix printer	Software
Execute	User-friendly
Floppy disk	Volatile
Flowchart	Word processing
Hard copy	

Add ten more words and definitions of your own choosing to this list. Compare your list and definitions with those of other members of your group. Are there discrepancies? If so, discuss the discrepancies and develop a common definition. Show your list to your instructor for feedback.

☐ **Comments**

B. Computer History

Listed below are the names of people and inventions that are important in the history of computing. Write a short statement to explain the importance of each.

John Napier	Herman Hollerith
Blaise Pascal	John von Neumann
Joseph Piccard	Transistor
Charles Babbage	Integrated circuit (IC)
Ada Augusta Lovelace	VLSI (Very Large Scale Integration)

What source did you use? Can you think of any others? Could you use this source with children?

☐ **Comments**

C. How Computers Work

There are three basic stages in the operation of all computers. The following exercise will help you become familiar with these stages and what happens in each. To do this activity, you will define some terms, see how they relate to a specific stage, and then explain what happens in that stage. You may also do some outside reading on the topic. Remember to keep it simple. You are trying to understand how a computer works on a basic level, not on an engineering level.

Look at the three boxes and their labels to see the stages of operation. Then define the terms and answer the questions that follow.

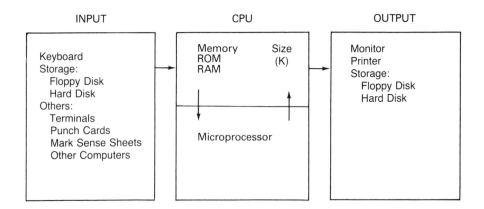

1. Input

a. Define input.

b. What is the purpose of input?

(1) Instructions (program):

(2) Data (information to be processed):

c. Define input devices.
    (1) Keyboard:

    (2) Disk drive:

       You may also define those terms listed as "others" in the input box.

d. Explain what happens in the input section.

2. CPU (Central Processing Unit)
    a. Define CPU.

    b. Define memory.
       (1) ROM:

       (2) RAM:

    c. Explain memory size (example: 128K) and why it is important.

3. Output
    a. Define output.

b. Define output devices.

(1) Monitor:

(2) Printer:

(3) Disk (floppy or hard):

c. What is the purpose of the output section?

d. Formulate a mental picture of what the computer does. With your group, discuss the following questions.

(1) How does the computer know what to do?

(2) How does the computer get information?

(3) What does it do with the information?

(4) After the computer has processed the information, how do you get the results?

☐ **Comments**

ACTIVITY 8.2: LEARNING WITH COMPUTERS

This is a simple hands-on experience with the microcomputer and different types of programs. You will experience different uses of the computer. Your instructor will either provide the software or tell you where to obtain it. Run the programs and see how they work. Think about how a child would react to the program. What are your reactions?

A. Drill and Practice
   Obtain a drill-and-practice program and load it into the computer. Follow the instructions as a child would. Try some incorrect as well as correct answers to see what happens.

   1. Name of the program:
      Appropriate grade level:
      Brief description:

   2. Was it easy, or difficult, to load and use? Explain:

   3. What was your reaction to this program?

   4. How do you think children will react to this program?

B. Simulation
   Select a simulation program and load it into the computer. Follow the instructions and go through the simulation.

   1. Name of the program:
      Appropriate grade level:
      Brief description:

   2. Was it easy, or difficult, to load and use? Explain:

3. What was your reaction to this program?

4. How do you think children will react to this program?

C. Word Processing
Select a word-processing program, preferably one designed for beginners.

1. Name of the program:
Write something or copy a paragraph from a book. You might even do this assignment on the computer. Be sure to try some *editing,* and then print what you have written. Once you try word processing, conventional typing will never be the same.

D. Data Base
Select a data-base program. You might use a *utility program* that contains a data base, word processor, and a spreadsheet for this activity. Read the manual first; then try it. Make up some data, or your instructor may provide you with a data sheet to use. Enter your data; then see what you can do with it.

1. Name of the program:

2. What problems did you encounter? What did you do about them?

3. Explain what you did and the results:

4. How could you use this in a science class?

E. Charts and Graphs
Select a program that produces charts and graphs. Read the instructions; then try the program. You may have to create some data to use. Make a graph and print it. Can you change it to a different type of graph?

1. Name of the program:

2. Could children use this program easily?

3. Were the charts and graphs it produced easy to understand and use? Explain.

ACTIVITY 8.3: SOFTWARE

You will need to look at some software catalogs for this activity. Check with your instructor to find where to obtain them. Do not forget to look at public domain software from MECC. Part C will require the use of a computer and a program.

A. Science topics

Choose a topic from those listed below. You may choose a different topic if approved by your instructor. Look through computer magazines, software catalogs, and software guides to find as many software titles as you can (or an appropriate sample) for your topic. Indicate the title and grade level and give a short summary of each program.

TOPICS:

weather	astronomy
biology (animal)	geology
biology (plant)	physical science

Title:
Grade Level:
Summary:

Title:
Grade Level:
Summary:

Title:
Grade Level:
Summary:

Title:
Grade Level:
Summary:

Title:
Grade Level:
Summary:

Title:
Grade Level:
Summary:

B. Grade Level

Pick a grade level (K–8), and see how many titles you can find for that grade level.

Grade Level:
Titles:

C. Software Evaluation

Pick a program to evaluate. You will need a program and a computer for this activity, as you cannot always rely on what the catalogs say about a program. You may use one of the programs (drill-and-practice or simulation) that you used in Activity 8.2 or a different one.

Evaluating software should not be a traumatic experience. Try the program to see if you like it, and decide whether or not it would do the job you want it to do. Do not try to look for hidden meaning or subtle inferences. Respond to the following questions with more than a simple yes or no. Make comments that say something.

1. Describe the documentation that goes with the program. What was your impression of the documentation?

2. Was it easy to load and execute? Were the instructions adequate? Based on your experience, what suggestions would you make?

3. Did the program follow good, sound teaching practice? If so, give an example. If not, give an example and explain what you would do to correct it.

4. Describe what the program was trying to teach. Give reasons why you think it would or would not be effective.

5. Explain why you did or did not like the program. Why do you think children would or would not like it?

☐ **Comments**

SUMMARY

The development of the microcomputer has opened new instructional and management possibilities to teachers. It can be a helpful tool, with unlimited capabilities, or it can be an expensive toy. We are in the state of infancy in developing the potential of computers in the classroom. Hardware is barely on the market before it becomes obsolete, being replaced by newer, better, and cheaper hardware. Software is being developed at a phenomenal rate, becoming more sophisticated and usable with each new program. One note of importance: in this chapter we have given very few specific references concerning available hardware and software. This is because of the constant change. Good recommendations today are obsolete in six months. But do not let the rapid growth deter you from using this new teaching aid. Those who wait for the final revisions in fear of purchasing hardware and software that may soon be obsolete will ultimately be left behind.

REFERENCES

Please keep in mind that software is constantly being developed, upgraded and replaced. The programs included here are representative samples. Use a good source such as TESS (see list) for current software. NASA Teacher Resource Centers are an excellent source for videotapes on many aspects of science. For the center nearest you, contact the Lewis Research Center at the address given for *Launching a Dream* (see list).

All About the Solar System [Computer program; tutorial]. Newbury Park, CA: Ventura Educational Systems. (3440 Brokenhill Street, Newbury Park, CA 91320).

Kinzer, C., Sherwood, R., & Bransford, J. (1986). *Computer strategies for education.* Columbus, OH: Merrill Publishing.

Launching a Dream [Videotape]. Cleveland, OH: NASA Lewis Research Center. (NASA Lewis Research Center, Teacher Resource Center 8–1, 21000 Brookpark Road, Cleveland, OH 44135).

The Observatory [Computer program; simulation]. Berkeley, CA: Lightspeed Software. (2124 Kittredge Street, Berkeley, CA 94704).

Odell Lake [Computer program simulation]. St. Paul, MN: MECC-Minnesota Educational Computing Corporation. (3490 Lexington Avenue North, St. Paul, MN 55126).

Planet Hopping [Computer program; game]. Uniondale, NY: Bergwall Electronic Publishing. (106 Charles Lindberg Boulevard, Uniondale, NY 11553).

Rendezvous [Computer program; simulation]. (1982). San Francisco: Edu Ware Services. (185 Berry Street, San Francisco, CA 94107).

Science Tool Kit [Computer program; utilities for science]. San Rafael, CA: Broderbund Software. (17 Paul Drive, San Rafael, CA 94903).

The Solar System (in 3-part package, *Your Universe*) [Computer program; skills and practice game]. Garden City, NY: Focus Media. (389 Stewart Avenue, P.O. Box 865, Garden City, NY 11530).

TESS: The Educational Software Selector. (1986–1987). Southhampton, NY: EPIE Institute. (Southhampton, NY 11968).

SUGGESTED READINGS

Bennett, R. E. (1987). *Planning and evaluating computer education programs.* Columbus, OH: Merrill Publishing.

Bramble, W., & Mason, E. (1985). *Computers in schools.* New York: McGraw-Hill.

Bright, G. *Microcomputer applications.* (1987). Boston: Allyn and Bacon.

Bullough, R., & Beatty, L. (1987). *Classroom applications of microcomputers,* Columbus, OH: Merrill Publishing.

Collis, B. (1988). *Computers, curriculum, and whole-class instruction.* Belmont, CA: Wadsworth Publishing Company.

Hunter, B. (1984). *My students use computers.* Reston, VA: Reston Publishing Company.

Schall. W., Leake, L., Jr., & Whitaker, D. (1986). *Computer education: Literacy and beyond.* Monterey, CA: Brooks/Cole Publishing Company.

Taffee, S. (Ed.). (1986). *Computers in education* (2nd ed.). Guilford, CT: Dushkin Publishing Group.

Turner, S., & Land, M. (1988). *Tools for schools.* Belmont, CA: Wadsworth Publishing Company.

Troutman, A., and White, J. (1988). *The micro goes to school.* Pacific Grove, CA: Brooks/Cole Publishing Company.

White, C., & Hubbard, G. (1988). *Computers and education.* New York: Macmillan Publishing Company.

The rapid development of the computer in education makes reading materials dated, even obsolete, very quickly. We suggest that you check your library for current literature. There are also several good periodicals available.

CHAPTER 9

Metric Measurement

Goals

After completing this chapter, you will demonstrate competence in the following:

1. The ability to estimate using common metric units.

2. The ability to use appropriate measuring devices to quantify data in metric units.

3. The ability to use the metric system of measurement in describing, explaining, and comparing natural phenomena.

Objectives

In completing this chapter, you will do the following:

1. Identify common usage metric units.

2. Estimate in appropriate metric units the linear dimensions of an object, the volume of a liquid, the mass (weight) of an object, and the temperature of a subtance.

3. Use linear measuring devices marked in metric units to obtain data about natural phenomena.

4. Measure the volume of various amounts of liquids in different containers by using a container marked in metric units.

5. Use a balance and standardized weights to measure in metric units the mass of various objects.

6. Measure the temperature of various substances using a thermometer with the Celsius scale.

7. Describe, explain, and compare substances and objects using metric units of measurement.

INTRODUCTION

Skill in measuring is essential to any effective science program. Even in the early grades, science activities involve students in collecting data because measurement is the tool that allows learners to describe and explain natural phenomena. It is used to make comparisons among objects and to determine how much, or how little, change has taken place over a specified time period. Furthermore, it allows students to make predictions and establish controls. Measurement provides students with a referent or standard that can be used to compare an unknown.

The process of measuring is a learned skill. Therefore, you, the teacher, must plan instruction that involves learners in this process. These planned experiences must take into account the students' physical, cognitive, social, and emotional development. Generally, the measuring process proceeds from very concrete comparisons to more abstract ones.

This chapter introduces you to the metric system, a system of measurement that has evolved over almost 200 years. The Systeme International, or SI, adopted in 1960, is the modernized version. It provides the basis for the units needed for everyday usage. The SI units of kilogram, meter, and liter are gradually replacing the familiar measures based on the English pound and pint.[1]

On December 23, 1975, President Gerald Ford signed the Metric Conversion Bill, which called for a gradual conversion to the metric system. Subsequently, preparing learners to deal effectively with a metric world has become a major responsibility for our educational system. The individual classroom teacher has to assume the primary responsibility for implementing a practical sequence of activities for learning this system of measuring.

In this chapter, you will be introduced to the overall process of measuring as well as to the specific units of the metric system. Also included is a description of the relationship of the various metric units and a rationale for learning this system. A teaching philosophy that is centered around "thinking metric" is stressed.

The aim here is to provide preservice and inservice teachers with appropriate background information and practical activities so that they can begin to develop competence in the common use of metric measurement. This chapter is divided into four sections on measurement: linear, volume, mass (weight), and temperature. These four areas of measurement are most common in elementary school science. A fifth common area of measurement is time. It is not dealt with here because the units of time (seconds) will not be altered by the conversion to the metric system.

In each section, you will be given specific information about that particular area of measurement. Terms that identify the appropriate metric units are included, appropriate measuring devices are examined, and opportunities for you

---

[1] The National Bureau of Standards uses the spellings *meter* and *liter*. The British spellings *metre* and *litre* have been adopted by many groups. Both spellings are correct.

to work concretely with the various metric units are provided. Unlike other chapters, most of the informational material is integrated within the activities, rather than preceding them. This meshing of information with practical experiences should help you begin to *think metric*. It is hoped that this chapter will provide you with a good foundation upon which you can continue to build in the area of metric measurement.

Before you become involved with the four specific areas of metric measurement, you should receive some background information on the process of measuring. The simplest form of measurement involves concrete perceptual comparisons of a particular characteristic of an object to a known referent. Learners must have many concrete experiences in making perceptual observations with various objects. In the area of measurement, we are most interested in guiding beginning learners to observe characteristics such as length, volume, mass (weight), and temperature. Nonstandard referents are commonly used in the beginning stage. "As heavy as my pencil," "longer than my arm," and "colder than tap water" are some examples. As the learner matures and develops, measurement concepts begin to be more abstract. Standard referents with numerical representations are used to describe and compare observations: three meters long, 23° Celsius, between five and six grams.

It is important that teachers and learners alike understand the process of measurement. Simply put, a basic referent must be identified. For beginning learners and those who have not had appropriate experiences, the use of concrete, nonstandard referents is suggested in order to help the learner understand the process. A method must be devised for counting how many of the referents or what portion of one equals the characteristic of the object being measured. The unknown is then described by comparing it with the referent. Beginning learners use terms such as *more, less,* or *the same as.* But as they gain experience and develop cognitively, they can make more precise measurements.

Many times, learners become skilled in measuring but are unable to make decisions concerning what to measure, which measurements to make, and how best to use the measurements once they have them. Teachers must help students establish a purpose for measuring. One way is by providing many science experiences in which measuring helps describe and explain natural phenomena.

SUGGESTED ACTIVITIES

ACTIVITY 9.1: LINEAR MEASUREMENT

A. Each area of measurement in the metric system has one basic unit associated with it. The *meter* (m) is the basic unit for linear measurement. Larger and smaller quantities of the basic unit are indicated by using prefixes. A meter can be subdivided into smaller units of 1000 *millimeters* (mm), 100 *centimeters* (cm), and 10 *decimeters* (dm). the prefix *milli* means one-thousandth, *centi* means one-hundredth, and *deci* means one-tenth.

    Obtain a meterstick and examine the metric scale marked on it. You should notice that the meter is divided into 1000 small units. Each of these units is called a millimeter (mm) and represents 1/1000 of a meter. After every group of 10 millimeters, there should be a numeral. This unit of length (10 millimeters) is called a centimeter (cm). There are 100 centimeters in a meter. These 100 centimeters can be divided into groups of 10. Each group of 10 centimeters is called a decimeter (dm). There are 10 decimeters in a meter.

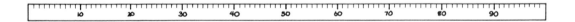

B. It should be evident to you now that the metric scale is based on a decimal system. This logically conceived system has been designed so that all measures are related through a factor of 10. This means that conversion from any one unit to any other unit within the same area—millimeters to centimeters, for example—can be made by dividing or multiplying by 10 or powers of 10. This is much simpler than our present system, which employs a multiple of conversion factors. For example, in the English system of measurement, to convert feet to inches, the factor is 12. To convert feet to yards, the factor is three. With each conversion, a different factor is necessary. In the metric system, the conversion factor is always 10 or powers of 10.

The important thing you must remember in the metric system is the order in size and the relationship of the units. The following shows the order in size of the units mentioned so far and their relationship:

1 meter = 10 decimeters = 100 centimeters = 1000 millimeters

C. In order to convert from centimeters to millimeters, you would multiply by 10 because you are going from a larger unit to the next smaller unit. You would divide by 10 to convert centimeters to decimeters because you are going from a smaller unit to the next larger unit.

  1. The following questions will give you a chance to use the information just presented:

  a. How many centimeters are in 60 millimeters?

  b. How many millimeters are in 15 decimeters?

  c. How many decimeters are in 60 centimeters?

  d. How many decimeters are in 640 millimeters?

  e. How many millimeters are in 4.5 decimeters?

  f. How many centimeters are in 1000 millimeters?

  2. Use a meterstick to check out your answers. You might want to compare them with your classmates' answers. If there are any conflicts, try to resolve them. If you have trouble, ask your instructor for help.

D. There are three other common linear metric units with which you will want to be familiar. These units are all larger than the basic unit of the meter. The *decameter* (dkm) is equal to 10 meters; the *hectometer* (hm) is equal to 100 meters; and the *kilometer* (km) is equal to 1000 meters. With the metric system, the distances between cities will be measured in kilometers.

E. The following activities are designed to give you some concrete experiences in using linear metric units.

  1. Look around you and find at least three objects that you estimate to be about one meter in length, width, or height. *Do not measure these.* Record your answers.

  Objects estimated to be approximately one meter:

  a.

  b.

  c.

  2. Obtain a meterstick and check your estimates by comparing them with the meterstick. Record the results as being more than a meter, less than a meter, or about the same as a meter.

  Results

  a.

  b.

  c.

3. Find three objects that you estimate to be about equal to two meters. Record them.

Objects estimated to be approximately two meters:

a.

b.

c.

4. Use the meterstick and check your answers. Record the results as being more than two meters, less than two meters, or about the same as two meters.

Results

a.

b.

c.

5. Try to estimate the length and width of your classroom in meters. Then use a metric tape to check your answer. Record your results.

Estimate   *Actual Measurement*

6. Try some other estimating in meters; then measure to see how accurate you are.

Estimate   *Actual Measurement*

F. Activities involving estimating and measuring objects of one meter are best to use in beginning measurement experiences. Once you have conceptualized the meter length, you are ready for other activities that focus on estimating and measuring larger and smaller units of the meter. By associating the various metric lengths with the length of common things, you can more easily conceptualize the units.

G. The following activities involve you in estimating quantities smaller than a meter:

1. List three things that you estimate to be approximately equal to one millimeter.

a.

b.

c.

2. List three things that you estimate to be approximately equal to one centimeter.

a.

b.

c.

3. List three things that you estimate to be approximately equal to one decimeter.

   a.

   b.

   c.

4. Use a meterstick as a guide, and mark off a strip of stiff paper into 10 centimeters. Divide each centimeter into 10 equal units to represent millimeters. Use this ten-centimeter strip to check the estimates you made. Indicate next to your answers in Part G whether your estimate was more, less, or approximately equal to the specific unit indicated.

5. Compare your results with others. See if you can find other things that are approximately equal to a millimeter, centimeter, and decimeter. What different parts of your body are approximately equal to any of the units?

H. The larger quantities of distance measurement—decameter, hectometer, and kilometer—do not lend themselves to concrete, in-class activities; so no planned activities involving these larger units are included here. However, there are activities that you could use to help yourself conceptualize these larger units. Activities outside the classroom involving cars, bicycles, or track and field events can be used to acquire a concrete idea of these longer distances. Making a scale drawing of a neighborhood, university campus, or elementary school playground using metric units is also helpful.

   Many different kinds of materials can be used to construct metric tape measures—ropes, adding machine tape, plastic webbing, or drapery tape. These materials can be marked off in metric units (generally one-meter lengths with decameters and hectometers indicated) using a commercial tape as a guide.

   You can probably think of many other ideas for teaching the metric system. Share these with others interested in becoming more familiar with the metric system. You might want to start a file of ideas to use when you work with elementary children.

   Avoid converting from the familiar English units—mile, rod, acre—to metric units with elementary children. It is much better to give them many concrete experiences so that they can think in metric terms.

I. To get more practice in using linear metric units, measure the following items using the meterstick for large measurements and the 10 centimeter strip for smaller ones. Record your answers.

   1. The length of your shoe in centimeters.

   2. The height of an average door in meters.

   3. The width of a desk in decimeters.

   4. The thickness of a nickel in millimeters.

5. The length of your outstretched arm in centimeters.

6. The length and width of your bed.

7. The length and width of your room.

8. Make several other measurements and record them.

   a.

   b.

   c.

   d.

   e.

J. You should be well on your way to acquiring a concrete understanding of the common metric units of linear measurement. Jot down any comments or notes you wish to make. If you feel you need more feedback or help, ask your instructor to discuss this section with you.

☐ **Comments**

ACTIVITY 9.2: VOLUME

A. The metric unit for describing the volume of liquids and gases is the *liter* (l). The liter is composed of 1000 equal subunits. Each subunit is called a *milliliter* (ml). The milliliter is the referent for volume and has a logical relationship with linear measurement units. One milliliter can be described in linear terms as one cubic centimeter (cm^3). This means that volume—how much space something occupies—is directly related to linear measurement. One milliliter is equal to 1 cm $\times$ 1 cm $\times$ 1 cm, or 1 cm^3.

   Since there are 1000 milliliters in 1 liter, and each milliliter is equal to 1 cubic centimeter, a liter would be equal to 1000 cubic centimeters or 1 cubic decimeter (1 dm^3).

B. Obtain several graduated cylinders and examine them carefully. Notice the scale markings on each cylinder. These markings indicate the measurement intervals. Some cylinders have a double scale marking the zero point at the top on one side and at the bottom on the other. Generally, 50 ml and 100 ml cylinders are graduated in 1 ml intervals.

   Determine the volume of liquid each interval on the scale measures for three different-sized cylinders that you are examining. Record your findings.

These students are learning how volume relates to linear measurement.

Maximum volume measured by selected cylinder	*Volume of liquid each interval on scale measures*
1.	
2.	
3.	

C. Obtain a liter box and examine it carefully. The inside dimensions of the liter box are 1 dm × 1 dm × 1 dm, or 1 dm³. You can verify this by using a meterstick or a 10 cm strip. Most liter boxes are graduated in 100 ml intervals. The liter box can help you visualize concretely the relationship between linear measurement units and volume measurement units.

    1. Select one of the graduated cylinders and a liter box. Make several practice measurements by pouring different amounts of water into each. Be sure the top surface of the water is at eye level when you make a reading. If you are using a glass cylinder, you will notice that the top surface of the water curves downward from the sides of the container. Water particles tend to cling to the glass sides of the cylinder, which causes the surface to be curved. In order to obtain an accurate reading, this curve, called the *meniscus,* is kept at eye level and the lowest part of the downward curve is used in making the measurement. If you are using a plastic cylinder, the surface should be level and not curved downward. Nonbreakable plastic cylinders and liter boxes are recommended for elementary classrooms. The measurement intervals should be clearly marked and easy to read.

2. Select several of the containers provided and use the graduated cylinders to determine the amount of liquid each will hold. *Suggestion:* Fill the graduated cylinder with water and note the amount. Pour the water from the graduated cylinder into the selected container, instead of filling the container and pouring the water into the graduated cylinder. When the water level is flush with the top of the container, the container is considered full. Record your findings.

Container selected   *Amount of liquid held when full*

a.

b.

c.

d.

3. Now that you have had some experience with measuring volume using metric units, estimate, in metric units, the amount of liquid some familiar containers will hold when filled. Some suggestions are listed to get you started. List others of your own choosing in the space provided. Record your estimates and the actual volume measured.

Description of container   *Estimate of volume*   *Actual volume*

a. a juice glass

b. a coffee mug

c. a medium-sized pitcher

d.

e.

f.

g.

4. You may want to calibrate some familiar containers in metric measurement intervals. This can be done by using the referent of 1 ml. Pour 1 ml of water into the selected container and mark the water level. Continue this procedure until you reach the desired volume. Larger containers can be marked in 100 ml intervals. You can effectively use these "homemade" graduated containers with elementary children to involve them with metric measurements. Older children can construct their own graduated containers for measuring volume.

5. The volume of solids can be measured by displacement. The cubic centimeter (cm^3) is normally used instead of the milliliter (ml) in describing solid volume measurements. Practice making volume measurements using the solid objects provided. Pour a measured amount of water into a graduated container. Place the solid object into the container of water and

measure the water level. The amount of water displaced—the second reading minus the first reading—will equal the volume of the solid. Record your findings.

Solid object used	Volume of water before adding object	Volume of water after adding object	Volume of solid object
a.			
b.			
c.			

D. You may want to discuss the activities done in this section with a group of your classmates. Compare your findings and talk about any difficulties you had in understanding the information presented or in doing the activities suggested. Jot down comments, questions, or notes concerning volume measurement. If you feel you need more guidance or feedback, ask your instructor for help.

☐ **Comments**

ACTIVITY 9.3: MASS (WEIGHT)

A. In the elementary grades, usually no distinction is made between the terms *mass* and *weight*. In this section, you will see the term *mass* followed by the term *weight* in parentheses. The mass of an object is the amount of matter or material it contains. The weight of an object is the amount of force being exerted on an object. The force being exerted on an object is determined by the pull of gravity. The following example will illustrate how the two measurements can differ. On the moon, the force of gravity is much weaker, about one-sixth the force on the earth. Because the force of gravity is less on the moon, the weight of an object would be less if measured on the moon than if measured on the earth. Mass is not affected by the force of gravity. Therefore, the mass of an object would always remain constant whether measured on the moon or on the earth.

The *newton* (N) is the standard metric unit that indicates the weight of an object. A spring balance with either a rectangular or dial-shaped face, on which the graduated scale is located, is used for measuring the weight of objects. When an object is attached to the spring scale, the spring will be stretched according to the amount of force the object exerts. In the metric system, one unit of force is equal to the distance of one centimeter.

These students are learning about mass (weight).

The *kilogram* (km) is the common unit of measurement for mass. A kilogram is composed of 1000 equal units. Each of these units is called a *gram* (g). Even though grams indicate the mass of an object, they also indicate weight. This is acceptable because there is a direct relationship between the mass and weight of any given object. As long as the gravitational pull on an object is constant, the weight of the object is directly proportional to its mass. This means that an object with more mass will have more weight and one with less mass will have less weight. Therefore, for general classroom use, the terms *mass* and *weight* can be used to indicate either.

An equal arm balance and standard masses or weights are used to measure mass (weight) of objects. All operate on the principle of the lever or teeterboard. An object is placed in a pan that is attached to one side of the basic beam. At an equal distance from the center balancing point on the other side is another pan attached to the basic beam. When a second object of equal mass is placed into the pan on this side, the basic beam should return to a horizontal or balanced position. If the two objects do not have the same mass, the beam will slant downward toward the object with the heavier mass. A spring balance with a scale calibrated in grams rather than newtons can also be used for measuring mass (weight).

Obtain several equal arm balances and examine them. Practice using one of the balances by selecting an object and placing it on one side of the balance. Find another object that has the same mass as the first. Place the second object on the other side and see if the balance returns to the horizontal position. Continue trying various objects until you find one with the same mass as the first. Next, balance the first object with two or three objects.

B. Now that you have had experience in using the equal arm balance, let's examine the standard masses or weights that are used to measure mass (weight). As you learned earlier, the gram is the unit for measuring mass (weight). This unit was determined by weighing one milliliter of cold water. Therefore, one gram is equal to the mass of one milliliter of cold water. Remember that 1 ml is equal to 1 cm³, or 1 cm × 1 cm × 1 cm. This logically conceived relationship among mass (weight), volume, and linear measurement allows for easy movement from one measurement to another. The following illustrates the relationship among volume, linear, and mass (weight) metric measurement units.

$$1 \text{ cm}^3 = 1 \text{ ml} = 1 \text{ g}$$

1. Obtain a set of standard masses or weights from your instructor. There are several different kinds. The plastic stacking discs and cubes are appropriate for the early elementary grades. They are relatively inexpensive and accurate enough for early experiences in measuring mass (weight). For the upper elementary grades, a brass gram mass set is more appropriate. These sets are more expensive but are much more accurate. Place one of the mass pieces in your hand and feel the weight. Try to find an object in the room that feels about the same weight. Put the selected object on one side of a balance scale and the standard mass on the other. Are they the same weight? Try this procedure with several other standard mass pieces and objects.

2. Find the mass (weight) of the following items. Also add some items of your own choosing.

	Items	*Measured mass*
a.	Your pencil	
b.	This textbook	
c.	An empty soft drink can	
d.	A piece of chalk	
e.	A nickel	
f.		
g.		
h.		

3. If there are some spring balances available, you might want to use them for practice in measuring the mass (weight) of several selected objects. Just attach the object to be measured to the spring scale. The measurement units are located on the face, and a marker indicates the mass (weight) of the object. Record your findings.

	Items	*Measured mass*
a.		
b.		
c.		
d.		

C. If a metric bathroom scale is available, weigh yourself. You will find that your weight is measured in *kilograms*. Compare your weight with that of several other people. After you have some experience with this, try to estimate the weights in kilograms of several people of different sizes; then compare your estimates to their actual weights.

   If a metric scale is not available, you can convert one that measures in pounds by recalibrating the scale. To get to the scale, you must remove the plastic covering and the top. The top is usually held in place by very strong springs, which must be pulled up to release their hold on the top. Once the top is off, remove the dial plate and glue a clean piece of paper over the old scale. Mark off the new scale in 5 kilogram intervals. Each 2.2 pounds equals 1 kilogram; therefore, 11 pounds equals 5 kilograms; 22 pounds is equal to 10 kilograms; 33 pounds is equal to 15 kilograms, etc. When the new scale is finished, replace the top, making sure you get each spring through the top.

D. You may want to discuss these activities with a small group of your class-mates. Compare your findings, and talk about difficulties you had in under-standing the information presented or in doing the activities suggested. Jot down comments, questions, or notes concerning mass (weight) measure-ment. If you feel you need more guidance or feedback, ask your instructor for help.

☐ **Comments**

ACTIVITY 9.4: TEMPERATURE

A. The unit for measuring temperature is a *degree.* The term *degree* is used in both the familiar Fahrenheit (F) scale and the metric scale, Celsius (C), but the unit of measurement a degree represents on the Celsius scale is *not* the same as a unit of measurement on the Fahrenheit scale. The Celsius scale, which was called the centigrade scale for a number of years, has 100 degree units. The two extremes, 100° and 0°, represent the boiling point and freezing point of water under standard pressure conditions.

A thermometer is used to measure the temperature of an object or system of objects. Temperature can be thought of as the degree of hotness or coldness of things. You can help young children develop the concept of temperature by involving them in concrete experiences in which they are able to "feel" the hotness or coldness. For example, prepare several containers of water—one warm, one cold, and one very warm. The learners can use the sense of touch to feel the temperature of the water, and then you can use a thermometer to quantify the observations and to help the children understand how the thermometer operates. For instance, a child puts his hand into a container of cold water. Then you place the thermometer in and make a reading. Associate the reading with the feeling of coldness the child experi-enced when his hand was in the water. The child can also observe that the red liquid goes up when the thermometer is placed in warm water and down when it is placed in cold water. Many concrete experiences such as these are necessary for children to develop the concept of temperature.

1. Obtain a thermometer with a Celsius scale. Examine it carefully. Notice the degree markings on the side of the scale. Generally, student thermom-eters with a C scale are marked in one-degree intervals, which are easier for elementary children to read than those of the F scale, which are marked in two degree units.

**These children are using a thermometer to learn about
temperature.**

2. One of the best ways to begin to think about temperature in metric terms
   is to establish a reference point. Room temperature serves this purpose
   well. Place your thermometer in a spot that you feel will give the most
   accurate reading of the temperature in the classroom. If possible, sus-
   pend the thermometer to minimize its contact with objects. This contact
   can sometimes affect the reading. Wait about 3 minutes before taking a
   reading. If you feel that thermal equilibrium—the point at which the liquid
   column becomes stationary—has not been reached, leave it for 2 additional minutes and take a second reading. Record your finding.

3. Now that you have measured the room temperature in degrees Celsius,
   make some observations that you can associate with that reading. These

observations will help you begin to "think metric." Use the following questions to help you in making some observations:

    a. How do you feel? Warm? Cool? Comfortable?

    b. What kind of clothing is most appropriate for staying comfortable in the temperature recorded?

    c. Are there other observations you can make to associate with the recorded temperature?

B. Room temperature can provide a reference point for thinking about temperature in metric terms. Generally, comfortable room temperature is approximately 22°–23° C. Consequently, temperatures higher than that will be warmer, and temperatures lower than that will be colder. It is a good idea to establish the degrees Celsius that you consider cool, cold, and hot and to make observations associated with each.

    1. Use the thermometer to measure the temperature of the following in degrees of Celsius.

Items	Temperature
a. Tap water	_____°C
b. Warm water	_____°C
c. Water from water fountain	_____°C
d. Outside air	_____°C
e. Mixture of ice and water	_____°C

    2. Make some other measurements of your own choosing using the Celsius scale.

Items	Temperature
a.	
b.	
c.	
d.	

C. All of us will need many concrete experiences in which we can associate the various degrees Celsius with our own observations. Activities for children should involve them in making observations about themselves in relation to the temperature. The following are examples:

    1. How do I feel in this temperature, cold? Hot? Cool? Warm? Comfortable?

    2. What clothes do I feel most comfortable wearing in this temperature?

    3. Can I see my breath in this temperature?

    4. Should I wear gloves in this temperature?

    5. Do I perspire easily in this temperature?

D. You might want to make a metric profile for yourself. Following are some suggestions.

height	_____ cm
weight	_____ kg
body temperature	_____ °C
neck	_____ cm
shoulders	_____ cm
arms	_____ cm
wrist	_____ cm
chest	_____ cm
waist	_____ cm
hips	_____ cm
legs	_____ cm
calf	_____ cm
feet	_____ cm

E. You may want to discuss these activities with a group of your classmates. Compare your findings and talk about difficulties you had in understanding the information presented or in doing the activities suggested. Jot down comments, questions, or notes concerning mass (weight) measurement. If you feel you need more guidance or feedback, ask your instructor for help. Remember, think metric!

☐ **Comments**

SUMMARY

The metric system of measurement is really very simple to learn and use. It is less complex than the English system and much more logical. The best way to become familiar with the system is to think in metric terms. The terms and the type of measurement they represent must be committed to memory—meters for linear measurement, liters for volume, gram for mass (weight), and degrees Celsius for temperatures. The prefixes of *milli-* for one-thousandth, *centi-* for one-hundredth, *deci-* for one-tenth, and *kilo-* for one-thousand indicate measurements that are more or less than the basic unit. Remember that all the metric units are related through a factor of ten. Linear, volume, and mass (weight) units are all related in the following way:

$$1 \text{ cm}^3 = 1 \text{ ml} = 1 \text{ g}$$

The best way to learn the metric system of measurement is to *think metric*. Don't convert the familiar English units to metric units or vice versa. Try to visualize metric units in terms of familiar objects, not as so many inches, pints, or pounds. Make measurement in metric units as often as possible. Estimating before you measure is also helpful. For everyday use, the units that you worked with in this chapter will serve you well. There are several publications available that give a more complete and in-depth description of the metric system. These are listed in the "Suggested Readings." Furthermore, many states have a metric resource guide available for teachers. Many school systems are beginning to develop their own metric resource materials. You will want to begin *now* to think metric so that you will feel comfortable in helping elementary students to learn and use the metric system of measurement.

SUGGESTED READINGS

ANMC metric editorial guide—Interim guide to accepted metric practice (11 pp.). American National Metric Council, 1625 Massachusetts Avenue, N. W., Washington, DC 20036.

Carin, A., & Sund, R. (1989). Chapter 10. *Teaching science through discovery* (6th ed.). Columbus, OH: Merrill Publishing.

ISO Recommendation R 1000, *Rules for the use of units of the international system of units* (21 pp.). American National Standards Institute, 1430 Broadway, New York, NY 10018.

NBS Guidelines for use of the metric system (1974, November). Metric Information Office, National Bureau of Standards, Washington, DC 20234.

Rowe, M. B. (1976). *Teacher resource guide for metric education.* Lansing, MI: Michigan Department of Education.

CHAPTER 10

Projects and Science

Goals

After completing this chapter, you will demonstrate competency in developing and using science projects as a teaching technique for elementary science.

Objectives

In completing this chapter, you will do the following:

1. Identify science projects as teaching activities.

2. Describe how science projects can be used to learn about local resources.

3. Describe how science projects are used in science fairs and special programs.

INTRODUCTION

Throughout this book the emphasis has been on learning science by doing it. This can happen only if the student is actively involved in the process. There are two ways that this involvement can occur. The first is by using the activities in the textbook. The student reads the text for information and then does activities to apply the knowledge and to reinforce the concept. This teaching strategy has merit as it provides a structured program.

A second way to involve the student in active learning is through the use of special projects. The basis of inquiry teaching is to give students (or help them to select) a problem to solve or a topic to investigate. The topic may come from the text, student interest, or the local community. The important thing to remember is that you want to get the students involved in the experience. You may choose to do class projects, group projects, or individual projects depending on your goals. The main objective is to get everyone involved in doing something other than just reading about a topic in the text.

Special projects can be either a part of, or in addition to a regular lesson. As a *part* of the lesson, you will select a project that corresponds to the content being taught. For example, in a fourth-grade unit on volcanoes the students might research volcanic geology or make models showing the various features they have discovered. Thus, you may choose to use the topic from the text, but not the text itself, to develop an inquiry lesson. Or a special project might be used to amplify the text. For instance, the text specifies a unit on sound, but rather than just read the text, your students make string, percussion, and wind musical instruments to learn about sound. The important point to remember is that you are teaching the material to be covered, just doing it a different way.

You may also do special projects as an extra unit in *addition* to the regular curriculum. Usually these projects relate to a special event, a local concern, or a teacher's interest. A special event such as a space launch might call for a special project in which the students set up their own simulated launch, perform experiments, simulate astronaut training, and/or undertake a multitude of related activities. A local concern such as oil drilling and production or a local problem such as the closing of a landfill can also be an effective source for a special project. These issues are of interest to the student as well as pertinent to their education. Local concerns are not usually brought into the classroom, but they should be (see the discussion of "Local Science Resources" later in this chapter). A teacher's particular interest is also a source of special projects. The teacher who has an interest in or sees a need for a topic may use a special-project approach.

Be sure to select activities that are appropriate. Pay particular attention to the abilities of your students as well as to the demands of the activity. An activity may be a great project, but if students cannot carry it out, frustration rather than learning will take place. In addition, be sure that the activity is appropriate for your objectives. A project may work well, with a lot of learning taking place, but if the learning is not relevant to the objectives, it is still not appropriate. Moreover, use projects that are current. A project that teaches obsolete information or skills may be fun but a waste of time. Use care and common sense in selecting your involvement activities.

In this chapter you will learn about

1. Science fairs

2. National and state programs

3. Local science resources

4. Projects - short term and long term

SCIENCE FAIRS

Let's have a science fair! Whether this suggestion comes from the teacher, the class, or the district, it evokes an air of excitement. What is a science fair? Whatever you want it to be. Usually it is a display of science projects accompanied by written and/or oral descriptions. Often the projects are judged, and awards of ribbons or certificates are presented. Science fairs come in all sizes and descriptions. You may have a small fair consisting of only your class, or a large district-wide fair with students representing all grade levels from all of the schools in the district. The fair may focus on a single topic such as a physics fair, or it may be open to many topics. Whatever the size or format, a science fair gives students an opportunity to show their work and be judged on it.

A science fair requires careful planning, a lot of which can be done by upper grade students. There are several points to consider for a successful fair.

This teacher and his students are planning a science fair.

Choosing a Topic.   You must decide on the topic(s) of the fair. Will it be limited to projects on a topic you are currently studying (the culmination of a unit), or is it going to be open to any topic (an open fair at the end of the year)? Will you have categories for entries? How many?

Setting Rules.   The rules of the fair must be established. They may be simple, but the rules should be known to all. Some things to consider are

1. **Date and time**—Students need to know how much time they have to get ready. Also, many parents may want to come.
2. **Individual or partnership projects**—How many students will work on a project? You may choose to use individual projects with each person doing his own, or allow two or three students to work together.
3. **Outside help**—Decide if the project will be completed in class or at home. If it is being done outside of class, how much help from parents or others is acceptable. A real concern is who does the outside project, the parent or the student.
4. **Criteria for judging**—If the project is to be judged or graded, set the criteria and rules before the students start to work. They need to know what is expected and acceptable. Hidden requirements or unexpected changes lead to frustration and a feeling of unfairness.

Explaining the Project.   The project must be explained, especially if it is the first time the students have participated in a science fair. You have to let them know what you expect. They must also know how the project is to be presented and what type of documentation goes with it. Do you expect a display of the project with a written explanation? An oral explanation? Do you want posters describing the project?

Judging and Awards.   If the projects are to be judged, what criteria will be used? Who will be the judge? You may judge the fair yourself or bring in an outside judge such as another teacher or the principal. Be sure they know the criteria before they start judging. Awards in the form of ribbons or certificates are appropriate. You may want to be sure you have enough "Honorable Mention" ribbons so that everyone gets an award. One teacher we know always had enough project categories so that there were never more than three projects in each category, ensuring everyone a first, second, or third place award. Do not let competition ruin your fair, but at the same time, good work should be rewarded.

STATE AND NATIONAL PROGRAMS

Several state and national programs are available for your students. Some are based on competition, whereas others are not. A state science fair may attract

Model rockets are a part of the *Young Astronaut* program.

winners from various local fairs with a scholarship or some such prize to the winners. Usually elementary students do not get such valuable awards, but the ribbons and certificates do mean a lot to them. Noncompetitive programs stress learning about special topics and provide resources, activities, and projects for that purpose. Participation in these programs allows students to know what other students their age and grade level are doing and, in some instances, compete with them. Two examples of national programs are *Odyssey of the Mind* and *Young Astronauts.*

Odyssey of the Mind stresses creative thinking in the arts and sciences. Teams compete in various structured events. The general format is for a school to develop teams for each event. The teams meet after school and work on ideas until they have developed their best solution. They then compete with other teams in local or area meets; winners go on to state competition. A national meet is held in the spring, usually on a university campus.

The *Young Astronaut* program was established by President Ronald Reagan in 1984 as a privately sponsored, nonprofit educational organization to promote space-related curriculum materials. Local chapters receive a variety of space-related materials and suggestions for their use. Unlike many programs, there are a lot of activities for lower elementary as well as for upper elementary and junior high levels. (For more information, write The Young Astronaut Council, P.O. Box 65432, Washington, DC 20036.)

LOCAL SCIENCE RESOURCES

One of the most neglected sources of science topics for projects is your own local area. The first thing you should do when you take a teaching position is to inventory the local area. Look for community strengths as well as unusual resources. Look at the following examples and think of additional activities that you might do with them.

Lakes, Rivers, and Streams

1. Collect and study aquatic specimens.
2. Learn how they were formed and how they change.
3. Do a study of water quality and physical pollution. Do something about it.

Forests

1. Learn to identify different kinds of trees.
2. Study the forest as a habitat: What animals live in the forest and where do they live?
3. Learn about forest products. List everything you can think of that can be made from a tree.
4. Set up a lumber camp, assign roles, and prepare to harvest a stand of timber.

Deserts

1. Study the ecology. Learn what plants and animals live there.
2. Learn how the desert was formed.

Agriculture

1. Learn what crops are grown in your area.
2. Study pesticides, herbicides, and fertilizers. Predict results if one or more of these were not used.

Manufacturing

1. Find out what products are made, what raw materials were used, and where they came from.
2. What happens to waste products? Make suggestions for pollution controls.

Mining

1. Study the effect of mining on the ecology.
2. Look for fossils and try to identify them.
3. Photograph and then study the strata in an open mine.

Oil

1. Learn who looks for oil and what they look for. Bring in a geologist or geophysicist.
2. Learn about seismographs, shock waves, and strata.
3. Learn about a drilling rig and what safeguards are employed to prevent oil spills and ground water contamination. What is a "blowout"?

Local Businesses

1. Interview business people, and find out how science is used in their business.
2. Pick a business that generates a lot of trash and try to develop better ways of disposing of the trash. Maybe you can make suggestions to decrease the amount of trash generated.

Utility Companies (Electric, Gas, Telephone)

1. Find out where the gas and electricity come from and how they get to the customer.
2. How is electricity made? Assign teams to debate the pros and cons of generating electricity by using water power, nuclear energy, coal, gas, and wind.

A map game is a starting point for a project on energy.

3. Learn how sound travels from one place to another by telephone. Does it always travel by wire, or are there other ways? For a big project, could you put a telephone or intercom in every room in the school?

Radio and Television Broadcasting

1. Make a mural showing how a person's voice and image get from the studio or remote site to you.
2. Make a crystal radio. This may not be too easy, as the simple, old-fashioned parts may not be available. Can a radio repairman help you?
3. Bring in an amateur radio operator (a ''ham''). He may be able to bring in a transmitter and receiver, show you how the equipment works, and let you talk to someone.

Local science has unlimited potential. The people associated with the resource are usually more than happy to work with schools as this cooperation is good public relations and education. Field trips can usually be arranged, except in hazardous situations. People can bring equipment, pictures, charts, graphs, and diagrams to explain a process and then answer questions. You may be able to coordinate some local science with your textbook science. On the other hand, local science is a good supplement to your regular curriculum.

PROJECTS

The easiest way to involve students in learning is to have them do projects. Children enjoy planning the project and then carrying it out. As they work on a project, they develop a sense of ownership ("Here is *my* project") and a sense of pride ("Look at what *I* did") that can carry over into your regular science program.

Do not forget the parents. A lot of public relation work is done with the home as students do projects. We want parents to know what we are doing at school, and we need their support. There are several ways to involve parents in projects. Often we will need materials such as boards, nails, screws, and tools that are not readily available at school but are common at home. It is not expensive or difficult for parents to supply materials for their child's project. Sometimes adults are needed to help as chaperones on a special visit, to act as judges for science fairs, or especially to assist if we are doing something that might prove dangerous for a small child such as actually cooking food (cookies, donuts, etc.) that they have prepared. Parents enjoy helping in the classroom and are a resource that we do not utilize often enough. Another way to involve parents is by giving them the projects. Projects can be designed so that the finished product is a special gift. When you schedule a unit on growing plants, can you plan it so that the plant can be a Mother's Day present? Sending projects home also solves the problem of what to do with them when you are finished using them.

One other point on public relations: Any favorable publicity that you, your class, or the school can get helps future programs. If your students are doing something interesting or unusual, call the local newspaper. Parents like to see their children's name and picture in the paper when their children are doing something special. Administrators especially like to see good press about their school. If you can get good publicity for students' projects, you can get more support in the future from the administration.

As in any good lesson, you will have to do a lot of planning to have a successful learning experience. The students may be doing the project, but the teacher must advise, guide, prod, and evaluate to keep it moving in the appropriate direction. It may seem redundant to restate the obvious, but when using projects, have specific goals in mind. Write objectives; then keep students on track and task to achieve those objectives. Once your objectives are set, and the decision to use projects has been made, you need to follow through with four steps.

1. Choosing a topic
2. Doing the project
3. Presenting the project
4. Evaluating the results

Choosing the topic

Several decisions must be made before starting a project, each of which has a direct effect on the others. The first and foremost consideration, obviously, is what you are trying to teach and what is the best way to do it. This is a part of initial planning. Once this has been done, there are some other decisions to make.

Is this a long- or short-term project?   Some projects such as making a model volcano may take only a few days or a week to complete, whereas others such as decomposing objects may take an entire semester. Long- and short-term projects will be examined in detail later in this chapter.

Will the topic be related to the textbook?   A project may be a part of the textbook curriculum and used to enhance a lesson or unit. On the other hand, you may use projects to teach material not found in the text. An example might be a project on a community resource such as finding and drilling for oil. This topic is not in the textbook, but it is important to students whose parents either work in the oil industry or are dependent on it.

Will this be a class, group, or individual project?   Each has its own potential. A class project can involve everyone in a single purpose, allowing each person to contribute individual talents. Group projects allow a team to develop the project, using the various talents of the members to produce a result. Individual projects force each student to produce her own project. Individual projects also give freedom to the student, allowing her to create her own project in her own way.

Who chooses the project, the teacher or the student?   There are several possibilities. You may assign each student a project or pick the class project. You may choose a topic, allowing a choice of projects on that topic, or you may even give free choice of topics. The purpose for the project will dictate who makes the choice.

Doing the Project

Now the work begins, but there are still decisions to be made.

Will the projects be done in class, at home, or both?   You can allow class time to be used for the project either by scheduling time blocks for everyone to work on projects or by using free time when other work is completed. Some projects can be completed at home and brought to school. You need to make clear how much help the child can get from parents or others. Parents want good projects and sometimes may even do the work for their child. You may have to remind the parents that it is the child's project, not theirs. On the other hand, parental help allows the parents and child to work together, sharing the learning experience. Too often we cut parents out of the learning experience.

How much time will be spent on the project?   Some require a short amount of time (a day or two), but others may last a long time. You may do a lot of work for a short time and then use only a small amount of time each day or week making observations.

What are the deadlines?   When are the projects due for presentation, or, in the case of a class project, when is the completion date?

Presenting the Project

When students do a project, you should do something with it. A class project should be shown to someone such as parents, other students, or the general public. Call the newspaper or local TV station. Let others know what your children have accomplished. A Texas teacher, John Johnston (Francone Elementary School, Cypress-Fairbanks ISD, Houston, Texas), and his fifth-grade students made two telescopes to observe Halley's Comet. They had nightly viewings for students, parents, and the general public. They also were the subject of several newspaper articles. Can you imagine the pride these children had in their project?

When you assign a project, part of the assignment must focus on presenting the finished product. There may be a written report on background research, an oral presentation and demonstration of the project, or the entry of the project in a science fair. Whatever the choice of presentation, let the students know what is expected of them and what they can expect of you.

Evaluating the Results

You must evaluate the students' projects, using criteria that were established when the assignment was made. More importantly, from a teaching/learning standpoint, you should evaluate the idea. Did the project work? Did it achieve the desired learning outcomes? Would you do it again? What changes would you make next time? Try to find the weaknesses so that you can eliminate them. Look back at what was done and start looking ahead for the next time your students do projects.

Short-Term Projects

The obvious difference between short- and long-term projects is the amount of time taken to complete them, but there are other differences. Short-term projects are most often based on the material in the textbook. The textbook will have activities for the students to do as a part of the lesson and may suggest supplemental activities or projects to extend the lesson. You may decide to do a project of your own choosing as a different way to teach the material. These projects usually take a few days or a week to complete. They may be done either in the classroom or at home. Students may have some freedom in how they proceed or in the choice of variables, but everyone will be doing nearly the same thing. What they do and what they learn is directly related to the textbook lesson. Quite often projects extend beyond a single lesson, using material from the entire unit. This is a good way to pull the unit together.

Long-Term Projects

There are two types of long-term projects: those that develop slowly and those that are big projects. Some projects just take time. You will do a lot of explaining, planning, and doing for the first few days, and then the class will settle back either to gather data or to wait for something to happen. For example, students may plant seeds. You will teach about seeds and plants, explain the project, and supervise the planting of the seeds. The class must wait for the seeds to germinate and grow. The students will observe their plants as well as water them as needed. You will be doing other teaching about plants and may even finish the

Animals in the classroom is a good project.

plant unit and start something else, but plant growth goes on. Students continue to make observations and take care of the plants. They may even perform some experiments. This goes on until the project is completed. As another example, you may decide to have the students set up a weather station. After the preliminary teaching, the students start collecting data. Periodically they will record the temperature, barometric pressure, humidity, and wind speed and direction. These data can then be analyzed and used in some form. This can easily be a semester project.

Some projects are big. A lot of time is needed to explore many avenues and to complete the project. A science fair is a good example. You cannot do a science fair in a week. You must make the assignment, explain the rules, and discuss possible projects. The students need time to choose, plan, and carry out the project. Then the fair takes place. All of these steps take time.

Another example might be a class project. Suppose the class decides to make a video tape movie of mining, a local resource. Class discussion will start the project as the students decide what will be in the movie. They may bring in a resource person to help them get an overall picture of the industry. Teams have to be formed and assignments made. Research must be done before writing teams and camera teams can do their work. Editing may require some rewriting and more camera work. After the tape is finished, it must be shown to someone such as parents or other students, or you may have a team present the film to civic or social organizations. Then the final critique must be made. A lot of time is used, but a lot of learning takes place.

Two potential problems that you should be concerned with are those of *maintaining interest* and *attention span*. Projects are high-interest learning experiences, especially in the early stages, but as time passes interest can begin to lag. This can happen easily when the pace is too slow; you may need to speed up some. Even when everything is going well and interest remains high, a progress review and a pep talk will help keep the project moving. Attention span varies from grade level to grade level and from child to child. Projects lasting one or two weeks may be all that lower elementary children can handle, whereas an upper grade class might be able to maintain interest for six weeks or more. Watch carefully, and when your students start to lose interest and you cannot easily revive it, it is time to start looking for a way to end the project.

Above all, it is important to remember that whatever the project—be it long or short term, big or small, involving local resources or special programs, exploring physical or life sciences—students must be involved in the learning experience. Learning science through involvement is concrete. Look for appropriate ways to involve your students in sciencing and monitor their interest in the project so as not to exhaust your students before you exhaust the subject.

SUGGESTED ACTIVITIES

These activities are designed to involve you in project science. As you go through an activity, think of what you would do to make it work with children. Think of new ways to involve students in science. Analyze each activity to determine what the role of the teacher and of the student would be.

ACTIVITY 10.1: SCIENCE FAIRS

In this activity you will plan and/or participate in a science fair. Your instructor will decide whether or not to have a fair. If so, you will get to do a project for the fair. Activity B will allow you to plan your own science fair.

A. In this activity you will plan and do, if your instructor requires, a science project to be entered in a class fair. Select a topic from the following list. Plan two appropriate projects: one for an upper grade and one for a lower grade. Your instructor will inform you if you are to complete the projects for a fair.

Topics

Weather	Rockets	Our Bodies
Planets	Computers	Simple Machines
Nature	Dinosaurs	Electricity
Transportation	Food	Geology

Upper Grade Level: _____   Lower Grade Level: _____

TOPIC: _____

Describe the project:
What does it do?

What do you learn?

What materials do you need? Where will you get them?

What is the source of your project?

      Make a poster to go with the project. The poster may show how your subject works or give supplemental information to help the viewer to better understand the project.

      Prepare your project for the class Science Fair if required.

B. Plan a science fair for a specific grade. You may need to examine a science textbook for appropriate topics and projects.

Acceptable topics:

Requirements:

To be completed at home or at school?

How much help can students get and from whom?

Where will students get the materials?

Make a one- or two-page handout that you would give to the students and/or parents explaining the science fair and the project.

ACTIVITY 10.2: SPECIAL PROGRAMS

This activity will require some library work. You are to find out all you can about the following programs.

Young Astronauts:

Odyssey of the Mind:

Your choice (find other programs that might be appropriate and useful):

ACTIVITY 10.3: LOCAL SCIENCE RESOURCES

To be aware of the local outside resources, it is necessary to go outside of the classroom. You may use the resources around your campus or those around your home. Indicate which.

A. Interview a resource person. Select a person that has expertise in an area appropriate to elementary level science. You may want to record the interview for playback to your group or to the class.

Name of the resource person:

Topic:

A brief description of what you learned:

How valuable would this person have been?
   Strengths:

   Weaknesses:

Would this person be appropriate for
   Upper grade: Why or why not?

   Lower grade: Why or why not?

B. Make an inventory of local resources. Name the resource and give a brief annotation describing the value of the resource. You may want to do this on file cards to start a collection for future reference.

People:

Places:

Industries:

Natural Resources:

Other:

ACTIVITY 10.4: PROJECTS

Science teachers never have enough activities and projects on hand, no matter how many they collect. You can start your collection now. As you collect ideas for projects and activities, you should field test some to see if they are really as good as they look before you use them in class.

A. Make a file collection of science activities and projects and a bibliography of sources for activities and projects. Be sure to give title, topic, description, and source. You should also write some comments to remind yourself of why you liked the idea. Your instructor will probably assign a minimum number for this activity. If not, start with a minimum of 10 in each of the following categories. Add other categories as they are needed.

1. Develop a bibliography of sources. Find books and magazines that are good sources of activities and projects. The books listed in the "Suggested Readings" at the end of this chapter are good sources and worth investigating.
   Bibliography of Sources:

2. Use these sources to select activities and projects in the following areas:
   Physical Science
   Earth Science
   Biology—Nature
   Biology—Health and the Human Body

B. Do a project. There are several long-term life science projects in *Activity 10.5*. Choose one and carry it out. These projects take time, so start early. Read the instructions carefully before you begin.

ACTIVITY 10.5: LIFE SCIENCE PROJECT IDEAS

Young children are fascinated by living things, whether plants or animals. They like to see them grow and change form as they mature. Almost all elementary teachers have something alive in their classrooms (besides students). Sometimes the room may resemble a zoo, at other times an arboretum. Sometimes there may be only one plant, but almost always, there is something living in the classroom. In this way, teachers use whatever is available to teach students about living things. The purpose of this activity is to acquaint you with some projects that you might use with your students, as well as to give you firsthand experiences in observing and reporting.

Involvement projects are fun activities designed to give you an opportunity to do some life science activities on your own that you probably would not ordinarily think of doing. Most of the activities that you have done or will do in the other chapters of this book are centered around the physical sciences for two obvious reasons: physical science activities can be done more quickly than life science activities, and the equipment is easier to maintain and store. It takes time for something to grow or to collect observational data. That is also the reason why any, or all, of the activities presented in this activity should be started early in the semester. You will need at least three or four weeks to get much out of them.

Four activities are presented here. The format for each will be slightly different, ranging from a nonstructured set of directions to a very complete, record-keeping set of directions. This variety will allow you to learn several ways of presenting activities to your students.

You may want to do one, two, three, or all four of these activities. Each one is completely different from the others so that learning will not overlap if you wish to do them all. Your instructor may choose to require one or more of these activities, and if this is the case, follow her requirement. If you are working on your own, do as many as you like.

Read the general instructions before attempting the activities. Doing so will save you some embarrassment later, especially in reporting your work.

These activities will get you to look closely at some life science phenomena that you may have seen only superficially before. If you really want to learn about something, get involved. Here is your chance.

General Instructions

You will find that if you really get involved, you will enjoy these activities and will learn many interesting things that you did not know before. You probably have read about most of the activities suggested or have seen them casually but have never really taken a close look at them.

Now is your chance to watch a seed actually break through the ground, to see snail eggs as they get ready to hatch, or to observe some other equally fascinating phenomena. The key word is *involvement*. You can read for background information or to help you understand your observations, but you cannot read for the answers—you must experience them. You will get out of these activities only what you put into them. With this in mind, here are some general instructions for all the activities. Specific instructions relating to each activity will be given with the activity.

1. Read all instructions before you begin. Ignorance of the directions is no excuse for not completing an activity to the satisfaction of the instructor. Incomplete activities result in incomplete credit from your instructor. If, after reading the instructions, you have questions, ask for help.

2. Select the activity or activities that you are going to do. Do not do activities that you have done before in another class because you already know what will happen. Try something new. Be adventurous. Do not turn up your nose at mold simply because you have always thrown moldy food away when you found it in your home. Take time to really look at some mold. Have you ever really seen red or yellow mold? It can be quite pretty. Look at all four activities before you decide which one(s) you want to do.

3. Look at the format of each of the activities. Each one is different. The reason for using the specific format is explained in the introduction to the activity. By reading the materials given for each activity, you will find out several different ways that you can structure an activity for your students.

4. Do the activity. You are to work alone, not with partners or a group. However, you can talk to others, compare your project with theirs, and swap information. You will have to obtain your own materials. Your instructor may or may not provide some of them, but involvement includes gathering materials.

5. Allow yourself plenty of time to complete the activity. You cannot do any of these in a few days. Think in terms of weeks, usually about four or five, with an absolute minimum of three. Mold may be the exception, depending on how fast it grows.

6. Success or failure? What happens if nothing happens? This is where the actual learning takes place in these activities. If everything goes well, you watch, wonder, and then report what happened. If not, you have a better learning opportunity than those who have immediate success because you must find out why the activity did not work and try it again until you are successful. If your seed, for example, does not grow, find out why and plant another (and yet another, if need be). If you were to use any of these activities, or variations of them, in your classroom, you would have to know what to do if nothing happened. You must have success in these activities, and sometimes the greatest success arises from initial failure. One exception might be with your snails. If they do not lay eggs, repeating the activity still may not bring success: we do not know how to make them lay their eggs. But, you can check around for information about how, when, and under what conditions they are supposed to reproduce and report that.

7. You are to report your activities in two forms: written and oral. The written report will follow the format established by the particular activity, but it is not limited to that format. In other words, you are expected to do more than just fill in the blanks. The blanks, where there are some, only report the factual observations of the process being carried out. Use your imagination to supplement your report. Make it *interesting* for you and your instructor. Then present information about the activity as a teaching tool. How could you use it in a classroom situation? Did you enjoy it? Would children enjoy it? What were your reactions? Did you change your outlook on the subject of the activity? Think about what you have done and the implications for teaching. Then write down your thoughts before you forget them.

The second portion of the report requires that you present your written report and discuss it. You may be asked to bring your plants, mold, or whatever along with your report. Check with your instructor about this requirement. Now is your chance to show off your project and to ask some of those questions that came up but that you could not answer.

If you have read these general instructions thoroughly, you are ready to start the activities. Remember, they are to be done out of class, on your own.

Activity 10.5a: Seeds

This activity uses seeds as a method of involving students in observing how a plant grows. You will plant, water, and observe the seeds. You can conduct various experiments on the plants to verify some of the things that you have read or heard about, such as how light affects plants or how much water plants need. This will give you some experience in formulating a question, devising an experiment, and then carrying it out to answer your question. Remember to control all of your variables when you do an experiment. You cannot start two plants, put one in the light and water it regularly and the other in the dark without water, and expect to get valid results. Do you know why? If you do not, you should refer to some of the previous chapters, especially the SAPA II activity on variables, and find out.

You will be given only a minimum of structure in this activity, and it will be up to you to set up your experiment, explain it, carry it out, and report it. No format for reporting your data is given. You will have to devise your own. You might want to present your data as you would to a group of first-grade students, to college biology students, or to a group somewhere in between. The choice is yours. Two important items to remember are

1. **You must devise a written report of your experiments and observations.** Your instructor might also want to see your actual plants, so check before you get rid of them.

**An excellent involvement activity consists of giving
students the opportunity to observe plant growth.**

2. **Use your imagination when reporting.** Do not use the old day-by-day diary
   approach. Be creative! Draw pictures, make graphs, write stories, and try
   anything else you can think of.

A. Equipment
   Seeds—Beans or peas work well, but others, such as flower or vegetable
   seeds, also work.
   Soil—Your choice, but commercial potting soil usually works best.
   Containers—Foam cups work well, but clear plastic cups allow you to see the
   root structure.

Hand lens (magnifying glass)—Optional but recommended. Makes the observations more interesting.

Water pitcher—You need something to water the seeds with.

B. Procedure

  1. Punch a small drain hole or two in the bottom of your cup(s). Drainage is very important to keep the seeds from rotting.

  2. Fill the cup(s) with soil. Pack it lightly.

  3. Plant two or three seeds in each cup. Do not plant too deeply.

  4. Water. A small amount might be better than a deluge. (This might be a variable worth investigating.)

  5. Start your observations. Do not forget to keep records.

C. Variations

You should do some experimenting with your plants. You may vary light, water, or temperature, but only one at a time. Remember variables? You may want to start your seeds between damp paper towels to see germination take place. Extra seeds may be started this way, and then cut open for examination. Be sure to record your variations and the observations you make.

D. Observing and Reporting

Prepare your report on separate sheets of paper, and remember to make it interesting. Be sure to include a section that gives your feelings and observations about this project. Did you like it or not? What would you do next time? How could you use this activity with children? Was it worthwhile?

☐ **Comments**

Activity 10.5b: Decomposition

Decomposition is one of the natural phenomena that people depend on very much but know very little about. "Ashes to ashes and dust to dust" refers to almost everything in nature, for after an object or organism has served its useful purpose, it eventually returns to the earth from whence it came. We accept this as a fact, but since most decomposition takes place slowly or out of sight, we are usually not aware of it taking place. Sometimes there is an exception to this rule, and we are made aware of it by our noses. But most decomposition takes place without our knowledge. In this activity, you will get the opportunity to experiment with decomposition and to become more aware of what materials will or will not decompose and how fast decomposition takes place. Do not be squeamish and overlook this activity; it is really quite interesting.

You will be given slightly more structure in this activity than you were given in "Seeds." It will still be necessary, however, for you to enhance the activity and your presentation by thinking of variations that you might try.

A. Equipment

For this activity, you will need four specific items and six or more items of your choice.

   1. *Container*—It should be at least 15 cm × 30 cm × 10 cm, or 6″ × 12″ × 4″ if you must use inches. This container should be reasonably sturdy and relatively watertight. A plastic shoe box is excellent, but a cardboard one can be used if you line it with aluminum foil.

One life science activity could be the study of decomposition.

2. *Soil*—Fill the container almost full. This should be dirt from outside, if possible, rather than commercial potting soil. Try to avoid beach sand or hard clay if you can. You might want to try different types of soil in different containers to see what happens.

3. *Small wooden stakes*—Ice cream sticks or small tree limbs work well to hold the paper markers that you will use to help keep track of your objects.

4. *Water*—It is important to keep the soil moist. Do not flood the soil, but keep it slightly damp. Do *not* let it dry out completely.

5. *Items of your choice*—You should choose a mixture of objects for this activity. Several possible choices are listed, and you should think of some of your own. Here are a few suggestions: a leaf from a tree; a sugar cube; or a piece of bark, fruit, meat, iron, aluminum, or plastic.

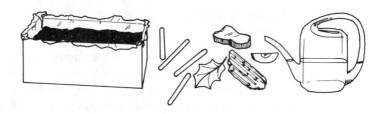

B. Procedure

This activity will take at least four to six weeks to complete; it cannot be hurried, so do not get impatient.

1. Fill the container to a depth of about 7 cm with soil.

2. Bury each of the items that you have selected about 3 cm deep in the soil.

3. Mark each item with a stick. Use a piece of paper or masking tape on the stick to identify each item. This step is very important. You must know what you buried and exactly where you buried it. This will be your marker.

4. Moisten the soil until slightly damp. Do not saturate the soil. Check periodically and add small amounts of water as needed.

5. Put the container in a safe place, preferably out of direct sunlight, and leave it undisturbed, except to add moisture.

6. Read some materials about decomposition while you are waiting. See if you can find out what to expect when you start to uncover what you have buried.

C. Observing and Reporting

1. At the end of four weeks or more—three weeks being the very minimum— check your box. Take a marker out, and uncover the item that you buried without disturbing the others. Record what you find. Do the same with the others.

2. Make a presentation for the activity. You will have to decide the format that you will use. Be imaginative. Use pictures, verbal descriptions, or whatever you can think of to make your presentation as informative and interesting as possible.

☐ Comments

Activity 10.5c: Snails

How many times have you seen a snail in an aquarium? Did you really look at it, or did you just see it? Have you ever wondered how a snail moves or eats? Probably not, because you never really had any interest in it. You know that snails are put into aquariums, but for what purpose? You watch the fish swim around, but does anyone ever watch the snail move around? You are going to, if you decide to do this activity.

This activity focuses on snails and their reproduction. You will learn to identify the parts of a snail, the function of each part, and where and how to locate snail eggs. You will also have to do some reading for background information. A unit of this type could be used to help the children learn to observe, to use a hand lens, to keep accurate records, and to understand that animals' offspring are like the parent animal.

You will be given a more structured format in this activity than was found in the two previous activities. Specific questions with blanks for answers are part of the activity. However, you can formulate and try other experiments and answer questions of your own making as a supplement to the activity, and you should do this to enhance the activity. Add these variations to your report. Allow yourself at least four or five weeks for the completion of this activity. You may finish it much earlier if your snails lay eggs quickly or if you find some eggs that have already been deposited on a leaf or in the container.

A. Equipment

Snail(s)—These may be obtained from a tropical fish dealer, a friend with an aquarium, or perhaps from your instructor. Try to get a large water snail. Very small snails are hard to observe.

Container—A mason jar with a top works very well. Punch holes in the top for ventilation. You need a top because snails can crawl out. Almost any container will work if it is transparent.

Snails in an aquarium are interesting organisms for observation.

Water—Important! Be sure to use aged water (water that has sat out overnight in a container) to eliminate the chlorine in the water and to allow the water to reach room temperature. Small quantities of water can be added as needed, but it is still best to age the water first, if possible.

Hand lens—This is an absolute necessity in this activity for close-up viewing. You should have one in your possession at all times since you never know when you might come across something interesting to look at. Your instructor may have one that you can borrow, or you may have to furnish your own.

Food—Snails do eat, and you have to feed them. A small piece of lettuce is a good start. You might experiment with a snail's eating habits or look up that information in a reference book.

B. Procedure

Use your hand lens to observe your snail; then fill in the first few blanks. This will help you get acquainted with the anatomy of the snail as well as some general characteristics. Read some information about snails. You will have to locate your own references. Then, based on some interesting facts that you read, develop and carry out an experiment with your snail. Meanwhile, look for snail eggs in your container. When you find some, mark them so that you can observe them, and record the information in the appropriate place on the chart. The following pages will constitute your report, but you can supplement what you write here with additional sheets if necessary.

1. Getting Acquainted with a Snail

   a. Draw a picture of your snail. Make it big enough to show the parts.

   b. Label the parts of your snail. Find the feelers (or antennae), shell, foot, eyes, mouth. Can you think of any other parts that need labeling? If so, be sure to label them on your picture.

   c. How do snails move around? Describe the motion.

   d. What happens if the snail is disturbed?

   e. Describe the habitat of your snail.

      What is the ideal habitat for your snail? (Answer this question before reading Part 2 of this activity.)

   f. How do snails eat? Draw a picture of the mouth; then describe how eating takes place.

2. Reading About Snails

   In this section, you will have to do some research. Go to the library and obtain some information about snails. You can use elementary- or college-level resources, but try to find out as much as you can about a snail. Here are some suggestions to guide your research:

   a. Describe a snail. How many different types are there?

   b. Identify your snail scientifically and by common name.

   c. Discuss the life cycle. How long does a snail live?

   d. What do snails eat?

   e. What is the ideal habitat for snails? What happens when conditions are not ideal?

   f. How do snails reproduce?

3. Baby Snails

   Most snails lay eggs, and if you can find them, you can watch them develop and hatch into baby snails. Look on the sides of your container or on floating material in the container. You will need a hand lens for this activity unless you have exceptional eyesight. Look for a small, clear mass, with a small black dot in each cell-like division. It will probably be a spot about one centimeter in diameter. This description fits some of the more common water snails but may not fit your snail. Refer to the research that you did in Part 2, "Reading About Snails," for more specific information. Keep a record of your observations using the chart in figure 10.1.

   a. When did you first start observing your snail? Color the day in green.

   b. When did you first see snail eggs? Color the day in red (a red-letter day). Describe what you found.

Week	Mon	Tues	Wed	Thurs	Fri	Sat	Sun
1							
2							
3							
4							
5							

Figure 10.1

c. What changes did you observe in the eggs between the time that you found them and the time they hatched?

(1)

(2)

(3)

d. When did the eggs hatch into baby snails? Color the day in pink and blue. Then describe the baby snails.

You have now studied a snail, and you may or may not have seen baby snails hatch. So what? Remember, the purpose of this activity is to give you some help in becoming a better teacher, not to make a "snail expert" out of you.

C. Reporting the Activity

Make your report on what you have done in this activity. Bring in any supplementary material you have to go with this written work. Make the presentation interesting and informative.

☐ **Comments**

Activity 10.5d: Mold

How many times have you found mold on something in your refrigerator or on a loaf of bread? What did you do? Did you look at it closely, or did you immediately throw it out? Generally, mold is not considered to be a very pretty sight, probably because it has spoiled something edible. But if you really take time to look at it, mold can be very pretty. It is also extremely important in our ecosystem.

In this activity, you will get a chance to make mold grow. There are many types of mold, and if you are lucky you will see several different kinds. You will be working with mold, but the real purpose of this activity is to give you some experience in experimenting and observing.

The format for this activity is slightly different from those of the other activities in that a structured reporting format is given to you, but you are on your own in devising your experiment. Some suggestions will be given, but you can also devise other experiments. You may need several weeks for this activity. The time factor will depend on how fast your mold develops. Allow at least two weeks from the time you first see mold. Do not forget that you should supplement this activity with some research in the library.

A. Equipment

Bread—The amount will depend on your experiments. Divide each slide into quarters for ease in handling. Commercial bread usually has preservatives that slow down molding, but it will work with a little time and care. White bread usually works best because the colors show up better.

Container—Plastic bags are excellent. You can tie them closed, and they are airtight. Small jars, such as baby food jars, also work well. You might find

The study of mold is a simple way to gain firsthand experience in experimenting and observing.

other containers that work just as well, but be sure that you can see both sides of your bread.

Water—Important! Bread needs to be moist (not wet) for best results. You might want to check this out as an experiment. Ten drops of water on a quarter of a slice of bread is recommended. Seal it to prevent evaporation. If the bread dries out, you will need to add more water.

Hand lens—This useful piece of equipment helps you see some interesting characteristics not usually seen with the naked eye. You might be able to learn some things about mold that you never knew before.

Other culture media—You might want to try growing mold on something besides bread, so you have a choice here. What will grow mold? How can you find out?

B. Procedure
  1. Cut a slice of bread into quarters. Put the pieces on a clean surface and do not touch them as you do this. Keep them as sterile as possible.
  2. Decide how you want to treat each one. Keep one untreated for a control. Suggestions:
     a. Rub one quarter between your hands or on your cheek.
     b. Rub one quarter on the floor or on the kitchen table.
     c. Rub one quarter on one of your textbooks.
     d. Your choice: use your imagination.
  3. Put 10 drops of water on each piece of bread.
  4. Put each piece into a plastic bag and seal. Attach a label to each bag describing the surface the bread was exposed to.
  5. Watch the samples and keep a record of what happens.
  6. Make up an experiment of your own and do it.
C. Experiment
  1. What was your variable?

  2. What were your controls?

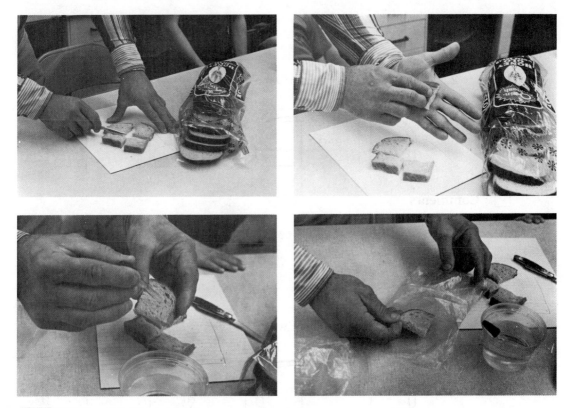

This teacher is preparing the pieces of bread for the mold experiment.

3. What problem are you trying to solve?

4. What do you think will happen?

D. Observations
Start your experiment and watch all of your samples daily. When you observe the first sign of mold on any of the samples, start recording the data for all of the samples. Data will be collected on the third, fifth, seventh, and tenth days after the first mold is observed.

1. How many days before you first saw mold?

On which sample?

2. Third day: Draw and color what you see.

☐ **Comments**

3. Fifth day: Draw and color what you see.

    a. How many colors do you see?

    b. Which grows the fastest?

    c. Which grows the slowest?

☐ **Comments**

4. Seventh day: Draw and color what you see.

BAG 1   BAG 2   BAG 3   BAG 4

    a. How many colors do you see?

    b. Has anything significant happened between your last observation and this one? What was it?

☐ **Comments**

5. Tenth day: Draw and color what you see.

BAG 1   BAG 2   BAG 3   BAG 4

    a. Which color seems to take over?

    b. What do you think will happen 5 days from now?

☐ **Comments**

E. Supplementary Work

1. Have you looked at the mold through a hand lens? Draw a picture of what you saw and describe it.

2. Have you done any reading about mold? What did you read?

What did you learn that interested you most?

3. What is one thing that you have learned about mold from your observations that you find most interesting?

4. Make any personal comments that you may have.

F. Experimental Variations

 1. Design an experiment that you could do with mold. Describe it briefly here, and develop it fully on a separate sheet. You need not actually do the experiment, unless (a) you want to satisfy your curiosity, or (b) your instructor wants you to.

 Description:

 Problem:

 Variable:

 Controls:

G. Use of the Activity in Teaching

 1. How could you use this activity in an elementary science classroom?

2. List three references that you could use with your elementary students. Give title, author, publisher, date.

a.

b.

c.

H. Present your results to your instructor. *Do not throw your mold away until after this check.* Your instructor might want to see it.

☐ **Comments**

Summary of Activity 10.5

This concludes Activity 10.5. You were given the opportunity to do some activities with living organisms. Each one used a different format so that you could learn different ways to present an activity to your students. Remember that children enjoy living organisms, large and small, and you can teach a great many things using this as a vehicle. In designing your own activities, think about the processes of science that you have used in these activities, as well as the subject matter (content). We hope you have had fun while you were learning and will construct activities for your students with this idea in mind.

SUMMARY

This chapter showed the importance of involving students in the learning experience. They are not passive vessels for us to fill, but active seekers of knowledge. Learning science through involvement is concrete. It is *doing,* not reading about or listening to, science. There are many ways to involve a child in science. You can start by doing the recommended activities in your textbook, but go further. Look beyond the textbook for ways to involve your students. Science fairs provide an opportunity to do a project and show it to someone. Special programs such as *Young Astronauts* provide resources and suggestions for you and your students. *Odyssey of the Mind* provides a challenge and an opportunity to compete against other students. Your local area is rich in resources. There are topics for study, resource people, and places to go in every locale. Projects involve everyone. There are ideas to develop, research to do, things to make, and a chance to share with others.

SUGGESTED READINGS

Several of these references are older but are included as they are good sources of science activities and projects.

Abruscato, J. (1988). *Teaching children science* (2nd ed.). Englewood Cliffs, NJ: Prentice-Hall.

Baybee, R., Peterson, R., Bowyer, J., & Butts, D. (1984). *Activities for teaching about science and society: Activities for elementary and junior high school.* Columbus, OH: Merrill Publishing Company.

Devito, A., & Krockner, G. (1980). *Creative sciencing* (2nd ed.). Boston, MA: Little, Brown and Company.

Friedl, A. (1986). *Teaching science to children.* New York: Random House.

Funk, H. J., Okey, J. R., Fiel, R. L., Jaus, H. H., & Sprague, C. S. (1979). *Learning science process skills.* Dubuque, IA: Kendall/Hunt Publishing Company.

Gega, P. C. (1986). *Science in elementary education.* (5th ed.). New York: John Wiley and Sons.

Harlan, J. (1988). *Science experiences for the early childhood years* (4th ed.). Columbus, OH: Merrill Publishing Company.

Headstrom, R. (1962). *Adventures with a hand lens.* New York: Dover Publications.

Henson, K., & Janke, D. (1984). *Elementary science methods.* New York: McGraw-Hill.

Hone, E., Joseph, A., & Victor, E. (1971). *A sourcebook for elementary science* (2nd ed.). New York: Harcourt Brace Jovanovich.

Jacobson, W., & Bergman, A. (1980). *Science for children.* Englewood Cliffs, NJ: Prentice-Hall.

Lunetta, V., Novic, S. (1982). *Inquiring and problem-solving in the physical sciences: A sourcebook.* Dubuque, IA: Kendall/Hunt Publishing Company.

Victor, E. (1980). *Science for the elementary school* (4th ed.). New York: Macmillan Publishing Co.

CHAPTER 11

Sciencing:
Looking into the Future

SCIENTIFIC LITERACY

A report released in 1989 by the American Association for the Advancement of Science revealed a core of scientific literacy goals for American students. A 26-member panel of educators and scientists compiled the report "Science for All Americans" for the Advancement of Science's Project 2061, named for the date of the next appearance of Halley's Comet.

The national council's recommendations address the basic dimensions of scientific literacy, which, in the most general terms, are:

- Being familiar with the natural world and recognizing both its diversity and its unity
- Understanding key concepts and principles of science
- Being aware of some of the important ways in which science, mathematics, and technology depend upon one another
- Knowing that science, mathematics, and technology are human enterprises and knowing what that implies about their strengths and limitations
- Having a capacity for scientific ways of thinking
- Using scientific knowledge and ways of thinking for individual and social purposes

These literacy goals are meant for all. They are not just for the students who plan science-related careers. Rather, all students are expected to be scientifically literate by the time they graduate from high school. In order to accomplish these ambitious goals, teams of 25 teachers in six different cities located across the country are developing model curricula.

This report supports the multitude of other studies done over the past several years that have pointed out the need for science reform. Nevertheless reform is slow, and students still graduate inadequately prepared to live in and contribute to an ever increasingly technological world. This reform must begin in the elementary schools, with you, the elementary teacher. This is where the foundation is laid for later science understanding. Elementary teachers must have a solid knowledge base from which to draw, coupled with an understanding of and support for the need for active involvement on the part of their students. Science activities that promote exploration, critical thinking, and doing—a sciencing approach—are necessary for achieving the challenge set forth in this report.

SCIENCING APPROACH

Sciencing is the term that has been used throughout this book to call your attention to the *process orientation* of science in the elementary grades. Sciencing is a verb—acting, doing, investigating—a means to an end. Sciencing is not

**Teachers must provide science experiences that promote
exploration, critical thinking, and doing.**

limited to memorizing facts. Teachers must recognize their role in providing
sciencing experiences that involve children in gathering, organizing, analyzing
and evaluating science content. The sciencing approach demands the active
participation of the student, with the teacher serving as guide and resource
person.

   In order for students to be actively involved in sciencing, they must develop
the ability to use the *tools* of sciencing, the process-inquiry skills. These skills
include observing, classifying, measuring, using special relationships, communicating, predicting, inferring, defining operationally, formulating hypotheses,
interpreting data, controlling variables, and experimenting. Process-inquiry skills
are basic to all later learning. They are not separate from science content; rather,
they provide the learner with the means to become actively involved in hands-on
science. Therefore, the focus of science in the elementary grades is on *how*
science content is learned. Verbal accommodation of science concepts, principles, and theories is simply not adequate. Children must experience these
concepts, principles, and theories concretely in order to truly understand and
build on them in later, more complex science experiences.

   The four components of science—process, content, attitudes, and technology—were identified and discussed in Chapter 1 to help you explore the nature
of science. These components provide structure and guidance for planning

The focus of science in the elementary grades is on *how*
science content is learned.

sciencing experiences for children. The nature of learning and the nature of the child were also examined. Findings in these two areas support the need for process-oriented sciencing. Teachers cannot ignore the impact of the learning process on the learning outcome. The domains of learning, the internal processes that enable a child to acquire knowledge, and the external factors that affect the learning outcome—all must be understood and utilized in making decisions about what to teach, how to teach, and when to teach. The work of Piaget, Erikson, and others provides considerable data to support the notion of providing hands-on, concrete learning experiences that help the child develop a sense of industry, productivity, and self-confidence. A sciencing approach provides those kinds of experiences.

In Chapters 2 and 3 you were introduced to the curricula materials that are available to help you in planning for successful sciencing experiences. These materials provide you with content information and activities. They also identify materials and equipment used in elementary science activities. The laboratory approach was the focus of Chapter 2. As you discovered in a laboratory approach, few reading materials are provided for the student. The child learns by doing. ESS, SAPA and SCIS are the best known laboratory programs. They are historically important because they represent the desire of science educators to break away from traditional textbook science. They are based on accepted child development theories and thus contain unique ideas and teaching strategies. As you reviewed these programs, you noticed that there were common bonds that produced similarities, but you found that they are all quite different also. Together they provide you with ideas, strategies, and activities that you can adapt to your own teaching.

In Chapter 3 the textbook approach was examined. You learned that science textbooks have evolved from "readers" to include the "concrete involvement" concept. Strengths as well as weakness of textbooks were identified. The major strength of the textbook is that it provides teachers and students with organized units of work that serve as excellent resources. The most serious weakness involves the reading of the textbook as a substitute for hands-on activities. Suggestions were provided to help you use the textbook effectively. These included using it as a reference or as a resource instead of allowing the text to dictate your program by following it page by page, from cover to cover. Additional help was provided by including some guidelines for reviewing and evaluating textbooks. Items to consider when reviewing a textbook included readability, content accuracy, presentation mode, and the inclusion of teaching helps or aids.

The sciencing teacher's role was examined in Chapter 4. You must see your role as one of active decision maker, manager, and coordinator, not just a recipe follower. Skillful management of your science program is necessary for meaningful science experiences. No program or textbook can be expected to fit the individual needs of all children.

The sciencing teacher's role is one of active decision maker, manager, and coordinator, not just recipe follower.

The teacher must be able to make adjustments and modifications in existing programs so as to use them in the best way possible. A teacher must be able to provide for individual differences of students whether they be cognitive, social, physical, or affective in nature. The physical environment in the classroom has both a direct and an indirect influence on the kind of learning that takes place. The teacher must be sensitive to the physical factors—lighting, room temperature, desk size, and distracting noises and sights—as well as classroom arrangements, both physical furnishings and grouping of students. The successful organization and storage of materials and equipment is vitally important to a science program. Identifying safety hazards and using techniques aimed at prevention of injury are also important factors in managing the physical environment. As a sciencing teacher, you must be aware of the profound effect, positive or negative, that you will have on those you teach. Therefore, you must be aware of who you are as a person and as a teacher, and of how you, your strengths, and your weaknesses fit into the whole scheme of providing successful learning experiences for children.

Systematic, creative planning is necessary for effective, successful learning experiences. Chapter 5 involved you in a step-by-step process of constructing a daily teaching plan that included behavioral objectives, teaching strategies, and methods of evaluation. The Hunter Model of effective instruction was integrated into the model provided in this chapter. This model is well known and provides guidance by giving teachers a step-by-step procedure for conducting lessons. However, the misuse of the model is causing many educators a great deal of concern.

Chapter 6 focused on various questioning strategies that help elementary teachers plan and integrate effective questions into their instructional strategy. The strategies based on the work of Bloom and Taba were examined. Guidance was also offered in responding to students' replies to higher level questions. Teachers must plan for and include questions that foster creative, thoughtful, high-level responses from their students. Teachers must be aware of the various instructional purposes for which they can use questions. Attention-getting, motivating questions can be used to begin a lesson. Questions can be structured to aid students in both data gathering and data processing. They can also help students reach closure in the final phase of the lesson. Questions can also be used to stimulate convergent or divergent thinking.

Areas of concern related to sciencing and special-needs students were explored in Chapter 7. Teachers must recognize the importance of science instruction for special-needs students. The hands-on process approach of sciencing is especially beneficial to special-needs students. Often the teacher must make modifications and adjustments for the various individual needs, and suggestions that were offered included (a) adapting reading materials, (b) adding extra training sessions for use of the equipment, and (c) building in multisensory experiences.

Current computer technology has opened an entirely new dimension in the classroom. The microcomputer came into existence in the late 1970s. Today the microcomputer can be found in most elementary classrooms. Chapter 8 provided some information about using the microcomputer in the classroom. Software is being developed at a phenomenal rate. Teachers must become computer literate and familiarize themselves with the various software that is available. The uses of the microcomputer are limited only by the imagination of the user. The computer is a tool of the teacher, a teaching aid that is still changing. But teachers must become comfortable with this new tool so that they can use it to provide meaningful science experiences.

Chapter 9 involved you in the metric system. Most science textbooks use metric measurement, and therefore teachers need to be familiar with it. The philosophy of "thinking metric" was stressed in this chapter. Learners need concrete experiences so that they can integrate the metric system into their way of thinking. Teachers must provide science experiences in which measuring helps describe and explain natural phenomena, thus providing a purpose for measuring. The metric system is really very simple to learn and use. The emphasis should not be on converting familiar English units to metric units or vice versa. Estimating before you measure is helpful.

Chapter 10 provided you with ideas for science projects. Long-term as well as short-term projects were suggested. Life science, physical science, and earth science content areas were included. All the suggested projects call for direct involvement of the learner. Science projects can be used to supplement your science program, to enrich it, or to become a complete program. This chapter also included information on science fairs. Whatever the size or format, a science fair gives students an opportunity to show their work and be judged on it. A science fair requires careful planning. First, you must consider the topic(s) for the fair. Will it be limited or open ended? How will you organize the entries? Rules must be established so that students know (a) when the projects are to be completed, (b) if the projects are to be done individually or in groups, (c) if the project is to be completed in class or at home and how much outside help is permitted, and (d) the criteria for judging or grading. The teacher must clearly explain the project to the students. Judging and awards must also be organized, keeping in mind the delicate balance between creating too much competition and rewarding good work.

This is an exciting time for science teachers. We have a great opportunity before us—providing students with science experiences that will lead to their being scientifically literate. It is hoped that this text has helped you gain insight into the teaching of elementary science and made you aware of your role in achieving a scientifically literate world for tomorrow.

This book began by asking the question "What is science?" How would you answer this question now?

ACTIVITY 11.1: SCIENCING ACTION PLAN

How will you continue to prepare for the exciting challenge of providing science experiences for students that will lead to their being scientifically literate? Prepare a Sciencing Action Plan for doing this. On a sheet of paper outline and describe how you intend to continue to prepare yourself for meeting the challenge of providing elementary students with valuable sciencing experiences.

A. Share your plan with a small group of your classmates. Ask for feedback and suggestions. Offer feedback and suggestions to others in your group as they share their plans.

B. Using the information gained from the interaction in the small group setting, refine and finalize your plan. Turn in your written plan to your instructor.

☐ **Comments**

REFERENCE

American Association for the Advancement of Science. (1988). Science for all Americans. In *Project 2061* (p. 4). Washington, DC: Author.

Supplemental Background Material for ESS, SCIS, and SAPA II.

A.1   ELEMENTARY SCIENCE STUDY (ESS)

Author: Developed by Education Development Center
                55 Chapel Street
                Newton, MA 02160

Publisher: Webster Division
                McGraw-Hill Book Company
                Manchester Road
                Manchester, MO 63011

                Currently Published by:
                Delta Education, Inc.
                P.O. Box M
                Nashua, NH 03016

History

In 1958, the Education Development Center was formed as a nonprofit organization devoted to the improvement of instruction in schools. It was originally funded by grants from the Alfred P. Sloan Foundation and the Victoria Foundation, and later by continuing grants from the National Science Foundation. In 1960, small-scale work began on a science program to be used from kindergarten through the eighth grade. This grew into the *Elementary Science Study* (ESS) materials. These materials were constantly revised, although no new units have been developed recently. New supplementary materials, based on research projects and classroom usage, were either incorporated into existing materials or published as supplemental materials.

The developers (there are no authors as such) of the ESS program came from all sectors of the scientific and teaching communities. Chemists, physicists, mathematicians, biologists, engineers, and teachers representing every level of public and private education from kindergarten to the university contributed to the program. Probably the most important developers were the school children who tried and criticized the ideas and materials presented to them.

There were several steps in the procedure for developing a unit. Someone, either a teacher or a scientist, would get an idea for a unit that he or she would then try in a classroom. Critiques by the users—teachers and students—helped either to discard the idea or to develop it further. After numerous critiques and rewritings, the final unit emerged for publication. Eventually, 56 units, which included physical science, biological science, earth science, and mathematics, were developed. Constant feedback by users helped keep the program current.

Conceptual Background

The conceptual framework for ESS was based largely on the work of Jerome Bruner (1961). He stressed that every topic can be taught in some intellectually honest form to any student. The secret is to match the level of the material with the level of the student. He also stressed the act of discovery, which he defined as obtaining knowledge for oneself by the use of one's own mind. The teacher is considered, by Bruner, to be the key to learning. It is the teacher who provides the opportunity for learning to occur. All of this suggests that a good science program should have a teacher who can use almost any topic to provide the students with the opportunity to discover.

Program developers, from the very beginning, insisted upon "units which satisfied two criteria: their scientific content is significant, and the activities, materials, and subject matter make children curious about some part of their world and encourage them to learn more about it."[1] Simply put, elementary science should be fun but should also be informative and accurate.

The following five major goals found in the ESS program reflect a blending of cognitive, affective, and psychomotor skills.

I. Rational Thinking Process
   A. Observation
      The student will develop skills in the identification of objects and their properties, changes in properties, controlled observations, and ordering of a series of observations.
   B. Classification
      The student will develop skills in classifying objects, actions, and phenomena.
   C. Measurement
      The student will demonstrate the ability to measure length, area, volume, weight, temperature, force, and speed.
   D. Data Collection and Organization
      The student will organize information pertaining to a scientific investigation, describe it verbally or graphically, and present the data in such a way that trends can be analyzed.
   E. Inference and Prediction
      The student will predict an outcome from a trend in data using inference, extrapolation, or interpolation.
   F. Variable Identification and Control
      The student will identify the independent and dependent variables in experiments and describe how variables are controlled and interrelated.
   G. Making and Testing Hypotheses
      The student will identify a scientific question, describe procedures to be used toward answering it, carry out the procedure, and evaluate the result.

H. Process Synthesis
   The student will utilize all rational thinking processes by designing and carrying out a scientific investigation and reporting its results.

II. Manipulation
   The student will be able to assemble and use the appropriate tools and apparatus needed to investigate a scientific problem.

III. Communication

A. The student will develop communication skills by describing orally, in writing, or nonverbally his conclusions about and reaction to science and its process.

B. The student will communicate scientific information by organizing and presenting data in graphic or mathematical symbols.

IV. Concepts
   The student will be able to recall and/or apply the knowledge of facts, theories, laws, structures, or concepts of science.

V. Attitude

A. The student will demonstrate individual curiosity and persistence in the study of science.

B. The student will participate willingly in science activities, accept evidence gathered through the scientific methods, and value critical thinking.

C. The student will develop self-confidence in the study of science by being involved in a variety of activities. Through personal participation in the ESS program activities, the students will develop a positive self-image and an "I can do it" attitude toward the study of science. (Aho et al., 1974, p. iv)

The conceptual framework can be summed up in a simple statement taken from the *Elementary Science Study, A Working Guide to the Elementary Science Study*:

> Basic threads of scientific investigation—inquiry, evidence, observation, measurement, classification, deduction—are part of the fabric of all ESS units, but they are not the whole cloth. No unit aims solely to teach individual skills, nor are any units intended primarily to illustrate particular concepts or processes or the like. Instead, by presenting interesting problems and real materials to explore, the units invite children to extend their knowledge, insight, and enjoyment of some part of the world around them. (p. 2)

Program Description

The ESS is different from most science programs in that it is composed of individual units. It is based on the assumption that all schools in Texas, for example, do not have the same needs as rural schools in Michigan, and neither group has the same needs as large urban schools. Therefore, why assume, as most textbooks do, that one program can fit all schools? Using ESS units, each school system can tailor a program to fit its own needs. There are 56 units (or modules, if you prefer) available, and each one can stand alone. Refer to the chart on the following pages for a list of these units and the wide array of subjects to choose from. Each is designed for a grade range rather than a specific grade level, making it adaptable to various grade levels or ability levels within a specific grade. This format allows flexibility in devising a program to fit individual needs.

The preferred implementation format is that of a total, tailored program for the school. An ESS consultant works with school personnel to help them decide which units would be appropriate to their curriculum. Usually five or six units per grade level are selected. Each teacher then teaches those units selected for that grade level. Sometimes a unit is used at a lower grade level and repeated in more depth at another level, but, generally, units used in one grade level are not used in others. Since an orderly, preplanned program is the goal of this format, all 56 units are not on hand at the school and available for random selection by individual teachers.

An alternative to the complete program implementation of ESS material is widely used. Individual teachers use various units to supplement existing programs. A teacher might prefer a complete program, but for various reasons, the change may not be feasible. A newer program might already be in existence, the school might be locked into a textbook program with little chance of change, the staff of the school may not want to change, or, as is so often the case, money may be limited. If so, teachers can obtain one or two kits and use them to supplement their materials. They can also modify their teaching strategies to that of the ESS program. Consequently, ESS can be used as a complete program or as a supplemental program, and it is effective either way.

Since ESS is a kit program, usually each unit is composed of a teacher's guide and the materials needed to teach the unit. However, this is an oversimplification because each unit is distinct. All units have a teacher's guide, but in some units, such as *Clay Boats* or *Tangrams,* the guides are very short and simple; whereas, in other units, such as *Small Things* and *Batteries and Bulbs,* the guides are very detailed and extensive. Some units, such as *Microgardening,* have supplementary manuals for reference, and others, such as *Bones,* have picture books for discussion. Materials included in each kit also vary. A general rule is that easily obtainable items are not included, but specialized or hard-to-obtain items are usually supplied.

ESS Units Grouped by Principal Subject Matter

UNITS	K	1	2	3	4	5	6	7	8	9
Biological Sciences										
Animals in the Classroom	▓	▓	▓	▓	▓					
The Life of Beans and Peas	▓	▓	▓	▓	▓					
Butterflies	▓	▓	▓	▓	▓	▓				
Eggs & Tadpoles	▓	▓	▓	▓	▓	▓	▓			
Growing Seeds	▨	▓	▓	▨						
Brine Shrimp		▓	▓	▓	▓					
Changes		▨	▓	▓	▓					
Pond Water		▨	▨	▓	▓	▓	▓			
Mosquitoes				▓	▓	▓	▓	▓	▓	▓
Animal Activity					▓	▓	▓			
Bones					▓	▓	▓			
Budding Twigs					▓	▓	▓			
Crayfish					▓	▓	▓			
Earthworms					▓	▓	▓			
Small Things					▓	▓	▓			
Tracks					▓	▓	▓			
Microgardening					▓	▓	▓		▨	▨
Starting from Seeds				▨	▨	▓		▨		
Behavior of Mealworms					▨	▨	▓	▨	▨	

UNITS

Physical Sciences

UNITS	K	1	2	3	4	5	6	7	8	9
Light and Shadows	■	■	■	■						
Printing	■	■	■	■						
Mobiles	■	■	■	■	■					
Musical Instrument Recipe Book	■	■	■	■	■	■	■	■	■	■
Spinning Tables		■	■							
Primary Balancing	▨	▨	■	■	▨					
Sand			■	■						
Structures			■	■	■	■	■			
Sink or Float			▨	▨	■	▨	▨	▨		
Clay Boats			▨	■	■	▨	▨			
Drops, Streams, and Containers				■	■					
Mystery Powders				■	■					
Ice Cubes				■	■	■	■			
Colored Solutions				■	■	■	■			
Whistles and Strings				▨	■	■	▨			
Batteries and Bulbs			▨	▨	■	■				
Optics					■	■	■			
Pendulums					■	■		▨	▨	▨

UNITS	K	1	2	3	4	5	6	7	8	9
Senior Balancing					▧	■	■	▧	▧	
Water Flow					▧	■	■	▧	▧	
Heating and Cooling						■	■	■		
Balloons and Gases						■	■	■		
Batteries and Bulbs II						■	■	■	■	
Gases and "Airs"						■	■	■		
Kitchen Physics							■	■	▧	▧
Earth Sciences										
Rocks and Charts				■	■	■	■			
Where is the Moon?				■	■	■	■			
Stream Tables					■	■	■	■	■	
Mapping						■	■	■		
Daytime Astronomy						■	■	■		
Mathematics										
Match and Measure	■	■	■	■						
Geo Blocks	■	■	■	■	■	■	■	▧	▧	▧
Pattern Blocks	■	■	■	■	■	■	■	▧	▧	▧
Attribute Games and Problems	■	■	■	■	■	■	■	■	■	▧
Tangrams	■	■	■	■	■	■	■	■	■	▧
Mirror Cards		■	■	■	■	■	■	▧	▧	▧
Peas and Particles				■	■	■	■	■		

A unit such as *Pond Water* contains only two items: a teacher's guide and a set of pond-water cards (enlarged photos of pond water microorganisms). On the other hand, a unit such as *Batteries and Bulbs* contains a teacher's guide, bulbs, wire, batteries, wire strippers, bulb holders, compasses, clips, brads, rubber bands, trays, students' prediction sheets, test cards, and project sheets. Replacement packages for the expendable items are also available. For the *Pond Water* unit, the teacher must supply everything; for the other unit, nothing. All of the units fit between these two extremes, but the best way to really see what is in each kit is to go through an ESS catalog. They may be obtained directly from McGraw-Hill or from your local Webster/McGraw-Hill representative. Check with your instructor to see if one is available for your use.

Note: The categories under which the units are listed do not encompass the total contents of the units. Activities in all of the units extend into and combine elements from a number of subject areas, both in science and other studies. A few units are essentially interdisciplinary. For information about each unit, see the unit descriptions. From *Elementary Science Study, A Working Guide to the Elementary Science Study* (Newton, MA: Education Development Center, 1971), pp. 8–9. Used with permission.

The cost of this program is comparable to other science programs. Some units are expensive and others are inexpensive, but a really balanced program will have some of each. The catalog gives an accurate cost analysis of this program.

Teaching Strategy

Probably the most important difference between traditional science programs and laboratory programs is in the teaching strategy employed. The teacher's role in the ESS program is very different from the traditional role. In ESS, the teacher acts as a guide and resource person. The activity is initiated through a discussion, a demonstration, or a question. Students then develop problems and devise

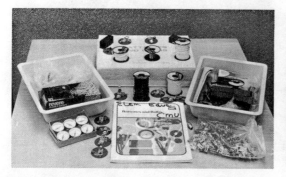

Two ESS kits.

solutions. The teacher raises questions but does not answer them. He may verify answers or ask leading questions to provoke thought or challenge data and solutions, but always he is trying to get the students to think and to understand what they are thinking about.

Students also have a different role in ESS science. They are involved participants, not passive receptors. What is learned depends upon what the student does, not on what she reads or hears the teacher lecture about. Students are expected to raise questions and then to devise methods of answering them. They develop experiments, collect data, and interpret their findings. Most importantly, students determine the direction and depth of each ESS unit. General directions are suggested by the ESS teacher's guide, and the teacher steers the investigations, but the curiosity and ability of the students are the final determinants of what is done with each unit. The flexibility of the program allows a curious student to explore any of the numerous problems that arise in the same unit. The students' active participation makes them partners in the learning situation.

The unit *Bones* illustrates how ESS is taught. There are three distinct portions of the unit: (a) "Mystery Bones," (b) "Bone Picture Book," and (c) "Bone Puzzle." To start the unit, the teacher takes one of the mystery bones, shows it to the students, and asks them to describe it and to speculate on it. Where did it come from? What kind of animal? Size? Function? As the various bones are presented, the teacher directs the discussion toward function and then leads the discussion to the bones in the students' bodies. They can feel them, try the different joints, or speculate on their use. In reality, they are developing an awareness of function. Then the "Bone Picture Book" is introduced. The students

This group is learning using the ESS unit *Bones*.

look at the pictures and discuss them. They learn through their discussions and observations that they can tell a lot about an animal from its skeleton. Without realizing it, they begin doing what a paleontologist does—taking a bone, studying its structure and size, and determining its function. Application of this knowledge is put to work in the third phase, "Bone Puzzles." A complete cat, mink, or rabbit skeleton is given to a small group of students. They are directed to lay it out in a tray in its natural order. There are no pictures or directions for them to follow. They must take each bone, determine its function, and place it in its proper place. This can be a real challenge, but one that fifth- or sixth-grade children can easily master if they have worked up to it. The teacher leads the early discussion and then acts as a consultant, but the students do the work. When they finish the unit, they have a good idea of what the skeleton does and how it works.

The procedure of discussion, speculation, experimentation, and application is carried out in virtually all of the units. The teacher acts as a guide and the students investigate. In ESS, learning is an experience shared by the students and the teacher. At this point, you might want to look at one of the teacher's guides. You will get the opportunity to review several when you start on the activities section of this program.

Evaluation of Student Performance

The ESS program is not a traditional type of program; therefore, it cannot be evaluated in the traditional manner. Pencil-and-paper exams on specific subject matter are not advisable since the focus of the program is on problem solving and "doing" science, not content. It is necessary to develop a different approach to students' evaluation. Actually, two methods of evaluation are recommended. The first, and most widely used, is the honest appraisal approach; and the second is the behavioral objective approach.

The honest appraisal approach is very simple. The teacher considers the student's effort, contributions, and performance; the teacher then makes a judgment as to what the student has learned from the experience. It is a very subjective evaluation, but probably the most honest, if the teacher takes the task seriously.

Many teachers do not feel competent to develop their own criteria and have considered this a weak area of the program. As a result, ESS developed a manual called *McGraw-Hill Evaluation Program for ESS* (Aho et al., 1974). It contains unit and evaluation objectives for each of the 56 ESS units and a sample check sheet for the teacher. This manual does help the teacher better understand the objectives of each unit and, for this reason alone, should be in his hands. Evaluation is simplified, or at least made more objective, since the teacher does have a definite list of objectives that can be marked "achieved" or "not achieved." This can establish a basis for an evaluation of the student. However, the teacher still must consider the honest appraisal in determining a grade or report because evaluation is not just a number on a test in the ESS program. It is an honest

By participating and observing, this teacher can make a good evaluation of each student's performance.

effort to determine what the child has accomplished during the course of the unit.

Implementation

Implementation of ESS is flexible. The program can be put into a school curriculum all at once or on a piecemeal basis. It does not need a stairstep approach, as is recommended with other programs. Sometimes a school will pilot some of the units one year to get the feel of the program, then completely implement the program the next year. Other schools may put in the whole program all at once. Still other schools will use one or two new units each year until they have developed a program. All three methods work equally well.

One major point needs to be stressed. ESS teaching is not like the traditional methods of teaching, and if it is to be successful, the teachers using it must be taught how to use it effectively. More than one new program has failed because the teachers did not know what was expected or what was to be accomplished. Therefore, it is imperative in this program, as in others that you will become familiar with, that some type of teaching training be provided. The publishers do not stress this point, but it is important. Preservice sessions to show the teachers how to use the materials before implementing the program or inservice sessions to answer questions as they use the materials are highly recommended by schools who have implemented the program.

Provisions for Special Education

One of the most recent additions to the ESS program is the *ESS/Special Education Teacher's Guide* (Ball, 1978). Thirty-one of the ESS units have been selected as appropriate for the child with learning difficulties. The guide was designed primarily for use by teachers of educable mentally retarded (EMR) students, but other teachers also will find it useful.

The units are divided into three categories—perceptual, psychomotor, and other appropriate units—and their formats follow the same sequence. First, the "Audience" section describes what type of child and grade range the unit is best suited. The "Overview" section describes the unit and explains what it can do for the child; then the "Objectives" section specifies the desired outcome. "Ways of Getting Started" offers suggestions to the teacher to help initiate the unit. This is followed by suggestions for "Keeping it Going." "Other Classroom Tips" provides extra help or insight into classroom management. An "Evaluation Checklist" is provided to help in evaluating the unit, and "Time Required" provides guidelines for scheduling. Finally, "Ordering Information" describes the ESS materials necessary for the unit.

Teachers who work with the exceptional child will find this addition to the ESS program very helpful. The flexibility of the ESS program makes it easily adaptable to all children.

Summary of ESS

The Elementary Science Study (ESS) is a nonsequential, modular science program based on the assumption that science can be fun as well as informative and accurate. Units in physical science, biological science, earth science, and mathematics are available for grade levels K through nine. Schools can choose units appropriate to their science program to develop a science curriculum tailored for their school. Teaching and learning are in partnership as the teacher and students work together to determine the direction and depth of the units. Little or no reading is required of the students since learning takes place by doing science, not by reading about it. Each unit consists of a kit of materials and a teacher's guide. The materials are for the students to manipulate, and the guide directs the teacher. As the program is not taught in the traditional manner, teachers need to learn how to use the material, and this can be done through a preservice workshop. The program is effective, but it does require a flexible, secure, and understanding teacher who is willing to let students learn.

A.2   SCIENCE CURRICULUM IMPROVEMENT STUDY

Authors: SCIS   The Science Curriculum Improvement Study
                        Robert Karplus, Director
                        University of California, Berkeley, California

               SCIIS   Herbert Thier, Robert Karplus, Chester Lawson, Robert Knott, and Marshall Montgomery (all were members of the original SCIS team)

               SCIS II   Lester Paldy, Leonard Amburgay, Francis Collea, Richard Cooper, Donald Maxwell, and Joseph Riley

Publishers: SCIS and *SCIIS* were originally published by
Rand McNally
P.O. Box 7600
Chicago, IL 60680

SCIS II was originally published by:
American Science and Engineering, Inc. (AS&E)
Education Division
20 Overland Street
Boston, MA 02215

All currently published by:
Delta Education, Inc.
P.O. Box M
Nashua, NH 03016

At the present there are three versions of the *Science Curriculum Improvement Study* on the market. In 1978, *SCIIS* and SCIS II were published to update and replace the original program. The original SCIS program will be discussed first, in detail, to give the background of the project and to describe the basic program. A section on each of the revisions will follow, explaining their similarities to and differences from the original version.

History

The *Science Curriculum Improvement Study* officially came into existence in 1962, but its beginnings go back to 1957. The central figure in the development of the SCIS program has been Dr. Robert Karplus, a theoretical physicist at the University of California at Berkeley. In 1957, Karplus's children entered the public schools, and he soon became interested in working with their science classes. At the same time, the National Science Foundation (NSF) showed a willingness to support the development of elementary-level science programs. The *University of California—Elementary School Science Project* (UC—ESSP) was born. As work continued, a new program began to take shape, and in 1962, it was separated from the parent (UC—ESSP) project. A new name, *Science Curriculum Improvement Study* (SCIS), was adopted.

    Karplus worked with the *Elementary Science Study* (ESS) program and with the *Minnesota Mathematics and Science Teaching Group* (Minnemast), gaining new ideas and insights that he would later incorporate into his own

This student is learning science from hands-on experience.

SCIS program. In 1963, Karplus began to choose the staff that would write, develop, and test the new SCIS program. This staff was composed of university professors, public school curriculum specialists, and classroom teachers. The classroom teachers were considered the indispensable backbone of the program development.

Much work went into the development of an SCIS unit. The SCIS *Final Report* describes 15 steps that were followed in the preparation of each unit. The three key teaching steps are underlined.

1. Brainstorming to create ideas for activities and investigations compatible with the conceptual organization of the units.

2. Laboratory investigation by project staff of phenomena and devices proposed for inclusion in the unit. Redesign or elimination of materials that appear too

difficult to manipulate, too hard to observe, or too unreliable using the equipment and facilities available in elementary school classrooms.

3. Exploratory teaching based on a teaching outline and discussion within the development team.

4. Preparation of a written draft for the trial edition teacher's guide and student manual. (Sometimes this step accompanied the exploratory teaching.)

5. In-house review, revision, and editing of the trial edition manuscript. Design and manufacture of trial edition equipment for about three hundred students.

6. Trial teaching in the Berkeley area by regular classroom teachers.

7. Evaluation of the trial teaching based on observer reports, teacher feedback, used student manuals, and testing of students.

8. Redesign of the conceptual organization, teaching activities, student manual, and/or equipment, accompanied by exploratory teaching, and leading to preparation of a new manuscript for the preliminary edition. (Some units were published in a revised trial edition and were cycled through steps 5, 6, 7, and 8 a second time.)

9. In-house review, revision, and editing of the preliminary manuscript.

10. Publisher's editing of the manuscript and apparatus maker's design of commercial equipment for the preliminary edition.

11. Field test of the preliminary edition in the five national SCIS trial centers.

12. Evaluation of the field test based on observer reports, recommendations of trial center coordinators, suggestions from trial center teachers, review of used student manuals, and testing of students. (The upper-grade units, which were not published in a preliminary edition, were field-tested in the final edition.)

13. Redesign of the conceptual organization, teaching activities, student manual, and/or equipment, accompanied by exploratory teaching, and leading to a new manuscript for the final edition.

14. In-house review, revision, and editing of the final-edition manuscript.

15. Publisher's editing of the manuscript and apparatus maker's design of commercial equipment for the final edition.[2]

All units, in final form, were available for distribution in the fall of 1971 with the completion of the *Energy Sources* unit for fifth grade. A kindergarten unit has since been developed. The project team has been disbanded, but several projects having roots in the SCIS programs have been developed or are in progress. Probably the most interesting is the *Science Activities for the Visually Impaired* (SAVI) program in which science activities are being adapted for use by visually impaired students. All copyrights for the SCIS program passed from the copyright holders (The University of California) to the public domain on January 1, 1978.

Conceptual Background

The conceptual framework for the SCIS program is basically Piagetian as adapted and applied to American education by Bruner and Stendler. These

authors stress that even though children go through sequential stages, they do not suddenly pass from one stage to another. For instance, they may be able to use conversation logic but may not be able to reason about abstractions without concrete analogies. Therefore, a science program for the elementary grades should provide a diverse program with emphasis on concrete experiences.

However, providing concrete experiences is not sufficient to ensure learning. The experiences must be presented in such a way as to build a conceptual framework that children can use with abstractions. In other words, through the concrete experiences, children collect data to interpret and act upon. As they learn to abstract, they are able to assimilate data collected by others. When this assimilation process occurs, it can be said that the children have developed "scientific literacy." This is the goal of the SCIS program.

Scientific literacy results from basic knowledge, investigative experiences, and curiosity. In the SCIS program, basic knowledge is gained through four major scientific concepts: matter, energy, living organisms, and ecosystems.

Matter is tangible. It can be perceived by the senses, and it has properties. Students become aware that matter can be identified by its properties and can change and interact with other matter.

Energy is not so tangible, but it can bring about change. Energy sources are studied as are energy receivers, culminating in the interaction that is a result of energy transfer.

Living organisms are plants and animals that are composed of matter and are able to use energy for their own benefit. This represents a combination of matter and energy.

Ecosystems are the interrelationships of all of the living organisms. This concept considers the diversity of organisms as they interrelate to each other. Every living organism is dependent upon other organisms (e.g., the carbon dioxide cycle illustrates this).

Investigative experiences are an integral part of the SCIS program. The theme might easily be "Don't tell me, I'll find out." Activities are the core of the program. Students are given problems to solve and the materials to solve them with. Furthermore, they are encouraged to investigate any new problems that may arise from the original investigation. Students ask themselves, "What would happen if . . . ," and then try to answer the questions.

SCIS also recognizes the importance of teaching the science processes of observing, describing, comparing, classifying, measuring, interpreting evidence, and experimenting. Four concepts—property, reference frame, system, and model—are used to help the student understand these processes.

Program Description

The SCIS program is designed as a complete K-through-six science program. It does not need additional texts, references, or other supplementary material. This does not mean that the teacher cannot use supplementary material.

There are thirteen units in the SCIS program. One unit, *Beginnings,* is an introduction to science for kindergarten. The remaining twelve units are divided into two groups, life science and physical science. There is one unit of each group for grades one to six. To best understand what is taught in each unit, here is information from a SCIS promotional brochure.[3]

Level 1—Overview

The first-year units have certain common objectives: to sharpen children's powers of observation, discrimination, and accurate description. The objectives are accomplished as children care for aquatic plants and animals, raise seedlings, and investigate the properties of a broad range of nonliving objects. The units can be taught in either order.

Life Science Concepts *ORGANISMS*		Physical Science Concepts *MATERIAL OBJECTS*	
organism	habitat	object	serial ordering
birth	food web	property	change
death	detritus	material	evidence

Level 2—Overview

In both second-year units the theme is change, observed as evidence of interaction or by the development of an animal or plant. The two units therefore require children to add the mental process of interpreting evidence to the observational skills they developed the first year. In their laboratory work children use magnets, batteries, wires, various chemicals, eggs, and fruit flies. The units can be taught in either order, or simultaneously.

Life Science Concepts *LIFE CYCLES*		Physical Science Concepts *INTERACTION & SYSTEMS*
growth	generation	interaction
development	biotic potential	evidence of interaction
life cycles	plant & animal	system
genetic identity	metamorphosis	interaction at a distance

Level 3—Overview

Children observe and experiment with increasingly complex phenomena as they build on the first two years of the SCIS program and move toward understanding the energy, matter, and ecosystem concepts. In the physical science unit children experiment with matter in solid, liquid, and gaseous forms, and make and analyze measurements. In the life science unit the children observe the interactions of various organisms within a community of plants and animals and consider the interdependence of individuals and populations within the communities.

Life Science Concepts		**Physical Science Concepts**	
POPULATIONS		*SUBSYSTEMS & VARIABLES*	
population	plant eater	subsystem	solution
predator	animal eater	histogram	variable
prey	food chain	evaporation	
community	food web		

Level 4—Overview

In the life science unit, children consider for the first time some of the physical conditions that shape an organism's environment. These investigations make use of the measurement skills and scientific background developed in the physical and life science units during the first three years. The physical science unit introduces techniques for dealing with spatial relationships of stationary and moving objects.

Life Science Concepts	**Physical Science Concepts**
ENVIRONMENTS	*RELATIVE POSITION & MOTION*
environment	reference object
environmental factor	relative position
range	relative motion
optimum range	rectangular coordinates
	polar coordinates

Level 5—Overview

The conceptual development of the SCIS program continues as examples of energy transfer are introduced in the physical science unit and of food transfer in the live science unit. Children apply the systems concept, the identification of variables, and the interpretation of data with which they have become familiar during the earlier years of the SCIS program.

Life Science Concepts		**Physical Science Concepts**
COMMUNITIES		*ENERGY SOURCES*
producer	community	energy transfer
consumer	food transfer	energy chain
decomposer	raw materials	energy source
photosynthesis		energy receiver

Level 6—Overview

The last year of the SCIS program contains both a climax and a new beginning. The life science unit integrates all the preceding units in both physical and life sciences as children investigate the exchange of matter and energy between organisms and their environment. The physical science unit introduces the concept of the scientific model and thereby opens a new level of data interpretation and hypothesis making. At the same time, the children relate matter and energy to electrical phenomena, acquiring a basis for their later understanding of the electrical nature of all matter.

Life Science Concepts ECOSYSTEMS	Physical Science Concepts MODELS: ELECTRIC & MAGNETIC INTERACTIONS
ecosystem	scientific model
water cycle	electricity
oxygen-carbon dioxide cycle	magnetic field
pollutant	
food-mineral cycle	

The key word to the SCIS program is *interaction*. As objects or living things interact with each other, change occurs. This change is natural and predictable. SCIS teaches children to look for change as evidence of interaction among objects.

The SCIS program is sequential. Each life science unit builds on prior units, as does each physical science unit. Students must have the information obtained at each level before they proceed to the next level. This brings up the question of transfer students. How do they fit into the program? Easily, says SCIS. The teacher works with the student, just as he would with any student who has been involved in a different program, and the student can quickly grasp the concepts and work patterns and move right into the class activities.

The materials for teaching SCIS science are in kit form. Everything needed to teach the unit is included, even live organisms and supermarket items. In each kit there are materials for 32 students, including students' manuals and a teacher's guide. A complete list of materials is included in the teacher's guide. SCIS kits can also be shared by several teachers, a practice sometimes necessary to cut back on costs. Refill kits are available so that each teacher has a set of consumable items but shares the basic kit.

The cost of implementing the SCIS program is comparable to any other program. Two kits for each teacher are obviously recommended, but kit sharing is an effective way to reduce costs.

Teaching Strategy

SCIS employs a unique teaching strategy called *exploration-invention-discovery*. It is a strategy well worth knowing and using. The teacher and the students assume different roles in each phase of this learning cycle.

Exploration consists of getting materials into the hands of the students, arousing their curiosity, and allowing them to find out what they have and what they can do with it. This is an often neglected, but vital, part of teaching. The students learn through their own spontaneous activities and experiments. The

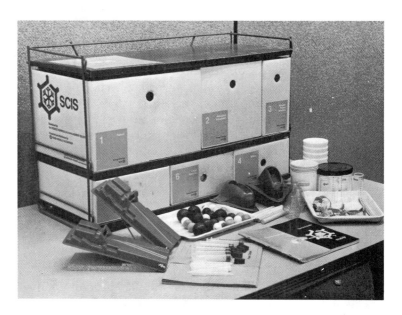

Materials for the SCIS Program are in kit form.

teacher's role in exploration is that of a guide who encourages the students but uses a minimum of specific instruction. The students are the active partners in this phase of the learning cycle. They handle the equipment, try out ideas, share ideas and results with each other, and develop new ideas of things to do. One thing to remember, though—it takes time for a student to explore. It is a process that cannot be hurried.

Invention is the structured teaching phase of the learning cycle. After the students have made some observations and discoveries in the exploration phase, they need help to develop the new concepts necessary for them to understand what they have learned. The teacher, acting as a resource and a guide, brings the class together to discuss their explorations and to "invent" the concept that they are working with. The teacher may ask questions, draw pictures on the chalkboard, lead discussions, or give verbal explanations during this phase. The student assumes the traditional role of learner but also participates in discussions by raising questions and suggesting answers. The goal is to use what was learned in the exploration phase to invent a concept previously unknown to the student.

Discovery can be called the application phase of the learning cycle. Students participate in activities that allow them to discover new applications for the concepts that they have just invented. The teacher may provide the applications or may depend on the students to furnish their own. The teacher again acts as a guide or resource person as needed. The students actively participate as learners by doing activities that reinforce the original concept.

As part of "Clues for Teachers" each SCIS teacher's guide explains these three phases of the learning cycle and describes where each can be found in the guide. Look for this when you review the teacher's guides in the activities section.

The teacher's guide tells you how to teach SCIS. Reading through the guide is, of course, the first step. Here you find a program overview; helpful hints on teaching called "Clues for Teachers"; a description of the kit listing all of the materials included; and the actual teaching unit, divided into chapters. For each lesson, the guide gives you an overview, materials needed and their location in the kit, advance preparation needed, and teaching suggestions. Follow the guide, and you will also follow the exploration-invention-discovery learning sequence.

Remember, take time to let your students *explore* before trying to *invent* the concepts. Then, let them *discover* new ways to use their newfound knowledge. This way, the students can gain investigative experience, learn basic knowledge, and keep curiosity alive, thus fulfilling the SCIS requirements for scientific literacy.

Evaluation of Students' Performance

SCIS is not a traditional, content-oriented program and cannot be evaluated as such. Written quizzes on factual material are not practical because there is very little factual information presented. The students work toward the goal of scientific literacy, and the teacher must be the judge of the progress being made toward that goal.

Evaluation in SCIS is considered to be an important ongoing process upon which the teacher bases teaching. Constant evaluation of each student's progress, based on a variety of feedback sources, allows the teacher to determine what each student is doing and what her needs are at the time. The teacher can then guide the student into discoveries that will bring her closer to scientific literacy.

Feedback is obtained in many ways. There are suggested feedback activities in each SCIS chapter to help the teacher determine what progress is being made toward the chapter goals. One of the easiest methods for obtaining feedback is simple observation of the students to find out their work habits, attitudes, and classroom participation. Written work on lab sheets and in the students' manuals also provides clues for the teacher.

SCIS also encourages the use of questioning as a means of evaluating pupils' progress. Convergent and divergent questions are recommended. Convergent questions tend to produce factual information and are effective when evaluating content knowledge. Divergent questions can be described as thinking questions. Various answers are possible, and each answer reflects the knowledge and interpretation of the student giving it.

Classroom teachers seemed to be happy with this more informal approach to evaluation, but school administrators were not. In response to the requests of the administrators, the SCIS project team developed a more formal evaluation program called *Evaluation Supplements*.[4] These areas are covered in this program: (a) students' perception of the classroom environment, (b) process content objectives, and (c) attitudes in science. Evaluation activities and charts for recording the evaluative outcomes are provided. Two other areas, general intellectual development and teacher's self-evaluation, were also considered important. But after field testing, these two areas were removed from the *Evaluation Supplements* and included in the *SCIS Teacher's handbook.*[5] Most of the teachers who use these supplements do not feel they add very much to their regular evaluation, and the increased record keeping takes time that could best be used for teaching. The *Evaluation Supplements* fulfill an administrative need but are not included extensively when SCIS is implemented.

In summation, the SCIS program is evaluated by teachers as they teach and by students as they learn. Conscious and subconscious observations lead teachers to adjust their approach to fit the needs of their students, and students respond based on their own perception of their needs and goals.

Implementation

The SCIS program can be put into effect all at once or in a graduated manner. The graduated approach allows a school system to implement the program over a period of two or three years. It also allows for the initial cost to be spread over a period of time. On the other hand, a school system may choose to implement the program all at once to get everyone involved in the program at one time. This way, no one is left out or has to wait for the new equipment. Variations of these implementation procedures can be devised to fit the specific needs of a school.

Some special considerations are required in the implementation of the SCIS program, but probably no more than should be made in the implementation of any new program. As mentioned in the ESS section, too often programs such as SCIS, SAPA, and ESS fail because the teachers are not properly prepared. They are simply given the materials and told to teach them without knowing what to do with the program, what to expect from it, or how to start. For this reason, preservice and inservice programs must be provided for the teachers who will be using SCIS. Help can be obtained from the publisher or from consultants recommended by the publisher.

SUMMARY OF SCIS

The SCIS program is a sequential program for grades one through six. A kindergarten program is also available. The program was developed by Robert Karplus under a National Science Foundation grant and was marketed by Rand McNally. Scientific literacy, defined as a functional understanding of scientific concepts, is the program's goal. The teacher uses the strategy of exploration-invention-discovery to develop scientific literacy. Two units per grade level, one on life science and the other on physical science, are taught, using the concept of interaction. Students are encouraged to learn through experimentation and to maintain their curiosity. There is very little material to be read by the student, but the teacher can encourage supplementary reading as necessary. The kit contains everything needed to teach the program, including supermarket items, consumable materials, live organisms, and reusable hardware. Refills are available for either kit sharing or for the beginning of a new year. Teachers need some training if they are to get the most out of the program. Delta Education now supplies the original SCIS program as well as the following two revisions.

THE RAND McNALLY SCIS PROGRAM

SCIIS was introduced in 1978 by Rand McNally to replace the original *Science Curriculum Improvement Study* materials that they had published since 1970. All of the authors of the new program were members of the original SCIS project team. The title *SCIIS* was chosen to indicate that even though the program was a revision of SCIS, the revisions were *internal* and not merely external appendages; hence the inclusion of the extra I (or Roman numeral II, if you prefer) in the title. *SCIIS* is not an acronym but is the title of the program.

SCIIS* is basically the same program as the original SCIS but with modifications that reflect the suggestions of the SCIS users. Almost all of the information concerning the conceptual background, program description, teaching strategy, evaluation of students' performance, and implementation given for SCIS can apply equally to *SCIIS.* Moreover, Delta Education, the current publisher, offers a conversion kit for changing SCIS kits into the *SCIIS* program.

The major changes found in the *SCIIS* program are as follows:

1. Earth science has been included in the program. The two major sequences have been renamed life/earth science and physical/earth science. New material has been added emphasizing the student's physical relation to the earth and the ecological nature of the earth.

2. Some activities have been changed. These new activities may incorporate hardier organisms than before, introduce new material not covered before, or be the result of suggestions of a better way to teach existing material.

3. The level-five physical/earth science unit has been expanded to include solar energy.

4. The level-five life/earth science unit adds *reproduction, the pyramid of numbers,* and *competition* to the original concepts for this level. Competition for food is stressed.

5. The level-six physical/earth science unit undergoes a major change, becoming *Scientific Theories.* Color, electricity, magnetic field, and light rays are covered.

6. The teacher's guide has been redesigned. It is larger and incorporates many more sketches to help the teacher understand the text material or equipment being used.

7. An appendix in the teacher's guide contains evaluation procedures for each chapter. This is completely new material.

8. *Extending Your Experience* (EYE) cards are a new addition to each unit. These cards provide activities to supplement the regular activities. Designed to be used by the individual student, the cards can provide enrichment, remediation, or extension of the basic topic. The teacher's guide provides suggestions for their use.

9. The design and packaging of the program have been modified for easier storage and handling.

10. Supply sources, delivery systems, and teachers' services have been improved.

In summation, *SCIIS* was designed as an improved version of the basic SCIS program. New material, new packaging, and improved support add to a solid core program.

THE AMERICAN SCIENCE AND ENGINEERING SCIS II PROGRAM

The federally funded SCIS program became public domain when the copyright expired in 1978. American Science and Engineering (AS&E) had been the exclusive designer and producer of all of the materials (except printed material) used in the SCIS programs during the copyright years. Because of their experience with the SCIS program, it was only natural that they would start publishing and marketing SCIS material when the copyright expired.

SCIS II uses the original SCIS program as a foundation, retaining the basic conceptual background, program description, teaching strategy, evaluation of students' performance, and implementation that describe the SCIS program. Its authors are respected science educators who have had extensive experience in training teachers to use SCIS as well as in implementing and managing SCIS in their own classrooms. Their experiences led them to turn SCIS into a more manageable program for the classroom teacher. A conversion kit allows present SCIS users to change to the newer SCIS II program with a minimum of expense.

The major changes or innovations in the SCIS II program are as follows:

1. The teacher's guide has been changed to emphasize classroom management. This change gives teachers help where they need it most.

2. New content has been introduced. The addition of earth science in the fourth and sixth levels is the most noticeable change. One or more additional concepts are introduced in each unit of the program.

3. The title of the fourth-level physical science unit has been changed to *Measurement, Motion, and Change*. The concepts of reference frame, change, distance, direction, and measurement were added to reflect the inclusion of earth science at this level.

4. The title of the sixth-level physical science unit has been changed to *Modeling Systems*. The concepts listed for this unit are electricity, model, magnetism, circuit, electrical energy, air temperature, barometric pressure, and atmosphere.

5. Activity cards are provided for use by individuals or small groups. These cards provide additional activities for enrichment and relate the science lesson to math and language arts.

6. The students' manuals have been replaced by duplicating master booklets. This cuts cost and simplifies classroom management of the materials.

7. The SCIS terms *exploration-invention-discovery*, used in describing the learning cycle, have been replaced in SCIS II by the terms *exploration-concept-application*. The learning cycle is still the same, but different terms describe the same step.

In summation, the AS&E SCIS II program is the basic SCIS program modified to include earth science and to make it more manageable for teachers. SCIS II is now available from Delta Education.

A.3   SCIENCE . . . A PROCESS APPROACH II

Author:	Developed by the Commission on Science Education of the American Association for the Advancement of Science (AAAS) 1515 Massachusetts Avenue, N.W. Washington, DC 20005
Publisher:	Originally published by: Ginn and Company 191 Spring Street Lexington, MA 02171 (Discontinued publication in 1981)
	Currently published by: Delta Education, Inc. P.O. Box M

History

In 1961, a group of science teachers and scientists working with staff members of the Commission on Science Education of the American Association for the

Advancement of Science (AAAS) undertook the task of developing a new elementary science program. The National Science Foundation encouraged the endeavor by providing necessary financial support. The format of the new program was the focal point of early discussions. Several proposals such as "major themes," or "selected topics for each grade," or "concrete and familiar" were suggested, but the decision was made to go with the teaching of the scientific processes. The name of the new program, *Science... A Process Approach* (SAPA), reflects this decision.

After the preliminary discussions and other basic decisions regarding the format, the hard work started. Writing teams were established, and they held four summer workshops to write the program. Trial centers were set up across the nation for field testing. After six years of writing, testing, and revision, the SAPA program was ready for public use. As the program was used and time passed, the need for a revision became evident. Important changes in science education, such as emphasis on teaching flexibility and the need for individualized learning, contributed to the need for revision, as did the development of a deeper national concern for the environment. The AAAS Commission on Science Education again accepted the challenge and undertook the task of revising the program. This time, Ginn and Company provided the financial support.

Input for the revision came from many areas. The major contributors were those classroom teachers who had used the program. Their experiences were the source of invaluable insight and suggestions. Trial centers also provided information and suggestions based on their experiences with the material. The Eastern Regional Institute for Education made several studies that helped provide concrete data. Finally, several special conferences and symposia were held to obtain additional ideas and suggestions. When the consulting, rewriting, and trial testing were completed in 1975, SAPA II was ready for use.

This preservice teacher is preparing a SAPA II lesson.

Conceptual Background

The major factor in establishing the conceptual framework of the SAPA II program was the decision to use science processes as the basis of the program. The traditional approach to teaching science is to use subject matter (content) as the base, bringing in the process skills as they are needed. SAPA II is unique in that it reverses this procedure. The process skills form the base of the program, and content is introduced as needed. The assumption is that if elementary children learn the processes, they can understand the content.

All together, 13 processes were identified to be used in the program. In the early grades, K through three, the following eight basic processes are developed:

1. *Observing*—Children learn to use their five senses to determine properties of an object.

2. *Using Space/Time Relationships*—Children learn that five categories (shapes, direction and spatial arrangement, motion and speed, symmetry, and rate of change) are used to describe spatial relationships and their change with time.

3. *Classifying*—Children learn to use classification schemes to impose order on collections of objects or events.

4. *Using Numbers*—Children learn that numbers are basic to science. Numbers allow scientists to make measurements, classify objects, and order objects.

5. *Measuring*—Children learn that they can quantify their observations by using the proper measuring device. Metric measurement is used exclusively.

6. *Communicating*—Children learn that they can use graphs, diagrams, maps, and mathematical equations as well as oral or written words to communicate.

7. *Predicting*—Children learn to make predictions based on observations, measurements, and certain inferences. They also learn the difference between a valid prediction and a guess.

8. *Inferring*—Children learn that an inference is an explanation of an observation and that more than one inference may be made in order to explain an observation.

After the child has learned to use the basic processes in the early grades, she is introduced to the integrated processes in the fourth, fifth, and sixth grades. There are five processes in this group.

1. *Controlling Variables*—Children learn to identify variables and then control them to manage the conditions of an experiment.

2. *Interpreting Data*—Children learn to use data to make predictions, inferences, and hypotheses. They also learn to collect data.

3. *Formulating Hypotheses*—Children learn to use observations and inferences to formulate generalizations (hypotheses) about all objects or events of the same class. They also learn to test their hypotheses.

4. *Defining Operationally*—Children learn to define terms in the context of their own experiences and to work with a definition rather than memorize it.

5. *Experimenting*—Children learn to use all of the previous processes to formulate and answer a problem.

The program's developers felt that as these process skills were mastered, the student would develop intellectual skills that could be used in all areas of science. What better way for a student to learn science than to do what a scientist does?

Underlying the development of the program were five criteria considered to be basic to a quality science program. Every effort was made to make the new program meet these criteria. From the SAPA II *Program Guide,* here are the criteria:

1. Science in the elementary school must contribute to the general education of every child.

2. A viable science program must enable children to reach a high level of achievement.

3. Children must be challenged by asking them frequently to think, to reason, and to invent.

4. Children's experiences must be broadened into many fields of science.

5. A good instructional program in science must be realistic in developing intellectual skills.[6]

A third factor also contributes to the SAPA II program. The developers felt that all children should be able to experience success and that major goals could be reached if pursued one step at a time. This thinking led to the establishment of a sequential program based on several small steps, each with objectives that could be easily achieved. The goal is for 90 percent of the students to achieve 90 percent of the objectives.

What about the graduates of the SAPA II program? The end products are the real proof of the program. What should the students be able to do when they have completed all of the modules? The goals of the program state that the graduates should be able to do the following:

a. Apply a scientific approach to a wide range of problems, including social ones, distinguishing facts from conjectures and inferences, and identifying the procedures necessary for verification of hypotheses and suggested solutions.

b. Acquire an understanding of the sciences he or she will pursue in junior and senior high school more rapidly and with less difficulty than would otherwise be possible.

c. Identify each of the following in a printed or oral account of a scientific experiment: the question being investigated; the variables manipulated, controlled, and measured; the hypothesis being tested; the relationship of such a test to the results obtained; the conclusions that can be legitimately drawn.

    d. Infer, where necessary, the question being investigated and the elements of scientific procedure in an incomplete account of a scientific experiment, such as might appear in a newspaper.

    e. Design and, under certain conditions, carry out one or more experiments to test hypotheses relevant to a problem, providing the problem is amenable to scientific investigation and the content is within the child's understanding.

    f. Show appreciation of, and interest in, scientific activities by choice made in reading, entertainment, and other kinds of leisure-time pursuits.

    g. Develop values, attitudes, value systems, and value judgment criteria not only applicable to science-related experiences but transferable to day-to-day experiences throughout life.[7]

In summation, the conceptual framework of the SAPA II program can be described as a conscientious effort to develop a quality science program based on the systematic teaching of the process skills.

Program Description

SAPA II is unique in that it is a sequential, but modular, program based on the assumption that all children, no matter where they may live, need to learn the processes of science. If school personnel choose to use this program, they are committed to the process philosophy for all grade levels up through the sixth grade. It cannot be used piecemeal because each activity builds on previous activities. However, there is an exception. If teachers cannot, or do not, want to change their science program but do want to include some process development, they can use some of the SAPA II modules to supplement their program. A module can be described as a unit of work involving a specific phase of a specific scientific process. In SAPA II, the unit of work consists of several, usually three or four, activities. The specific process taught may be any of the eight basic skills or five integrated processes. The specific phase refers to the concept of logical progression. Each process is taught in several steps, each step building on the step previously presented.

    Each module is designed to achieve specific objectives. There may be as few as one or as many as five, but every objective is important in the overall sequence of the program. To keep the objective simple and easily attainable, SAPA II uses 15 modules for each grade level, or a total of 105 modules. A list of these modules appears on pages 385–387.[8] As you look at this list, keep the following in mind:

1. Each module teaches only one process.

2. There are 15 modules per grade level.

3. The sub-letter beside each process denotes the number of that process; for example, *c* means that this is the third module of the particular process.

4. Modules in each stage can be taught in any order, but each stage must be completed before going on to modules on the next stage.
5. Ideally, modules should be taught in numerical sequence.
6. Asterisked numbers indicate the better modules for individualized usage.

Modules for SAPA II

Grade Level	Stage	Module No.	Process	Module Title
K	I	1	Observing/a	Perception of Color
		*2	Space/Time/a	Recognizing and Using Shapes
		*6	Space/Time/b	Direction and Movement
		7	Observing/d	Perception of Taste
	II	3	Observing/b	Color, Shape, Texture, & Size
		5	Observing/c	Temperature
		8	Measuring/a	Length
	III	4	Classifying/a	Leaves, Nuts, & Seashells
		9	Using Numbers/a	Sets and Their Members
		*12	Space/Time/d	Three-Dimensional Shapes
		*11	Observing/e	Listening to Whales
	IV	10	Space/Time/c	Spacing Arrangements
		13	Using Numbers/b	Numerals, Order, & Counting
		14	Classifying/b	Animals & Familiar Things
		15	Observing/f	Perception of Odors
1	V	*16	Classifying/c	Living & Nonliving Things
		17	Observing/g	Change
	VI	18	Observing/h	Using the Senses
		19	Observing/i	Soils
		20	Using Numbers/c	Counting Birds
		23	Measuring/b	Comparing Volumes
		25	Communicating/b	Introduction to Graphing
	VII	*21	Observing/j	Weather
		22	Communicating/a	Same but Different
		*24	Measuring/c	Metric Lengths
		*26	Measuring/d	Using a Balance
	VIII	27	Communicating/c	Pushes and Pulls
		28	Observing/k	Molds & Green Plants
		29	Space/Time/e	Shadows
		30	Using Numbers/d	Addition Through 99

Modules for SAPA II (continued)

Grade Level	Stage	Module No.	Process	Module Title
2	IX	31	Communicating/d	Life Cycles
		*32	Classifying/d	A Terrarium
		33	Inferring/d	What's Inside
		*34	Measuring/e	About How Far?
	X	36	Observing/l	Animal Responses
		37	Measuring/f	Forces
		39	Measuring/g	Solids, Liquids, and Gases
		*40	Inferring/b	How Certain Can You Be?
	XI	35	Space/Time/f	Symmetry
		38	Predicting/a	Using Graphs
		42	Classifying/e	Sorting Mixtures
		43	Communicating/e	A Plant Part That Grows
	XII	41	Measuring/h	Temperature & Thermometers
		44	Predicting/b	Surveying Opinion
		*45	Space/Time/g	Lines, Curves, & Surfaces
3	XIII	*46	Inferring/c	Observations & Inferences
		47a	Communicating/f	Scale Drawings
		*48	Predicting/c	The Bouncing Ball
		49	Measuring/i	Drop by Drop
	XIV	47b	Communicating/g	A Tree Diary
		*50	Predicting/d	The Clean-Up Campaign
		54	Measuring/j	Static & Moving Objects
	XV	52	Inferring/d	Plants Transpiring
		53	Predicting/e	The Suffocating Candle
		55a	Observing/m	Sprouting Seeds
		55b	Observing/n	Magnetic Poles
	XVI	51	Space/Time/h	Rate of Change
		56	Classifying/f	Punch Cards
		58	Inferring/e	Liquids & Tissue
	XVII	57	Communicating/h	Position & Shape
		*59	Using Numbers/e	Metersticks, Money, & Decimals
		60	Space/Time/i	Relative Motion
4	XVIII	*61	Inferring/f	Circuit Boards
		62	Controlling Variables/a	Climbing Liquids
		63	Interpreting Data/a	Maze Behavior
		65	Interpreting Data/b	Minerals in Rocks
	XIX	64	Defining Operationally/a	Cells, Lamps, Switches
		*66	Controlling Variables/b	Learning & Forgetting
		67	Interpreting Data/c	Identifying Materials
		70	Formulating Hypotheses/a	Conductors & Nonconductors

Modules for SAPA II (continued)

Grade Level	Stage	Module No.	Process	Module Title
	XX	*68	Interpreting Data/d	Field of Vision
		69	Defining Operationally/b	Magnification
		*71	Controlling Variables/c	Soap & Seeds
		*74	Defining Operationally/c	Biotic Communities
	XXI	72	Controlling Variables/d	Heat Rate
		73	Formulating Hypotheses/b	Solutions
		75	Intepreting Data/e	Decimals, Graphs, & Pendulums
5	XXII	76	Interpreting Data/f	Limited Earth
		77	Controlling Variables/e	Chemical Reactions
		78	Formulating Hypotheses/c	Levers
	XXIII	80	Defining Operationally/d	Inertia & Mass
		*83	Formulating Hypotheses/e	Chances Are
	XXIV	*79	Formulating Hypotheses/d	Animal Behavior
		81	Defining Operationally/e	Analysis of Mixtures
		82	Controlling Variables/f	Force & Acceleration
		*85	Interpreting Data/h	Contour Maps
	XXV	84	Interpreting Data/g	Angles
		89	Defining Operationally/g	Plant Parts
		90	Interpreting Data/k	Streams & Slopes
	XXVI	86	Interpreting Data/i	Earth's Magnetism
		87	Interpreting Data/j	Wheel Speeds
		*88	Defining Operationally/f	Environmental Protection
6	XXVII	*91	Defining Operationally/h	Flowers
		92	Formulating Hypotheses/f	Three Gases
		*95	Interpreting Data/l	Mars Photos
	XXVIII	93	Defining Operationally/i	Temperature & Heat
		94	Controlling Variables/g	Small Water Animals
		96	Experimenting/a	Pressure & Volume
	XXIX	97	Experimenting/b	Optical Illusions
		*98	Experimenting/c	Eye Power
		99	Experimenting/d	Fermentation
	XXX	100	Experimenting/e	Plant Nutrition
	XXXI	*101	Experimenting/f	Mental Blocks
		102	Experimenting/g	Plants in Light
	XXXII	103	Experimenting/h	Density
		104	Experimenting/i	Viscosity
	XXXIII	105	Experimenting/l	Membranes

In SAPA II, there is a kit for each module. Each kit contains most of the materials needed to teach the module and an instruction booklet. Such items as living organisms and perishable materials are not included. The teacher must arrange to purchase them locally as well as the more common items usually found around the classroom, such as construction paper, rubber bands, and scissors. On the other hand, most of the necessary laboratory materials, such as containers, metersticks, metric rulers, washers, chemicals, and thermometers, are included. Printed material furnished in the kit includes pictures, charts, transparencies, and 30 nonconsumable students' booklets. Spirit duplicator masters are also furnished so that the teacher can reproduce necessary worksheets. Some items are consumable and must be replaced as they are used. If kits are shared, each teacher will need extra packages of the consumables for the classroom. These are available for reorder.

The contents of a SAPA II kit vary with the topic. Some modules are supplied with many materials; whereas, other modules do not need much. For example, module 46, *Observations and Inferences,* needs only a small amount of equipment. It has 30 cartoon booklets, 3 wall charts, 10 footprint cutouts, 30 worksheets, and 5 nutcrackers. On the other hand, a module like module 103, *Experimenting,* needs more equipment: modeling clay; equal arm balances; five sets of gram masses; graduated cylinders; iron, lead, and aluminum samples; marbles; graph paper; and two kinds of booklets. The best way to know exactly what a kit provides is to look at some of the instruction booklets. You will have the opportunity to do this when you start the SAPA II activities.

The module instruction booklet is a unique feature of the program. It is a guide that tells the teacher what the child is expected to learn, why it is important, how to teach it, what materials are needed, and how to find out if the child learned what was taught. The teacher follows the booklet closely or uses it as a guide, depending upon her experience and the needs of the students. Theoretically, if the teacher follows the instructions in the booklet, 90 percent of the students will achieve 90 percent of the stated objectives for the module. Each instruction booklet contains the following information:

1. *Objectives*—Those minimal behaviors expected of each student who completes the module.
2. *Sequence chart*—Shows the prerequisites for the module as well as what comes next. (A large planning chart is available to show where each segment fits into the overall program.)
3. *Rationale*—Background information and sometimes advice on the module.
4. *Vocabulary*—New words that will be used in the module.
5. *Instructional Procedure*—The actual teaching strategy. (Included are an introduction, several activities, and a material list for each activity.)
6. *Generalizing Experiences*—Activities designed to allow the student to relate what was learned to different situations.

7. *Appraisal* (Modules 1–60)—A group activity used to determine if the students have met the objectives.

8. *Group Competency Measure* (Modules 61–105)—A group activity used to determine if the students have met the objectives.

9. *Competency Measure*—Individual testing procedure using test items directly related to each objective.

   The cost of the SAPA II program is comparable to other science programs. You can order the program as individual modules, by grade level, or as a total system. The cheapest way, of course, is to implement the total program. Remember that there is a yearly maintenance cost for expendable items as well as additional costs for living materials and perishable items. An actual cost breakdown can be obtained from Delta Education, Inc., Box M, Nashua, New Hampshire 03061.

Teaching Strategy

The SAPA II teacher acts as a guide, instructor, evaluator, and resource person. As a guide, it is the teacher's task to keep the students moving toward the goals of the program. She may allow them to wander a little, exploring side topics, but she keeps them moving toward their goals. This is done by asking questions, pointing out new information, presenting new material, or guiding discussions. As the instructor, she must also act as an evaluator. In this role, she keeps a progress record for each child and determines what needs to be done next. The teacher, as a resource person, answers students' questions or sends them to appropriate sources, such as charts or books, or helps them set up an experiment.

   The students also have a role in SAPA II. They are learners and, as such, are actively involved in the learning process. They must learn the process skills for themselves, with the teacher's help. Consequently, they do activities, discuss their ideas, and question what they have done. Faster students participate in optional activities, extending their understanding. Students also are involved in peer teaching, helping each other when necessary. They get their hands on the program, use the teacher when necessary, and learn. Obviously, students must be motivated to want to assume this role. SAPA II thinks that involvement in, and success with, the program provide the challenge and rewards needed to provide this motivation.

   How is a SAPA II module taught? The first step, of course, is for the teacher to read over the material in the instruction booklet, becoming familiar with the objectives, the activities, and the appraisal. The instruction booklet gives explicit instructions as to what to do and how to proceed. If necessary, she might also go through the activities to see if there are any problems.

To teach a module, the teacher should follow the directions in the instruction booklet as to how to introduce the unit and how to proceed through the activities. The booklet gives explicit directions: "Do this, then ask these questions," or "Have the students do that, then ask for their responses." Look for this when you review the SAPA II booklets in the activities section. The teacher can vary the approach or the questions asked if a change seems warranted.

After teaching the module, the teacher evaluates the students. Two evaluation activities are given in the instruction booklet—an appraisal and a competency measure—with specific directions. The results are recorded, and the module is completed. Teacher and students are ready to move on to the next module.

Evaluation of Students' Performance

The evaluation of students' performance is very structured in SAPA II. Specific behavioral objectives are given at the beginning of each module and are tested for at the end. If the students can perform them, they have achieved; if not, they have not achieved. Actually, this is an oversimplification of the suggested method of evaluating students' performance, but it is the central idea.

The teacher must do several things to evaluate a student's performance. She has to make anecdotal notes during the lessons and administer the "Appraisal Activities" and/or "Group Competency" measures. Individual records must also be kept for each student. This is usually done on SAPA II "Tracking Cards." These cards provide a continuous record of each student's performance from the beginning to the completion of the program.

Specific recommendations for evaluating students' performance are given by SAPA II in the *Program Guide*:

1. Use the *Sequence* chart on the first page of each *Instruction Booklet* to determine whether or not the children have the prerequisite skills; if not, provide the appropriate DEBUT modules, or review the module objectives identified as prerequisite.

2. After the modules have been taught, administer the *Appraisal* activity (Modules 1–60) or the *Group Competency Measure* (Modules 61–105) to measure the achievement of objectives by a group of children.

3. Administer the *Individual Competency Measure* to a small group of pupils for each module. In selecting students, you may wish to include some from the high- and some from the low-achiever groups and some from the group that you feel least certain about. This evaluation device may be waived if evidence warrants it.

4. Keep an individual profile sheet for each pupil, even though you do not have a competency score on each objective for each pupil. Many tasks can be scored from your observation of investigations by individuals and small groups of children, without use of the *Competency Measures. Tracking Cards* can be used here.

5. Keep an anecdotal record or diary of significant events in your teaching (failures as well as successes), including the involvement of individuals by name.

6. Administer check-point tests and end-of-the-year science tests if you like. Choose tests that measure individual performance rather than memory of facts.

7. Report to parents on the progress of their children in achieving competence in the processes of science. *Tracking Cards* may be discussed in the conferences with parents. In the periodic reports of student progress made in most schools, inclusion of statements about skills in the processes of science would be interesting and helpful to parents.

8. Encourage parents to report their children's comments in science experiences in school.

9. If your school requires reporting by letter or numerical grade, the *Tracking Cards* will provide an adequate basis for determining the children's grades. Devise scales that are appropriate for your school and for your groups of children.

10. Finally, the anecdotal record referred to in Step 5 can serve as a basis for describing student interest, attitudes, and character development. The use of varied instructional modes in SCIENCE . . . A PROCESS APPROACH II will help children see that learning can be fun, and that it sometimes proceeds best when you work with friends in one way or another.[9]

Implementation

Implementation of the SAPA II program is not at all complex. The first stage, as mentioned earlier in the ESS and SCIS programs, is to get the teacher ready for the program. Inservice training is recognized as an important part of the SAPA II program.

It is suggested that the SAPA II program be implemented totally at one time. This method allows all students to be involved in the program at once and causes fewer problems in the long run.

Teachers will have to provide extra background information to help the students develop the skills needed to master new modules. However, by using the implementation approach, everyone will be in sequence at the beginning of the second year.

Summary of SAPA II

The *Science . . . A Process Approach II* (SAPA II) program is a sequential, but modular, science program developed by the Commission on Science Education of the American Association for the Advancement of Science (AAAS), and now published by Delta Education. It is based on the assumption that young children should be taught how to do science rather than read and listen to science subject matter (content). Eight basic processes are taught from kindergarten through the third grade, followed by five integrated processes in the fourth, fifth, and sixth grades. Children are exposed to subject matter, but knowledge of the processes is the prime objective. Fifteen modules per grade level are taught in sequence with slight variation permitted. The teacher presents the material, leads discussions, evaluates the students, and keeps records of students' achievement. The kit comes packaged in individual modules with materials for 30 students and can be shared by several teachers, providing each has a set of consumable materials. A module instruction booklet provides behavioral objectives, activities, and appraisal for each module. Teacher's training material is available for purchase from Delta Education. The program has been proved effective, generally reaching its goal of 90 percent attainment of the written objective by 90 percent of the students, if taught as suggested.

ENDNOTES

1. Elementary Science Study, *A Working Guide to the Elementary Science Study* (Newton, MA: Education Development Center, 1971), p. 2. Available from the EDC Distribution Center, 39 Chapel St., Newton, MA 02160.

2. Reprinted with permission from the *SCIS Final Report* (pp. 64–65), published by the Science Curriculum Improvement Study. Copyright 1976 by Regents of the University of California. Limited copies are available from Delta Education, Inc.

3. *Science Curriculum Improvement Study* (Promotional Brochure R 10/71 90281) (Chicago: Rand McNally, 1971). All SCIS material is now supplied by Delta Education, Inc., Nashua, NH.

4. *Evaluation Supplements* (Berkeley: Science Curriculum Improvement Study, University of California, 1971–1975). Limited copies are available from Delta Education, Inc.

5. Robert Karplus and Herbert Thier, *SCIS Teacher's Handbook* (Berkeley: Science Curriculum Improvement Study, University of California, 1974). Limited copies are available from Delta Education, Inc.

6. From *Program Guide of Science . . . A Process Approach II,* Copyright, 1975, American Association for the Advancement of Science. Used by permission of the publisher, Delta Education, Inc.

7. Ibid.

8. Adapted from *Curriculum Catalog of Science . . . A Process Approach II,* Copyright, 1976, American Association for the Advancement of Science. Used by permission of the publisher, Delta Education, Inc.

9. From *Program Guide of Science . . . A Process Approach II,* Copyright, 1975, American Association for the Advancement of Science. Used by permission of the publisher, Delta Education, Inc.

REFERENCES

Aho, W., Alberti, D., Perkes, V., Sheldon, R., Thomas, T., & Ward, R. (1974). *McGraw-Hill evaluation program for ESS.* St. Louis: Webster/McGraw-Hill.

American Association for the Advancement of Science. *Curriculum catalog.* Washington, DC: Author. Now available from Delta Education, Nashua, NH.

———. (1975). *Program guide: Science ... A process approach II.* Nashua, NH: Delta Education.

Ball, D. W. (1978). *ESS/Special education teacher's guide.* St. Louis: Webster/McGraw-Hill.

Bruner, J. (1961 Winter). The act of discovery. *Harvard Educational Review, 31,* 21–32.

Elementary Science Study. (1971). *A working guide to the Elementary Science Study.* Newton, MA: Education Development Center.

Evaluation Supplements. (1971–1975). Berkeley: Science Curriculum Improvement Study, University of California. Limited copies are available from Delta Education.

Karplus, R., & Thier, H. (1974). *SCIS teacher's handbook.* Berkeley: Science Curriculum Improvement Study, University of California. Limited copies are available from Delta Education.

Science Curriculum Improvement Study. (1976). *SCIS final report.* Berkeley: SCIS, University of California.

SUGGESTED READINGS

Carin, A. A., & Sund, R. B. (1989). *Teaching modern science* (5th ed., pp. 182–192). Columbus, OH: Merrill Publishing Company.

———. (1989). *Teaching science through discovery* (6th ed., pp. 179–182). Columbus, OH: Merrill Publishing Company.

Karplus, R., & Thier, H. (1967). *A new look at elementary school science.* Chicago: Rand McNally.

Renner, J. W., & Ragan, W. B. (1968). *Teaching science in the elementary school* (pp. 258–279, 287–294). New York: Harper & Row.

Sample Packet, Science ... A Process Approach II. Nashua, NH: Delta Education.

Science Curriculum Improvement Study. (1971). (Promotional Brochure R10/71 90281) Chicago: Rand McNally.

———. (1970). *Teacher's Guides.* Chicago: Rand McNally. Now supplied by Delta Education.

———. (1976). *Final Report.* (1976). Berkeley: SCIS, University of California. Limited copies available from Delta Education.

Thier, H. et al. (1978). *Teacher's guides for SCIIS.* Chicago: Rand McNally. Now supplied by Delta Education.

Individual Education Program: Supplemental Material for Chapter 7 Activity 7.1

INDIVIDUAL EDUCATION PROGRAM
Total Service Plan

Name ___Brown, Tom___
    (Last)   (First)   (Middle)

Birth date ___6/1/80___

School ___Kennesaw Elementary___

Grade ___3rd___

Date of Program Entry ___9-1-88___

I have received and I approve of the Total Service Plan:

Parent's Signature _____ Date _____

Placement:

Learning Disabilities—Full-time Class

Summary of Present Levels of Performance

WISC IQ V 90 P 110 FS 100

WRAT Reading 1.8 grade

        Spelling 1.6 grade

        Arithmetic 3.0 grade

Very well coordinated, excellent in sports, tries hard, poor visual memory, learns well by listening

Regular Classroom Placement

Grade	Activity	% Time
3	Math	35
	Social Studies	
	Science	
	Lunch	
	P.E.	

Committee Members Present

Mrs. Brown, Parent
Miss Day, Special Ed. Teacher
Miss Jackson, 3rd gr. Teacher

Dates of Meeting ___5-30-89___

Chairman Miss Day, Special Ed. Teacher

Long Range Goals	Specific Educational and/or Support Services	Person(s) Responsible	Beginning Date & Review Dates	Evaluation Performance
To improve reading	LD Class	Special Education Teacher	9-1-89 6-1-90	Teacher-made tests
To improve spelling	LD Class	Special Education Teacher	9-1-89 6-1-90	Teacher-made tests
To improve independent work habits	consultation for regular class teacher	Special and Regular Education Teacher	9-1-89 6-1-90	Teacher-made tests

INDIVIDUAL EDUCATION PROGRAM
Implementer's Instruction Plan

Name ___Tom Brown___ Birth date ___6/1/80___

Teacher ___Miss Day___ Skill Area ___Reading___

LONG RANGE GOAL   date:

| TO ASSIST THE STUDENT IN: |
| Improving reading. |

INSTRUCTIONAL OBJECTIVES:
A. OBJECTIVE   date: 9/1

| THE STUDENT WILL BE ABLE TO: |
| Read a list of the Dolch Level I words selected at random. |

B. OBJECTIVE   date: 10/1

| THE STUDENT WILL BE ABLE TO: |
| Read the Dolch Level I words above. |

C. OBJECTIVE   date: 10/15

| THE STUDENT WILL BE ABLE TO: |
| Read the Dolch Level I words above in context in the basal reading text. |

D. OBJECTIVE   date:

| THE STUDENT WILL BE ABLE TO: |
| Read the Dolch Level I words above in context in content area texts. |

Evaluation Dates

Mastered Stated Objective	Progress Made Continue Objective	Objective is too Easy/Difficult (State which under Comments)	Student interest is High/Low (State which under Comments)	More time needed to meet Objectives	Dropped
10/15					
Comments					
Comments					
Comments					
9/30					
Comments					

ACTIVITIES

A.

| Flash card drill with teacher, peer. |

B.

| Drill on language master |

C.

| Cloze exercises |

D.

| VATK drill |

MATERIALS

A.

| Language master and cards |

B.

| Dolch popper words, games and workbooks |

C.

| Dolch puzzle books and readers |

D.

| Star chart |

I have reviewed this report and have been informed of its contents:

Parent Signature: _____ Date: _____

Comments: _____

INDIVIDUAL EDUCATION PROGRAM
Implementer's Instruction Plan

Name ___Tom Brown___ Birth date ___6/1/80___

Teacher ___Miss Day___ Skill Area ___Spelling___

LONG RANGE GOAL   date:

TO ASSIST THE STUDENT IN:
  Improving Spelling.

INSTRUCTIONAL OBJECTIVES:
A. OBJECTIVE   date: 9/1

THE STUDENT WILL BE ABLE TO:
  Spell orally 10 words from reading vocabulary
  words, given orally.

B. OBJECTIVE   date: 9/15

THE STUDENT WILL BE ABLE TO:
  Spell, orally, 10 words from social studies text
  terms, given orally.

C. OBJECTIVE   date:

THE STUDENT WILL BE ABLE TO:
  Spell, orally, 10 words from science text
  terms, given orally.

D. OBJECTIVE   date:

THE STUDENT WILL BE ABLE TO:
  Spell, in writing, 20 words from science and/or
  social studies text terms, given orally.

Evaluation Dates

Mastered Stated Objective	Progress Made Continue Objective	Objective is too Easy/Difficult (State which under Comments)	Student interest is High/Low (State which under Comments)	More time needed to meet Objectives	Dropped
9/15					
Comments					
Comments					
Comments					
Comments					

ACTIVITIES	MATERIALS
A. language master drill	A. reading text, social studies text, science text, dictionary
B. scrambled words	B. language master and cards
C. VATK drill	C. letter cards
D. drill with peer	D. VATK drill sheet

I have reviewed this report and have been informed of its contents:

Parent Signature: _____ Date: _____

Comments: _____

INDIVIDUAL EDUCATION PROGRAM
Implementer's Instruction Plan

Name __Tom Brown__ Birth date __6/1/80__

Teacher __Miss Day__ Skill Area __Work Habits__

LONG RANGE GOAL   date:

TO ASSIST THE STUDENT IN:
Improving independent work habits.

INSTRUCTIONAL OBJECTIVES:

A. OBJECTIVE   date:

THE STUDENT WILL BE ABLE TO:
Complete a 10 minute task, including reading directions, answering questions and reinforcing correct responses, with teacher assistance.

B. OBJECTIVE   date:

THE STUDENT WILL BE ABLE TO:
Complete a 10 minute task with immediate feedback after completion of the task and no more than one request for teacher assistance.

C. OBJECTIVE   date:

THE STUDENT WILL BE ABLE TO:
Complete a 10 minute task independently.

D. OBJECTIVE   date:

THE STUDENT WILL BE ABLE TO:
Complete a 15 minute task independently.

Evaluation Dates						
Mastered Stated Objective	Progress Made Continue Objective	Objective is too Easy/Difficult (State which under Comments)	Student interest is High/Low (State which under Comments)	More time needed to meet Objectives	Dropped	
10/30	10/1					
Comments						
	12/1					
Comments						
Comments						
Comments						

ACTIVITIES

A.
Have student read directions aloud.

B.
Have student check his own work.

C.
Set time and have student time himself on task completion.

D.

MATERIALS

A.
Star chart

B.
Math work sheets from text.

C.
Reading work sheets from text.

D.
Timer

I have reviewed this report and have been informed of its contents:

Parent Signature: _____ Date: _____

Comments: _____

INDEX

ABOUT THE AUTHORS

Dr. Sandra Cain is an Associate Professor of Teacher Education at Central Michigan University where she teaches undergraduate and graduate Science Education classes. She completed her undergraduate degree at the University of Georgia and taught elementary school in Georgia and Tennessee for six years. She received the Master of Education and the Doctor of Education degrees from the University of Georgia. Her activities include Interim Director of the Central Michigan University Science and Mathematics Teaching Center (1989), Project Director for the Science Education in Michigan Schools (SEMS plus) grant (1989), National Science Teachers Association (member and presenter), Michigan Science Teachers Association (member and presenter), Association of Supervision and Curriculum Development (ASCD), National Education Association (NEA), Michigan Education Association (MEA), Member of the Christa McAuliffe Fellowship Review Committee for the State of Michigan (1988), Institutional Representative for Central Michigan University to the American Association of Colleges of Teacher Education (AACTE), Member of the Central Michigan University National Council for Accreditation of Teacher Education (NCATE) Steering Committee (1988–89), President of the Central Michigan University Chapter of PHI DELTA KAPPA (1988–89). Dr. Cain has also presented numerous science workshops for inservice teachers.

Dr. Jack Evans teaches at Central Michigan University, currently holding the rank of Associate Professor. He did undergraduate work at Texas A&M and East Texas State University, and received the Master of Arts and the Doctor of Education degrees from the University of North Texas. He taught in the elementary school, junior high school, and at the university level prior to coming to Central Michigan

University. His activities include: Malone Fellowship (Egypt, 1988), National Science Teachers Association (NSTA) (member and presenter), Michigan Science Teachers Association (MSTA) (member and presenter), Association for Supervision and Curriculum Development (ASCD), National Education Association (NEA), Michigan Education Association (MEA), and educational consultant for Estes Model Rockets.